Praise for Griffith REVI

'An always vibrant mix of cr
and ideas, *Griffith REVIEW* ....
Adelaide Review

'Of all the small magazines in this country, *Griffith REVIEW*
is the one that's essential reading.' *The Australian*

'One of our best journals.' *The Age*

'*Griffith REVIEW* represents "the long game" in journalism,
providing quality analysis in an age of diminishing
journalistic integrity.' *Walkley Magazine*

'*Griffith REVIEW*, under the editorship of Julianne
Schultz, just keeps getting better and better.'
Australian Book Review

'*Griffith REVIEW* is a wonderful journal. It's pretty
much setting the agenda in Australia and fighting way
above its weight...You're mad if you don't subscribe.'
Phillip Adams

'A stalwart of best essays in recent years...arguably
the best of all the Australian literary magazines.'
Sydney Morning Herald

'*Griffith REVIEW* takes academic journalism out of
the ivory tower onto the street and into the countryside...
a refreshing and invigorating move.' *Courier-Mail*

'The indispensable read for literate Australians.'
Geraldine Brooks

SIR SAMUEL GRIFFITH was one of
Australia's great early achievers. Twice the
premier of Queensland, that state's chief
justice and the author of its criminal code, he
was best known for his pivotal role in drafting
agreements that led to Federation, and as the
new nation's first chief justice. He was also an
important reformer and legislator, a practical
and cautious man of words.

Griffith died in 1920 and is now best
remembered in his namesakes: an electorate,
a society, a suburb and a university.
Ninety-six years after he first proposed
establishing a university in Brisbane, Griffith
University, the city's second, was created. His
commitment to public debate and ideas, his
delight in words and art, and his attachment
to active citizenship is recognised by the
publication that bears his name.

Like Sir Samuel Griffith, Griffith
REVIEW is iconoclastic and non-partisan,
with a sceptical eye and a pragmatically
reforming heart and a commitment to
public discussion. Personal, political
and unpredictable, it is Australia's best
conversation.

GriffithREVIEW28
Still the Lucky Country?

Edited by Julianne Schultz

GriffithREVIEW28

Barrier Highway, NSW, 2005. Martin Mischkulnig, C-type Print, 100 x 80 cm. From the book *Smalltown,* published by Penguin, with text by Tim Winton. *Smalltown* was inspired by Martin's experiences growing up in a series of roadside motels run by his parents. www.martinmischkulnig.com

Griffith REVIEW gratefully acknowledges the support and generosity of founding patron Margaret Mittelheuser.

GriffithREVIEW27 AUTUMN 2010
GriffithREVIEW is published four times a year by Griffith University
in conjunction with Text Publishing. ISSN 1448-2924

Publisher	Marilyn McMeniman AM
Editor	Julianne Schultz AM
Deputy Editor	Erica Sontheimer
Picture Editor & Production Manager	Paul Thwaites
Associate Editor	David Winter, Text Publishing
Publication & Cover Design	WH Chong & Susan Miller, Text Publishing
Text Publishing	Michael Heyward, Kirsty Wilson, Sarina Gale, Megan Quinlan, Michelle Calligaro
Proofreader	Andrea Lewis
Administration	Andrea Huynh
Typesetting	Midland Typesetters
Printing	Ligare Book Printers
Distribution	Penguin Australia

Contributions by academics can, on request, be refereed by our Editorial Board.
Details: www.griffithreview.com

GRIFFITH REVIEW
South Bank Campus, Griffith University
PO Box 3370, South Brisbane QLD 4101 Australia
Ph +617 3735 3071 Fax +617 3735 3272
griffithreview@griffith.edu.au www.griffithreview.com

TEXT PUBLISHING
Swann House, 22 William St, Melbourne VIC 3000 Australia
Ph +613 8610 4500 Fax +613 9629 8621
books@textpublishing.com.au www.textpublishing.com.au

SUBSCRIPTIONS
Within Australia: 1 year (4 editions) $99.80 RRP, inc. P&H and GST
Outside Australia: 1 year (4 editions) A$149.80 RRP, inc. P&H
Institutional and bulk rates available on application.

FEEDBACK AND COMMENT www.griffithreview.com

 Griffith REVIEW
receives project
sponsorship
from Copyright
CAL Cultural Fund Agency Limited.

 **Australian Government**

 **Australia Council** for the Arts

This project has
been assisted by
the Australian
Government through
the Australia Council,
its principal arts
funding and
advisory body.

Cashing in the chips

A bountiful mirage beyond the Great Divide

Julianne Schultz

NAGGING curiosity about where the rivers originated lured Australia's great European explorers beyond the Great Dividing Range. Equipped with boats, drays and provisions they followed the rivers as far as they could, hoping against hope that the source would be a vast inland sea watering a continent as well endowed as North America. In their wake the land filled with sheep and cattle.

The grand vision of an inland sea defined Charles Sturt's public life and culminated in his final journey of exploration from Adelaide in 1844, pursuing, some say, seagulls that flocked north every autumn and returned in good condition each spring. It was an arduous trek; Sturt and his party were forced to camp just beyond a 'hog-backed hill' for months, waiting for rain. When the journey resumed they established, at great personal cost, that the inland sea was a tantalising mirage in country that seemed to be made up of unforgiving ranges, flatlands and deserts.

It was another three decades before settlers inspired by the Californian and Victorian gold rushes applied for leases and pegged out the site – near Broken Hill – hoping to find tin. They were disappointed when assays revealed lead and silver instead, but they did not have to wait long before the 'haphazard' and at times 'dangerously amateurish' enterprise brought them extraordinary wealth. What is now the world's largest resources company, BHP Billiton, was conceived in that hot, unforgiving land – not far from where it continues to make fortunes ripping precious minerals from the ground.

As Peter Thompson and Robert Macklin document in *The Big Fella* (Heinemann, 2009), the pastoralists who created the Australian narrative were battling drought and rabbits, unimpressed by the foreign prospectors chipping away in the sun. They readily traded their interests in the venture and passed up access to fortunes that would outlive their properties.

THIS SCEPTICAL VIEW entered the national mindset: mining was for gamblers – pastoralists were the colonies' true, hard-working aristocracy. In a gold rush fortunes may be made quickly, but they are also easily lost. During the 1850s gold accounted for a third of GDP and Victoria's population jumped from 77,000 to 540,000 in two years, but wages doubled, wool exports fell and manufacturing stalled. The colony enjoyed extraordinary wealth, but it didn't last and once the boom was over there was little to show for it – apart from grand buildings in Melbourne, Ballarat and Bendigo.

Economic historians agree that there have been four mining booms since – each, so far, marked by an equally spectacular crash.

The late-nineteenth-century boom made Broken Hill a national icon, enabled Charters Towers to run its own stock exchange and saw Western Australia's population almost quadruple to 180,000. It ended with a whimper, a victim of a global depression, rising costs, falling profits, capital drought and impoverished investors who learned, at their cost, that mining was for gamblers. In response city-based industries regained the ascendancy, aided by a protective buffer of tariff walls.

Through the first part of the twentieth century Australia muddled along with a mix of protected manufacturing and agricultural industries; even in the good years of the 1950s growth rarely pipped 2 per cent. The possibility that Australia could be a country that built its wealth on extractive industries, like the oil-rich Middle East, was not a serious part of the national conversation. Mining may have been the bedrock of the biggest companies, but it was remote and detached from the reality of most people's increasingly urbanised lives.

It took until the late 1960s before there was another mining boom of any consequence. Discoveries of coal, iron ore, bauxite and oil provided a focus for the new capital-intensive extractive industries; Japan was hungry for materials and conveniently close; export prices, employment and inflation soared.

True to the dominant image that boom, like the ones that preceded it, is best remembered for the gambling it inspired. A company named for the Greek god of the sea, Poseidon, reported discovering nickel in Western Australia. It did not take long for Poseidon to become derogatory shorthand for the boom that collapsed under the weight of its own hype. Speculators listed companies on the stock exchanges, rich with promise but little more. Mining shares reached an all-time high in January 1970, and then crashed – taking the savings of countless small investors with them. Poseidon produced little nickel; its sharp practice resulted in new corporate regulations, and reinforced the sense that mining is a gamble.

In the early 1980s global demand for coal, oil and gas produced another brief spike – ships lined up off the New South Wales coast, new coal loaders were commissioned and built, railway links were extended. According to the Reserve Bank Deputy Governor, Ric Battellino, this induced 'a sense of euphoria about Australia's future'. It too was short-lived. Yet the recession that followed provided the impetus to float the dollar, deregulate the economy, reduce tariffs, encourage global competitiveness and the services sector – the pre-conditions essential for the current boom, one that promises to break the mould.

SOMETHING EXTRAORDINARY IS again going on beyond the Great Divide, something that will profoundly change Australia in ways we have scarcely begun to imagine, something that demands fresh thinking and courageous policy innovation.

There are not enough clichés to describe the transformation of the outback into the economic heart of the nation. The scale of the new industrial mining is incomprehensible to those of us who spend our lives in congested, lush and well-resourced towns and cities on the coast. Yet last year mining and energy accounted for nearly 20 per cent of GDP, surpassing the export revenue from manufacturing for the first time, with 40 per cent of the total value.

Australia is the great pit enabling the industrialisation of the developing world – especially China. In the parts of the country where few of us ever venture there is an overabundance of the ingredients needed to build and power the cities of the future, not impossibly far beneath the surface.

Beyond the Great Divide the dusty outback, once divided between vast pastoral stations, is now dotted with mining operations of extraordinary scale and scope: Olympic Dam in South Australia is the largest underground mine in the world (and set to grow); there are open-cut pits so big they can be seen from space and change the local climate, piles of bauxite and iron ore that reach for the skies and would dwarf city towers if there were any nearby.

This is not simply the upswing of another boom. There may be a bust lurking, but mining is no longer the pursuit of gamblers and shysters, although it still has more than its fair share of colourful characters. It has been professionalised and internationalised; miners now talk about social responsibility, Indigenous rights and improving the lot of people in developing countries.

The descriptions all too easily wash over us: for a people with an obsessive attachment to *big*, things are about to get a lot bigger. Already it is known that Australia has the *world's largest* reserves of bauxite, uranium, nickel, *and* the second largest reserves of gold, *and* the third-largest supply of iron ore.

That is just the start. The country is also home to the sixth-largest supply of coal, the seventh-largest reserve of manganese, and even oil and gas comes in twentieth on the world league tables. It is not likely to run out soon; at current rates, copper is projected to last for at least three decades, oil and gas for half a century, iron ore a century, bauxite, coal and platinum much, much longer.

Australians may like to think of the country as a knowledge-intensive services economy – but at its core it is a giant mine, one that is about to become much bigger. As the chief executive of BHP Billiton, Marius Kloppers, regularly says, 'I doubt the average Australian understands how his prosperity is linked to resources.' Yet one way or another the new boom will force a fundamental transformation of the Australian economy. This is not something we can afford to ignore, or leave to luck, or the mining companies, investment bankers and economists to resolve – there is more at stake.

WHEN DONALD HORNE sat down in his Sydney backyard after lunch on a summer afternoon to write *The Lucky Country*, his concern that 'Australia is a lucky country run mainly by second-rate people who share its luck' was widely shared, but rarely expressed. Penguin's British bosses did not want to publish it; they did not think it was the sort of book Australians would want to read – a view they quickly corrected when it sold 18,000 copies in nine days late in 1964, and 260,000 within a few years.

Horne was concerned (among other things) that the easygoing nature he admired in his country folk fostered a lack of curiosity and ambition, and would result in a continuing decline in the standard of living. He had not anticipated the new boom, although in updated editions of the classic text he touched on the possibility that bauxite, iron ore, oil and coal might play a part in the country's economic future. He was pessimistic about the capacity for innovation and about foreign ownership, and no more of a seer than any other commentator or explorer.

The Australia Horne ironically described as lucky in the early 1960s is radically different today – some of the good things have been lost, but there is a sense of urgency, opportunity and global engagement. His throwaway phrase has now entered the national vernacular, and is increasingly used literally, even a tourism slogan, 'Say g'day to the lucky country'.

It was not just luck that Australia managed to navigate the recent global financial crisis better than those countries with which we like to be compared; it was not just luck that China's industrialisation requires what Australia can provide, or that government policies and corporate capacity and ambition combined to make it possible to satisfy this demand. These outcomes are a product of tough decisions over many years. The Australia Horne described lacked the intellectual, political, regulatory and capital requirements to engage on a boom of this nature with confidence, rather than a gambler's bluff.

But this does not mean that everything is sorted. Mining is by nature a finite activity – one day the mines will run out, and we need to be prepared. Although mining jobs pay almost twice as much as those in manufacturing, they don't raise the standard of living of those not directly involved.

Australia now has the opportunity to reinvent itself on the back of this extraordinary boom, digging into Sturt's mirage to produce untold wealth. This sort of opportunity does not happen often. Few countries are so fortunate – but with resources now accounting for a fifth of GDP and rising, that is the prospect on offer, if we are bold enough to grab it. The discovery of North Sea oil and the development of economically efficient means of extracting it, forty years ago, gave Britain a boost as its Empire died, but Norway – now the world's third-largest oil exporter – remade itself and created a sovereign wealth fund today worth $491 billion that will bankroll its future.

In calling for change Horne noted, 'The time might come when broad views of change that now seem impractical will seem sensible and to the point.' Once again we need to think carefully and boldly about the sort of place we want Australia to be, how the benefits of the buried treasure can be shared now and preserved for future generations, how we can develop diverse downstream industries that increase wealth and opportunity for all, how we can extract social as well as economic benefit from the bounty beyond the Great Divide.

10 March 2010

'I invest ethically because I don't want to make money from harming others.'

NADINE
Adelaide,
Environmental
Engineer.
New mum.

Tears of the sun

Mining fever and the making of a nation

Kathy Marks

AS you fly out of Perth, heading east, the wheat and sheep country cushioning the world's most isolated capital city quickly recedes. The already sparse signs of settlement diminish, and soft yellows and greens give way to the harsh rust-reds of the continent's interior. But this is not the mostly flat, mostly featureless landscape characteristic of much of central Australia – not nowadays, anyway. This is a landscape pockmarked with man-made hills, and gigantic holes gouged out of the earth. This is gold country.

Of all those holes, none other compares with the Super Pit, one of the biggest craters ever dug by man – so vast that it can be seen from space, and is even reputed to influence the weather in Kalgoorlie, the hard-bitten town crouched on its rim. One of the richest goldmines on the planet, the open-cut pit will be 3.6 kilometres long, 1.6 kilometres wide and 650 metres deep when a current expansion program is completed. The creation of Alan Bond, it is the thrusting symbol of the Australian mining industry, an industry that has shaped multiple aspects of the modern nation, while underpinning the economy and, recently, enabling the country to weather the global financial upheaval with little more than a scratch.

It was in this remote and desperately arid corner of Western Australia that Paddy Hannan and two fellow Irish prospectors made camp in 1893, after one of their packhorses threw a shoe. Ever alert to the potential of virgin ground, they kept their eyes firmly down and spotted several nuggets in a gully. Before long they had collected a hundred ounces of gold, and within three days hordes of men were pegging out claims on what became known as the Golden Mile. It was the beginning of Australia's last and greatest gold rush – 'the rush that never ended', as they call it in Western Australia, after the title of Geoffrey Blainey's classic history of the mining industry.

More than a century on, the goldfield that Hannan discovered – and the hundreds of ore bodies in and around Kalgoorlie – is still being worked with the same intensity: by thousands of lone prospectors, hoping for their own lucky strike, and by companies large and small. At the Super Pit, where hundred-metre-high slag heaps loom up against the horizon, the blasting, shovelling and crushing go on twenty-four hours a day, 365 days a year. As

---

PREVIOUS PAGE: JJ Dwyer (1869–1928), Dryblowing with dishes, c. 1896. Courtesy of the State Library of Western Australia and the National Trust of Australia (Western Australia).

I watched the oversized dump trucks, laden with rock, toil up the pit face, then descend, empty, to be loaded again, it struck me that this hole, evocative of unbridled ambition and perhaps even hubris, also represents something quite primal: man's millennia-old mania for digging up the treasures in the earth's crust, and the gamble upon which the mining business has always been predicated.

When Blainey's book was first published, in 1963, gold was in long-term decline, and by the mid-1970s headframe lights were dimming across the Golden Mile. However, new technology and the emancipation of the gold price resurrected a dying industry, and in the early 1980s another boom began. In recent times the price of gold has risen spectacularly, and all over Australia drill holes are being sunk, mothballed mines are being reopened and existing ones are being enlarged. Meanwhile, after a blip lasting barely a year, other mineral and energy resources are being shipped overseas as fast as they can be scooped out of the ground.

In Perth, the cafés are bursting and the traffic is beyond belief: a sure indication that the good times have returned. With China barrelling ahead in its industrial revolution and India not far behind, demand for Australia's raw materials is expected to climb even higher. Yet amid the euphoria – felt most keenly in Western Australia, the nation's resources powerhouse, but also beyond – there is an undercurrent of disquiet. How wise is Australia to stake its future on an industry reliant on finite reserves and fickle commodity prices? How sustainable is mining, with its colossal environmental footprint? And just who is reaping the rewards?

SOON AFTER 2010 dawned, I stood calf-deep in a tranquil creek, swishing gravel and sand around a dish while carefully watching for 'colour'. At this same spot in April 1851, John Lister and William Tom noticed gold glistening in a rock crevice, then, a little way downstream, came across a two-ounce nugget. Three years after the start of the California gold rush, they had found Australia's first payable goldfield, thirty kilometres north-east of Orange, in the undulating countryside beyond the Blue Mountains. The site was christened Ophir, after the biblical city of gold, by the man who had identified the area's promise: Edward Hammond Hargraves.

Gold. No other element on the periodic table – not platinum, nor carbon, the source of diamonds – has seized the imagination in the same way, nor ignited such passions. The Incas called it 'the tears of the sun'; the Egyptian pharaohs were buried with it; for thousands of years it has occupied a unique place at the heart of civilisations. Deposited in quartz veins hundreds of millions of years ago by fluids surging up from the earth's molten core, gold has driven people 'to travel the globe...to lie and cheat, to suffer and speculate, to risk their lives, to move mountains and reshape the landscape', according to *Gold: Forgotten Histories and Lost Objects of Australia* (edited by Iain McCalman, Alexander Cook and Andrew Reeves; Cambridge University Press, 2001). Symbolic of wealth, power, beauty and immortality, gold has tantalised and tormented men, fuelled and funded wars, propped up currencies, permeated languages, and spawned innumerable myths and legends.

Like most people, I'm familiar with the glamorous metal. But the first time I held a chunk of raw gold in my hand, fresh from the ground, I felt a little dizzy. It was so shiny, so yellow, so solid, and as I turned it over I caught a faint glimpse of what sends folk crazy. The shy, lanky man who showed it to me had sold his home and business in Perth in order to move to the Eastern Goldfields, around Kalgoorlie, and prospect full-time. I met Brad Parslow outside a shop in Boulder, Kalgoorlie's faded twin town; he was heading back out bush, and when I asked him if he'd had any luck, he reached into his canvas shoulder bag and took out a Tupperware box containing a three-ounce nugget – which, on that day in early December 2009, was worth US$3,624: not bad for an afternoon's work. (One troy ounce is 31.1 grams.)

In central New South Wales shepherds tending their flocks had been picking up gold long before Lister and Tom, but the metal's existence was apparently hushed up; according to one tale, Governor Sir George Gipps, on being presented with specks of gold by a geologist and Anglican clergyman, the Reverend William Branwhite Clarke, spluttered: 'Put it away, Mr Clarke, or we shall all have our throats cut.' His fears proved unfounded; however, when news did get out, 'a great excitement unhinged the minds of all classes of the community', writes Manning Clark in *A History of Australia* (abridged version, Pimlico, 1995).

There's not much gold left at Ophir; in fact, there's nothing much at all – just a commemorative obelisk; a few crumbling headstones in the overgrown cemetery; a landscape pitted with old shafts, mullock heaps and wide tunnels carved out of the hillsides; and the once richly endowed creek, still blithely babbling in the shade of gracefully inclined casuarinas. In 1851 there was a chaotic township, complete with school, post office, police station, apothecary, hotels and sly-grog sellers, while the diggings, according to a letter to the *Bathurst Free Press* in June that year, were so crowded that 'in some spots the miners stand so close together that their picks have to be very carefully used to prevent them from striking each other.'

An estimated three thousand people worked Ophir's stony ground at its peak; the frenzy was short-lived, though, and many miners decamped to the more promising Turon River, to the north-east. In August 1851 the bountiful goldfields of Ballarat were discovered, followed by those of Bendigo and Beechworth. Australia's first real gold rush was on, with fortune-seekers from around the globe converging on Victoria's so-called Golden Triangle. At home, police and soldiers deserted their posts to dig for alluvial gold; ships docking in Melbourne were abandoned by their crews. Geoffrey Blainey writes in *The Rush that Never Ended*: 'Shopkeepers and employers found the relationships of society reversed. Calling at the blacksmith to shoe their horse they found his door locked...Their children returned from school to report the master had gone...Preachers looked down from pulpits and denounced avarice to congregations empty of men' (fifth edition, MUP, 2003).

Although the rush was mostly over within twenty years, Victoria – and its capital city, which metamorphosed into 'Marvellous Melbourne' – would never be the same. For the other colonies, too, it was a turning point: the country's population nearly tripled during the 1850s, to more than a million, as migrants arrived not only from Britain and Ireland but China, the United States and all over Europe. At last Australia had the massive influx of free settlers it coveted; breakneck economic growth boosted the living standards of a society until then largely dependent on agriculture, and as major gold seams were located, in turn, in Queensland, the Northern Territory and Western Australia, each received an injection of wealth and people. Far-flung regions were opened up, with inland towns established and linked by railway to the coast. And Australia's international image was transformed: rather than a dreary outpost of Britain or a convict dumping-ground, it became a promised land.

Today it is the world's second-largest gold producer, behind China, and gold is its third-biggest export, after coal and iron ore, worth $17.5 billion in 2008–09. Yet gold, notwithstanding its allure, has relatively few practical applications, unlike, for instance, that most basic of industrial raw materials, iron ore. In the Pilbara region of Western Australia, iron ore is mined in prodigious quantities – and it is in the Pilbara that the reality of Australia being a quarry for Asia really hits home.

THE SKYLINE IN Port Hedland, 1,630 kilometres north of Perth, is dominated by towering red stockpiles: iron ore, awaiting shipment to China's steel mills. Red dust coats pavements and lawns in the small, somewhat unprepossessing town, where every other building seems to be a gleaming mine company headquarters. Port Hedland is often referred to as the engine room of the Australian economy; visiting for the first time, I found it hard not to think that the iron ore companies, particularly Rio Tinto and BHP Billiton, own the Pilbara. Need a motel in Tom Price, the spick-and-span mining community rising from a baked landscape 430 kilometres south of Port Hedland? You'll have to call Rio Tinto's reservations service. (All rooms are booked up months in advance.) Want to drive from Tom Price to the port of Dampier? Sorry, that road is owned by Rio Tinto, although they might let you use it if you ask nicely. Fancy a walk in the fresh air? Try the BHP Billiton Marapikurrinya Park in Port Hedland, where you can also ogle the enormous bulk carriers. Or, you could go hiking in Rio Tinto Gorge.

The rust-coloured gorges of the Pilbara's Hamersley Ranges caught the eye of the late mining magnate Lang Hancock in 1952, when stormy weather forced his plane to fly low over the area. One of the most significant deposits was unearthed at Mount Tom Price, where, three or four times a day, a 2.5-kilometre-long train departs for Dampier, carrying more than 16,000 tonnes of iron ore. (The railway is privately owned, naturally.) If that sounds like a lot of ore, consider this: Tom Price is only one of eleven Rio Tinto mines in the Pilbara, producing 220 million tonnes a year. Then there are BHP's seven mines – another hundred million tonnes – as well as the lesser players, chief among them Andrew 'Twiggy' Forrest's Fortescue Metals, which exported twenty-seven million tonnes in its first year.

Tony Dekuyer gave up his job as a maths teacher at a private Catholic boys' school in Perth in 2006 to drive trucks at Rio Tinto's West Angelas mine. Set against a billowing backdrop of saltbush, spindly trees and red sandhills, West Angelas consists simply of the mine, an airstrip and an accommodation camp. The nearest town, Newman, is 110 kilometres away. Dekuyer's wife, Janette, also worked at the site; for two years, the couple occupied adjacent huts at the camp, returning to Perth one week in three to watch their adult sons play sport, catch up on the gardening and enjoy the café lifestyle. Dekuyer, fifty-one, has now gravitated to a position in the operations centre in Perth, where he earns 'just over double' his teacher's salary.

Everyone at West Angelas has signed up for the 'fly in, fly out' (FIFO) regime that is increasingly the norm in the Australian resources industry, as new mines, many with short lifespans, open up in isolated spots. For the workers, FIFO means long periods away from home and life in a camp which, despite being well equipped – canteen, wet mess, gym, tennis courts, internet access – has no frills. The wages help to compensate (truck drivers earn about $150,000, including allowances; train drivers up to $210,000) – so much so that some miners commute from Brisbane and Sydney. Tony Dekuyer, who has bought himself a Ducati motorbike (Janette has a convertible sports car), reflects: 'Teaching was very rewarding in many ways, but mentally it was quite exhausting. Here, when the day finishes, it finishes, and you don't have to think about the job at all.'

At Rio Tinto's mines, nearly a third of truck drivers are women. Kylie Piggott spends her waking hours perched eight metres off the ground, driving back and forth to the West Angelas pits. Each trip she collects 240 tonnes of drilled and blasted rock, then, following instructions on a computer screen, transports it to the crusher, stockpile or dump. Piggott, twenty-five, has to climb three metal staircases to reach her cab; the vehicle's tyres alone are twice her height. She says: 'The cabs are air-conditioned and you can play your own music. It's like a little world of your own up there. It's pretty relaxing, although it can be lonely too.'

Young women like Piggott are the new face of the industry, according to mining executives. But you don't have to look far for a more familiar face. On a Sunday afternoon in Tom Price – 340 kilometres from the hottest town in Australia, Marble Bar – I meet Ross, Digger and Pirate in the crowded beer garden of the Tom Price Hotel Motel. Ross is a boilermaker from Queensland with a long, shaggy beard, grey ponytail, beer belly and eye-catching array of tattoos. He spends nine days of each month in Perth with his partner. 'Do I miss home? Hell, yeah,' he says. 'But it's very good money: that's the trade-off. I'm prepared to do the hard yards in the short term in order to pay off the mortgage and create a bit of wealth. But it can be really hard on your relationship, and the evidence is all around you.'

Digger, a short, voluble man who disappears to buy a round of drinks and returns with a blowsy girl on his arm, has three broken marriages behind him. A miner since the 1970s, he believes the industry is far more civilised nowadays. 'It was rough back then. It was all single men, and the wet mess was open twenty-four hours, and there were fights breaking out the whole time.'

What about the lifestyle now? Ross sighs. 'It's a small town in the middle of nowhere. It's stinking hot in summer and freezing cold in winter. If I could make the same money at home, I wouldn't be flying away.'

AT THE TURNOFF from the Albany Highway to Bannister Marridong Road, 115 kilometres south-east of Perth, a sign states: 'Boddington – A Golden Opportunity'. Another fifteen kilometres on is a country town that is holding its breath.

Boddington is a farming community sitting on Australia's biggest goldmine. The mine, owned by the American giant Newmont, opened in 1987 and was decommissioned in 2001; after the gold price rose, Newmont decided to restart operations, mining and processing lower-grade ore. The first bar was poured last October at the site, which was upgraded at a cost of US$3.2 billion and has a projected life of at least twenty-four years; the plan is to produce a million ounces of gold annually for the first five – even more than the Super Pit. The inhabitants of Boddington are, mostly, thrilled: investment is flowing into the once dozy town of 1,600, new businesses have been set up, and new health and recreation services are in the works. The jobless rate has dropped to almost zero (the mine will employ nearly nine hundred people), and the property market is boiling. In 2009 Newmont ploughed more than $70 million into the local economy.

Over the next four years the population of the town, situated in the Darling Ranges, on the banks of the Hotham River, is forecast to double: a trend that most rural communities can only dream of. However, residents are wary. They recall the high hopes of Ravensthorpe, six hours' drive south, when BHP opened its US$2.2 billion nickel mine in 2008. Eight months later, after the nickel price fell to below $11,000 a tonne – it was above $50,000 in mid-2007 – BHP walked away and 1,800 people lost their jobs. In Boddington, many miners have chosen to rent houses, or to live at the camp just outside town, leaving their families behind in Perth. And it is not only they who are hesitant. 'The problem we're having now is to convince the state government, the businesses and, particularly, the financiers that we're not Ravensthorpe,' says Paul Carrots, president of the shire council.

Yet mining has traditionally been a precarious business: for prospectors and companies, for mine workers and their communities, for investors and speculators. Booms are inexorably followed by busts; bubbles always burst. Of the hundreds of new Western Australian companies floated on the London Stock Exchange after Kalgoorlie's riches came to light, only a fraction survived. In 1969 the excitement whipped up by the discovery of nickel at Windarra, north of Kalgoorlie, spurred thousands of Australians to invest in a company called Poisedon; shares soared from eighty cents to $280, but the field did not live up to its hype, and Poseidon's stock, along with other mining shares, crashed. Despite such debacles, a gambling mentality has infused Australian mining since the early days. Geoffrey Blainey calls the gold rushes 'a gigantic lottery in which all had a chance…the magic formula in an age without football pools or state lotteries'; he also relates how, after their board meetings, the directors of Broken Hill Proprietary would play two-up with gold sovereigns.

For today's companies, the gamble is twofold: will the immense capital staked in the quest for new deposits pay off in the shape of a viable mine, and if so, will the commodity price be sustained long enough – and production costs remain low enough – to guarantee profits? Although the odds can be shortened through drilling, geophysics, aerial photography and the study of geological maps, they are still daunting. 'You back yourself to find stuff,' agrees Chris Banasik, exploration director of a small, recently formed goldmining company, Silverlake Resources. 'As a punter, you read the form;

as a geologist, you look at rocks and data and make an interpretation about where the gold is.' Campbell Baird, chief executive of Focus Minerals, which owns land at Coolgardie, forty kilometres south of Kalgoorlie, says: 'The high value of gold makes it a high-risk, high-reward business: that's the attraction. But only one in five hundred deposits makes it into production. It's reasonably easy to find gold mineralisation, but to prove up an economic deposit – that's the challenge. There are hundreds of companies out there, still looking after ten or fifteen years, and the faith and belief they have in themselves and the land is quite extraordinary.'

Tiny quantities of most minerals are found almost everywhere (even seawater contains minute amounts of gold); the difficulty is to identify abnormal concentrations. The line between success and failure can be fine – particularly with gold, where 'you're mining ounces in a vast landscape', as Chris Fraser, executive director of the Mineral Council of Australia's Victorian division, puts it. Chris Banasik observes: 'The hardest thing in mining is to stop, because there's always the chance you might have missed it. It's always, "Jeez, can we give it one more shot? Because look at the rocks – it's got to be here somewhere."' Jim Beyer, Boddington's general manager, says: 'You're putting drill holes down, and you could be centimetres away and you wouldn't know. The difference between a dry hole and a bonanza hole can be tiny. Then someone else comes along and finds it. It's heartbreaking, but that's the way the game goes.'

'OUR SKIMPIES THIS week: Holly, Sarah, Jamie, Danni', announces a blackboard sign outside the Exchange Hotel, one of the imposing gold-rush-era buildings that line Hannan Street, in central Kalgoorlie. Across the road, outside the equally historic Palace Hotel, with its stone facade and wraparound balconies, an electronic board flashes up the latest gold price. It is December 2009, and gold is about to hit US$1,217.40 – its all-time peak.

'The price is absolutely unbelievable,' exults Ashok Parekh, whose sprawling accountancy firm occupies almost an entire city block. He boots up his computer to check it yet again. He beams. 'Everyone in Kalgoorlie is happy; you can feel it in the air. I drink in the Tattersalls Club every Friday night with my friends – builders, taxi drivers, businessmen, pensioners – and we all talk about the same thing: the gold price and gold shares; which companies are doing well.' He rummages in a cabinet and brings out a 22-ounce nugget. 'That's worth US$26,000 today,' he confides. I suppress an urge to shrug; after a few days in Kalgoorlie, I've seen so much gold that, like everyone else, I've become blasé. In one pub, the barman produces a nugget as we chat; no one else looks up from their drink.

The gold price smashed record after record last year, as nervous investors sought a safe haven. The Perth Mint could not turn out coins fast enough, and even its souvenir shop was packed with people 'desperate to give us their money and buy gold', recalls Edward Harbuz, the Mint's chief executive. Six hundred kilometres inland, the global recession barely registered in this community of 30,000, or 32,000, or 35,000 – no one seems quite sure what the Kalgoorlie population is. A new $10 million retail development opened, Harvey Norman moved to more spacious premises and work proceeded on a $20 million golf course. 'The global financial crisis?' remarks Russell Cole, the Super Pit's general manager. 'We watched it on our new plasma-screen TVs and heard about it as we drove to work in our big new cars.' Across Western Australia, in fact, apart from the closure of Ravensthorpe and a clutch of other nickel mines, it was almost business as usual. 'The boom hit a speed bump. There was a hiccup, that's all,' says Tim Treadgold, a Perth-based mining journalist. Now, once again, all the talk is of skills shortages, and Perth airport is congested with men and women in steel-capped boots and orange shirts, waiting to catch charter flights to far-flung mines.

An effervescent character with thick grey hair and chunky gold jewellery, Ashok Parekh owns the Palace Hotel, as well as extensive mining interests. Keen to distance Kalgoorlie from its hard-drinking, hard-fighting, Wild West image, he declares: 'I've operated hotels and nightclubs here for twenty-two years, and the whole scene has become a lot more family-oriented. There are thirty-two hotels in Kalgoorlie, and only seven would have skimpies [scantily clad barmaids].' Parekh whisks me across to the Palace, to show me its restaurant ('The pepper steak is superb') and the newly renovated Gold Bar, a nightclub. 'Yes, we do have adult entertainment a couple of nights a week,' he says. 'But you're catering for different crowds, like anywhere.'

No doubt the miners of yesteryear would find it difficult to credit that book clubs, wine clubs and repertory theatre are now part of Kalgoorlie's social scene, or that the West Australian Ballet can fill the 750-seat Goldfield Arts Centre – or that the commercial sex business has become so sanitised that the few surviving brothels earn more from showing tourists around than from prostitution. Yet this is still a community with a preponderance of transient, cashed-up single men, and it retains a hard edge: alcohol-fuelled violence persists, and those who transgress Kalgoorlie's unwritten codes are quietly run out of town. Hannan Street on a Saturday night is not a place for the faint-hearted.

Families such as the Mahoneys avoid the pubs. 'The town's got everything for the kids, all the sports facilities you can think of,' says Lecky, who manages a gold dealership with her husband, Ted. Ashok Parekh, who is of Irish and Indian descent, feels 'the people are very welcoming of outsiders…They don't care who you are, or what you have or don't have.' Perhaps because of its remoteness – seven hours from Perth, four hours from the port of Esperance – Kalgoorlie has acquired the reputation of a resourceful, can-do place. In the early 1990s, frustrated at government delays in building a bypass road to divert heavy vehicles and equipment, residents got together and built it themselves over a long weekend.

Isolation, a common mission and the challenges of living in a semi-desert environment have forged a strong communal spirit. 'It's harsh conditions, and it attracts a certain type: a person who doesn't mind a bit of adversity,' says Ted Mahoney. But there are chasms within this society: between black and white; between 'old Kalgoorlie' and newcomers; between the beneficiaries of mining and those left behind. Propping up the bar of Boulder's decrepit Grand Hotel, a refuge from the forty-degree heat scorching the deserted wide main street, one old-timer, Malcolm Olden, laments: 'In the past everyone was born here, and we worked shoulder to shoulder at the mines. We were a harmonious community. Nowadays we've got a lot more itinerant workers, and they've brought their own morals and code of ethics.'

And while Kalgoorlie flaunts its multiculturalism, the legacy of migration from Italy and the Balkans, relations have not always been peaceful. In 1934 a miner died after a fight with an Italian barman; locals burnt down the pub, along with houses and shops belonging to southern Europeans; two people were killed as two days of riots climaxed in an onslaught on Dingbat Flat, an immigrant neighbourhood. It was one of Australia's worst outbreaks of racial violence, excluding the frontier wars between whites and Aborigines, and it is still remembered as Kalgoorlie's 'day of shame', according to Bill Bunbury in *Gold: Forgotten Histories and Lost Objects of Australia*.

Elsewhere, Chinese miners bore the brunt of the xenophobia. The Chinese, who landed in Victoria in the early 1850s and pursued the gold rushes anti-clockwise around Australia, were resented for their industriousness, the thoroughness of their mining methods, and their adherence to their own language and culture. The *Ballarat Star* warned in 1866: 'If these heathens who came here to pollute our blood and debauch our young children are not put under severe regulations we may reckon an epidemic sooner or later that may be as deadly as leprosy.' Colonial governments took steps to limit immigration, and the Chinese were banned from new goldfields. However, anti-Chinese protests escalated, and attacks by white miners culminated in a series of riots in 1861 at Lambing Flat (now Young), in central New South Wales.

The hostility unleashed by the presence of the Chinese miners, in particular, reached a high-water mark with the passage half a century later of the *Immigration Restriction Act 1901*, which formed the basis of the White Australia policy. That policy was not formally jettisoned until 1975, and the issues surrounding it – immigration, multiculturalism, racism, Australia's desired ethnic composition – continue to generate profound ambivalence. It seems ironic that China, as the biggest market for Australian minerals, and as a major investor, has become the backbone of the country's mining industry.

ROD WILSON IS driving back and forth across a patch of red dirt, shovelling up earth with his front-end loader. After stripping off a good layer, he jumps out and walks over the plot, slowly waving his metal detector. When his headphones squeal, he investigates with pick and shovel, but today the only spoils are scraps of lead and a rusty nail. 'That's the way it goes,' says Wilson, a former fox shooter from Deniliquin, in New South Wales. 'You find nothing for a week, then all of a sudden it's payday. I'll never be a multimillionaire, but as long as I can feed the animals and pay the bills, I'm happy.'

We're in a parched terrain dotted with stunted white gums, just outside Coolgardie, and the earthmoving machinery – not to mention the metal detector – seems about as far removed from the romance of gold as you could get. Wilson, though, is the contemporary embodiment of a tradition dating back to ancient Egypt, and probably before. So long as men have valued gold they have prospected, and the yellow metal has influenced exploration and settlement on every continent – indeed, mining of all kinds has been so important that the prehistoric ages of man are named after the principal toolmaking materials. In Australia, there would be no mining industry without the individuals who discovered the great ore bodies subsequently exploited by companies: Kapunda, Mount Bischoff, Mount Lyell, Broken Hill, Mount Isa and, of course, Kalgoorlie. But Wilson's predecessors not only located the first copper, gold, lead, silver, tin, iron, coal, diamonds and so on; they also, some historians believe, helped to mould the national character. Enterprise, optimism, rugged individualism, 'mateship', lack of deference to authority, belief in a fair go – such qualities, sometimes defined as quintessentially Australian, crystallised, so it is said, on the nineteenth-century goldfields.

And the love of a flutter – which, along with the hope of winning a fortune, drove people to forsake home and family for the hardships of life on the diggings. The early goldminers gambled with each swing of their pick, and for the diggers of today the motivations are not much different. Rod Wilson, who lives in a simple house shaded by peppertrees with his wife, Donelle, and one dog, three cats, two rabbits and a lorikeet, explains: 'We do gold prospecting during the week and Lotto at weekends, so we've got to have a win somewhere along the line.' One of Australia's most successful prospectors, Mark Creasy, spent two decades in the wilds of the Western Australian interior (on one occasion nearly dying of thirst) before uncovering an immensely rich lode which he sold in 1991, for $115 million. He says: 'It's the game that counts, not the actual pot that you get at the end of it. You just chuck the pot straight back on the table.' Creasy, who is still exploring, although nowadays he employs teams of geologists, adds: 'It's the ambition to succeed at what you've set yourself. It's an intellectual pursuit – you wonder if there's something out there. It's like doing a crossword puzzle or a quiz and getting all the answers right.'

The ground where Wilson forages is only metres from the site of the lucky strike that unleashed one of the world's final gold stampedes. In

September 1892 Arthur Bayley rode into Southern Cross, 190 kilometres west of Coolgardie, with 540 ounces of gold, which he and a mate, William Ford, had collected in an afternoon. Prospectors who followed the pair's tracks 'picked up gold as easily as mushrooms', according to Geoffrey Blainey, and despite Coolgardie soon being eclipsed by Kalgoorlie, the Eastern Goldfields had burst into being. The population of the Golden West, as the colony called itself, nearly quadrupled within a decade, and in 1900 migrants from the east swung an otherwise reluctant Western Australia into voting for Federation – a decision that many in the state, with its disproportionate share of the country's mineral wealth, still rue today.

Such was the lure of the new gold that men disembarking from ships walked cross-country from the coast, pushing a wheelbarrow of possessions through thick scrub for hundreds of kilometres. Many were seasoned prospectors, but here, in one of Australia's most distant and inhospitable regions, they encountered the harshest conditions yet. Unlike elsewhere, these goldfields had, for the most part, not been settled by pastoralists; they were thinly populated by white men, and quite apart from the dust, flies and punishing heat, water was so scarce that it was almost as precious as gold. Malcolm Olden, the long-time Boulder resident, says dryly: 'If you asked for a Scotch and water in those days, the publican would pass you the Scotch and keep his hand on the jug of water.' There were recurrent typhoid epidemics, and a visitor in the 1890s reported that 'one half of Coolgardie is kept busy burying the other half.'

The goldminers – whose lives were transformed by the construction of a water pipeline between Perth and Kalgoorlie, recently recognised by the American Society of Civil Engineers as one of the world's great engineering feats – had much in common with the early pioneers; indeed, one of the nation's most noted explorers, Ernest Giles, took to prospecting later in life and is buried in the Coolgardie cemetery. While the new generation of prospectors might be better equipped, the desert environment is just as tough, and the work is still backbreaking. 'But I'm a lot more fortunate than the old-timers: imagine digging a hole in this heat,' remarks Rod Wilson, who wears dirty jeans, a ripped checked shirt and no hat. Occasionally he finds old bully-beef cans. 'You can see where they [the first miners] had their little camps.'

Unlike iron ore, say, which involves huge capital investment, gold can still be mined by individuals. At its most basic, prospecting requires little more than a pick, shovel, panning dish and dolly pot (mortar and pestle); gold has a high value, and it can be liquidated straight away. (When I visited the Perth Mint, a slightly dishevelled man dressed for the bush wandered into the grand limestone building with a nugget for sale.) Not for nothing is gold known as the 'democratic mineral': a creator of hierarchies, it is also a great leveller. For similar reasons, it suits small companies. Silverlake's Chris Banasik says: 'We decided to go into gold – I'm pretty sure the decision was made over a flat white and a plum muffin in a Perth coffee shop – because, from a mining perspective, it was one of the least complicated things to turn into cash. You don't need squillions of dollars and a railway line; the beauty of gold is that within two days of seeing it underground you can pour a bar of gold, and the next day you can sell it to the Mint. There are very few industries or commodities that afford you that kind of instant karma.'

A century and a half after Ophir, gold continues to enthral; some prospectors still dream about Australia's El Dorado, Lasseter's Reef, claimed to have been found in Central Australia in the 1930s. Gold can be hammered into leaf so thin you can see through it. An ounce can be stretched for eighty kilometres without snapping. Nineteen times heavier than water, gold does not rust or tarnish, and it is almost indestructible: most of the gold mined to date – according to the Perth Mint a total of 160,00 tonnes, which could fit into an average family home – is still in circulation. Both currency and commodity, its primary use – apart from in jewellery – is as a store of wealth; much of the gold removed from the ground, at considerable expense, ends up back underground, in vaults.

And although most of the easily accessible gold has been dug up, it is still possible to hit the jackpot. Bill Powell prospects the old-fashioned way: loaming (tracking a gold source by sifting soil); panning off; dollying (crushing rock); and dry-blowing, using air to separate fine gold from dirt. In 1984 Powell made international headlines when he discovered McPherson's Reward, said to be the most significant find for forty years in the Eastern Goldfields. Powell turned down offers of up to $25 million (including one from Alan Bond) but eventually had to sell the mine, and recently resold it to Ashok Parekh and another Kalgoorlie businessman. Now seventy, Powell lives in a modest house in Coolgardie and drives a decade-old ute.

POWELL IS SOMETHING of a hero to members of the Eastern Goldfields branch of the 105-year-old Amalgamated Prospectors and Leaseholders Association, who gather monthly in a dusty premises in Boulder. The December 2009 meeting, held on a swelteringly hot evening, is sparsely attended; as the APLA's president, Sean Ashcroft, explains: 'A lot of the guys are out in the field, because the gold price is so high.' As flies buzz around, the dozen men and one woman discuss the latest metal detectors and swap rumours about outrageously sized nuggets. 'Anyone else heard about a thirty-ouncer found near Lake Carey?' enquires one veteran prospector, Stuart Hooper. I ask Hooper if he has ever stumbled across anything noteworthy himself. He shrugs and looks embarrassed. 'Not really,' he says. Later, back at my hotel, I notice a newspaper clipping about Hooper's discovery of a 56-ounce nugget, Little Darling, near Coolgardie in 1979.

Bill Powell's father was a prospector who gambled his gold away on the horses; were it not for the kangaroos and rabbits that Powell shot as a boy, his family would have starved. By the age of fourteen, he had his own little mine. 'I never worried about getting rich,' he reflects. 'At different times I've had quite a bit of money, but flash homes and flash motor cars never really interested me. All I wanted was to get a big mine off the ground. I've been wound up by that all my life. If you find a major ore body, you've really achieved something. It's in your blood and you can't leave it alone: you have to keep digging.'

Last year Powell announced he was hanging up his boots. A few months later he put them back on. 'A lot of my old prospector mates are in the cemetery,' he says. 'I used to see them sitting around, and the next thing you knew they were dead. I thought to myself: Don't do that. Get out there and look for a bit more gold.' Does he have gold fever? 'Christ, yes. That's what's wrong with me: I can't get rid of the gold fever; I can't shake it; it's like a bloody disease. I've often said to myself: Why don't I get a little boat and go fishing? But I never do, I just keep going out prospecting. When I finally get to the cemetery I'll still be digging, so long as they bury me standing up.'

At the APLA meeting, much of the conversation is about the array of fees facing prospectors – 'before you can even put your spade in the ground', Sean Ashcroft complains. There is no open talk of insurrection, but I'm reminded of the tumultuous events at Ballarat, on the Victorian goldfields, 155 years earlier. Heavy-handed policing of the licence system, in a place where the alluvial gold was particularly tricky to mine, is thought to have sparked the 1854 Eureka uprising, which saw diggers draw up a list of political demands, burn their licences, build a stockade and raise the Southern Cross. Up to thirty of them were killed during a dawn attack by the military, along with five soldiers; such was the strength of public feeling that juries refused to convict the thirteen men charged with treason.

White Australia's first and only armed rebellion against colonial authorities, Eureka led to the licence being replaced by a miner's right and miners being given the vote. Mark Twain declared: 'It was a strike for liberty, a struggle for principle, a stand against injustice and oppression.' Over the years Eureka has become loaded with meaning: hailed as the birth of Australian unionism, a milestone on the road to democracy and nationhood, and as the first stirring of republicanism. Some think it speeded up the process that saw every colony bar Western Australia gain 'responsible' self-government between 1854 and 1859. And at Ballarat another layer was added to the myth-making already inspired by the gold rushes. 'For many the diggers stand between the convicts and the Anzacs as landmarks on the road towards a national self-image,' the editors of Gold write, and they quote the historian Sir William Keith Hancock's observation in 1930 that Australians 'have acclaimed the diggers as their Pilgrim Fathers, the first authentic Australians...the fathers of their soldiers'. Australian soldiers are still known as diggers, reflecting the miners' heroic aura, but the navy and white Eureka flag – a version of which was brandished by the Europeans who drove the Chinese off Lambing Flat – has increasingly been commandeered by extremists. In January this year the Indigenous filmmaker Warwick Thornton, speaking just before Australia Day, expressed concern that the Southern Cross, used as a guiding beacon by Aboriginal people for forty thousand years, was being deployed as a 'racist nationalist emblem'.

EUREKA IS A white, male story, and so is the story of Australian goldmining, and of mining generally. Yet there were women on the goldfields, if in relatively small numbers, and there are plenty of female prospectors nowadays. As for the continent's Aboriginal inhabitants: they had been mining the land, for ochre and flint, for tens of thousands of years before the First Fleet arrived. Almost certainly they encountered gold, but since it did not appeal as an ornamental material they left it be. At first perplexed by the Europeans' passion for the yellow metal (according to Derek Elias in *Gold*, the Walpiri people called it 'white man's Dreaming' and equated its subterranean veins with Dreaming tracks), they soon realised its trading potential. Aubrey Lynch, a prospector and Wongatha elder, says: 'As a child in the 1940s I can remember walking around with my mother, speccing for gold, with our hands behind our backs, stooping down to look at the ground. We were speccing for gold to live on, to go and buy tucker. My mother, one of the old tribal ladies, had been doing that most of her life. We also told the mining companies where our people had been picking up gold, then the companies went out and got themselves tenements.'

Although Indigenous Australians are scarcely mentioned in accounts of early goldmining, they made some key finds, and no doubt others went unrecorded. In 1871 a stockman, Jupiter Mosman, came across gold-bearing quartz at Charters Towers, which became, for a while, Australia's largest goldfield; in 1932 a cattle hand found gold near Tennant Creek, in the Northern Territory. In addition, as Henry Reynolds writes in *With the White People* (Penguin, 1990): 'Frontier prospectors were often accompanied by, and dependent on, Aboriginal assistants in the same way that explorers and pioneer squatters had been before them. Their bushcraft, tracking ability, and skill at finding water, were all invaluable assets in the interior of the continent and could be directed at seeking evidence of mineralisation in the same way that they were used to find good pastoral country and easy tracks across unknown country.'

In a broad sense, the gold rushes were disastrous for Indigenous people, bringing them into ever worsening conflict with European settlers. They had already been displaced from their lands by the pastoral industry; now, that process accelerated as waves of fortune-seekers surged inland. In Western Australia, the migration of prospectors from the depressed east in the 1890s led to Indigenous workers losing their jobs on stations. By the mid-twentieth century some were employed in mining; Aubrey Lynch worked underground at the Sons of Gwalia mine, 230 kilometres north of Kalgoorlie, in the late 1950s. 'They were only employing non-Aboriginal people at the time,' he recalls, 'but me and another Aboriginal person turned up and asked for jobs and we were taken on. There were a lot of Italians and Greeks there; we were teaching them English.'

Until quite recently, Australian companies made little effort to engage with communities adjacent to mines. Instead, closed towns such as Tom Price – and, more recently, FIFO camps – were built, housing well-paid workers imported from urban centres. The traditional owners of the land that was being dug up were not consulted; sacred sites were mined willy-nilly, and people were prevented from entering leases to take part in ceremonies. Since the mid-1990s the culture has changed, chiefly as a result of the *Native Title Act 1993*, and nowadays companies, as well as negotiating land use agreements, establish community partnerships and set targets for Indigenous employment and training. However, employment levels are still low, and many native title deals have proved divisive, with just a few families receiving royalties. According to Simon Hawkins, chief executive of the Yamatji Marlpa Aboriginal Corporation, the Pilbara's native title representative body, payments to titleholders represent less than one-eighth of a per cent of total mining profits; moreover, royalties are paid only on post-1993 mines. 'Iron ore mining in the Pilbara had been going on for thirty years [before that], without any compensation for the impact on Aboriginal country and culture,' he says.

Projects such as the Ranger and Jabiluka mines, which are enclosed by Kakadu National Park, and the recent five-kilometre diversion of the McArthur River, in the Northern Territory's Gulf Country – designed to enable Xstrata to enlarge a huge zinc facility – were approved against the wishes of traditional landowners, and despite massive protests by environmentalists. Decades of uranium royalties from Ranger, amounting to more than $200 million, have failed to improve the lives of the local Mirrar people. As for the McArthur decision, Charles Roche, of the Minerals Policy Institute, which campaigns against environmentally and socially destructive mining, asks: 'Would a mine that involved the diversion of a river with a substantial white community next to it have happened in southern Australia? Would it even have been contemplated?' Just as the Howard government was endorsing the scheme, Roche notes, it was intervening to scupper a proposed mine in Papua New Guinea because it threatened the Kokoda Track.

In Kalgoorlie, not far from the Super Pit and the ceaseless excavations taking place below, is the community of Ninga Mia, with its run-down houses, packs of stray dogs and rusting abandoned cars. It is hard to imagine a greater divide between black and white, haves and have-nots, mainstream and alienated. Ninga Mia is not marked on town maps; no one from the community works at the pit and, according to Geoffrey Stokes, an Aboriginal pastor, the benefits of living next door to one of the world's biggest goldmines consist of 'sweet nothing, beside the pollution and the dust and the noise'. Stokes says: 'Every week we have a funeral in Kalgoorlie: that's our reality. We die of common diseases while the rest of the community gets fat and rich on our inheritance, our birthright.'

Bryan Wyatt, executive director of the Goldfields Land and Sea Council, was roundly condemned in 2001 when he called Kalgoorlie the most racist city in Australia. Wyatt says he was quoting a Murdoch University survey, and he is convinced that, despite a string of reconciliation-based measures, 'not much has changed'. He mentions a 2010 community calendar published by the Kalgoorlie-Boulder Shire Council, full of glossy photographs, not one featuring an Indigenous subject. The *Kalgoorlie Miner*, meanwhile, ran a cartoon last year portraying an Aboriginal man as a violent, drunken paedophile. Although I knew a little of the region's hard-boiled attitudes, I was unprepared for the casual – and sometimes brutal – racism of many of the white people I met there. One otherwise genial man told me: 'When I was a boy, niggers had to be out of town and they knew their place. Then they made them equal, gave them drinking rights, and look at the spin-off now. They breed like flies; they are totally non-contributing; they are unemployable.'

In Western Australia many Indigenous people feel that the industry, abetted by a royalty-hungry state government, is trampling their rights. Aubrey Lynch, the Wongatha elder, says: 'Exploration is killing a lot of our country, and our cultural ways are being destroyed. Wherever you go in the bush, you see mining pits and the land being cleared for miles around. They destroy our sites; the Super Pit was developed over Dreamtime tracks. Our people are afraid to go out hunting, because they think the kangaroos and goannas are being affected by mining activities – they think the meat will be poisoned.'

Aboriginal employment levels will remain dismal, Brian Wyatt predicts, unless a more imaginative approach is adopted. For instance, working hours in mining – typically, twelve-hour shifts for two weeks, then a week off

– effectively exclude Indigenous people, who need to participate in cultural business. Wyatt adds: 'But you have to remember there are two different cultures here. For Aboriginal people, it's never been about gaining maximum economic benefit from the land. People don't see why they should have to dig up the ground when they've lived on it and hunted on it and just want to be there on it. And it's very difficult to say to them: "You're living on a goldmine; dig it up, and all your worries will go away." Yet if they don't, someone else will come along, grab all the minerals and become quite wealthy.'

Robin Chapple, a Greens politician who represents the Mining and Pastoral Region in the Legislative Council, believes mining companies have 'never really engaged with the Aboriginal psyche'. By contrast, he says, on the Gove Peninsula, in Arnhem Land, an Aboriginal corporation contracted to truck waste from the Nabalco bauxite mine has many more drivers on its books than it requires – a recognition that some work only intermittently.

Yet the likes of BHP and Rio Tinto have made determined efforts in recent years to build constructive relationships; at the latter's Argyle diamond mine in the Kimberley, Indigenous workers make up about a quarter of the workforce, the highest proportion at any Australian mine. Then there are success stories such as that of Daniel Tucker, from the Eastern Goldfields, who – inspired by the High Court's Mabo decision – set up a mining and civil contracting firm, Carey Mining, in 1995. Tucker has become one of Australia's few Aboriginal millionaires; more than half of his employees are Indigenous, and he has contracts with some of the world's largest companies, including AngloGold Ashanti. Out in the bush, small bridges are built. Aubrey Lynch says: 'We sometimes make camp with the white prospectors. There's a bond between you, regardless of colour.'

SONS OF GWALIA, where Lynch was employed, opened in 1896 and was, for a long time, the biggest goldmine in Western Australia outside the Golden Mile. Beside it was a flourishing township, with a general store, butcher, bakery, barber shop, guesthouse, swimming pool and state-run hotel. The underground mine was in its early years managed by a young Herbert Hoover, at that time an engineer with a London firm, later to become the thirty-first president of the United States. Shortly before Christmas 1963 the mine closed down, and Gwalia, home to about 1,500 people, emptied almost instantly; with no other work available, the miners and their families left on a special train sent up from Kalgoorlie, taking only what they could carry.

Today Gwalia, three hours' drive from Kalgoorlie, is all but a ghost town, its peeling shopfronts and deserted cottages an evocative reminder of the transience of mining. Inside the corrugated-iron dwellings, with their sagging bare floorboards and rotting furniture, the remnants of lives lived half a century ago are preserved, thickly covered in dust: a transistor radio, a patchwork rug, an oil lamp hanging on a wall, a twisted iron bedstead, a cracked mirror, a child's bicycle.

The Eastern Goldfields are strewn with such towns: places like Kookynie, a red-dirt wasteland dotted with the smashed ruins of brick buildings, and tiny Broad Arrow, which in 1900 had eight hotels, two breweries, a stock exchange, two banks and a hospital; only one pub and a few houses remain. These 'shooting star' communities sprang up overnight and, as the gold-seekers moved on, died almost as swiftly. The larger towns have survived as administrative centres but have a similar air of decay: Coolgardie, Menzies and Leonora, with their broad, silent streets and handsome historic buildings standing next to boarded-up shops and empty lots.

Wandering through them, you marvel not only at the ruthlessness of boom-and-bust, but that this unforgiving region was settled at all. Much as the locals rave about Kalgoorlie ('It's only four hours from the beach,' several told me), they also admit it would not exist were it not for the gold in the ground. 'There'd be no cause to pitch a tent here; you would just keep on riding your horse past it,' declares Malcolm Olden. The same could be said of Mount Isa, Tom Price, Broken Hill and all the other remote towns established solely because of the presence of minerals, and where, over the decades, those born in or drawn to such places have learned to make the best of things. Without mining, the map of Australia would look quite different, and it is unlikely that the nation would have grown at the same pace, or enjoyed such prosperity. Resources accounted for 41.5 per cent of exports, worth nearly $160 billion, in 2008–09. The country is the world's biggest exporter of iron ore, black coal, lead, zinc and alumina. 'If Australia wasn't mining, it would be bankrupt,' says Tim Treadgold, the Perth-based journalist.

The average lifespan of an Australian mine is ten to twenty years. Gwalia's longevity was unusual, and so is the Golden Mile's, but even the Super Pit will not last forever – it is forecast to shut down in 2021. Communities such as Ravensthorpe know the risks of being a one-company town; while Kalgoorlie has diversified into tourism and the supply of mining services and equipment, and while there are dozens of lesser mines within a fifty-kilometre radius, Kalgoorlie Consolidated Gold Mining – KCGM, which manages the Super Pit on behalf of its joint owners, Newmont and the Canada-based Barrick Gold – wields enormous clout. At least twice it has threatened to close operations unless allowed to proceed with controversial plans: to enlarge a tailings dump, and to build a 3.5-kilometre-long conveyor belt.

Both times the company got its way: no one wants to jeopardise the future of a town which, despite laying claim to the richest square mile of earth in the world, has a history of wildly vacillating fortunes. The gold industry lost its gleam early in the twentieth century and, apart from a mini-revival in the 1930s, it ebbed steadily as other commodities took precedence within the Australian economy. In Kalgoorlie, rising production costs led to mine after mine closing, and in the late 1970s the Golden Mile was on the verge of extinction – saved only by the abolition of the fixed gold price and new processing techniques, which made it profitable to mine much lower grades. Mines reopened and the Super Pit was born in 1989, after Alan Bond conceived of buying up all the old underground leases. (Bond was forced to sell his stake when his business empire crumbled.) Bill Powell still recalls goats wandering through empty houses in Boulder; one of his contemporaries, Doug Daws, was among the nearly eight hundred people who lost their jobs one black day in 1978. 'It's a bloody devastating feeling,' says Daws. 'You got married in the church, you've got kids to bring up – where the hell do you go when you've got a town that is so overwhelmingly consumed by this giant set of mines on your doorstep?'

FOR NOW, THE Super Pit remains Australia's largest open-cut mine; on the opposite side of the country, Newcrest Mining's Cadia Valley gold facility, near Orange, is poised to be the biggest underground mine after an expansion plan was endorsed in January 2010. Generously endowed with minerals and metals, thanks to the age and nature of its rocks and the geological forces at play, Australia had, as of December 2008, the greatest known reserves of uranium, brown coal, nickel, silver, zinc and lead, while its stores of copper, gold, black coal, iron ore, bauxite and industrial diamonds were in the global top six. If a $20 billion development proposal is approved, BHP's Olympic Dam in South Australia – site of the world's largest uranium deposit, as well as gigantic quantities of copper and gold – will become the biggest open-cut mine on the planet: 4.1 kilometres long, 3.5 kilometres wide and up to a kilometre deep. Also on the horizon is the monumental Gorgon liquefied natural gas (LNG) project, off the Pilbara coast, expected to employ ten thousand people and channel $64 billion into the economy over three decades. The coalfields of central Queensland are humming, and geological surveys point to a new Golden Triangle in northern Victoria, with reserves of up to seventy million ounces: nearly as much again as the state's total output since the gold rush began. There is talk of mining space, and the seabed, for gold and minerals. Australia's future is secure, thanks to its natural resources. Or is it?

To say that mining is unsustainable seems to be stating the obvious. If only it were as simple as calculating what is left in the ground and how long it can last – although even that, as it turns out, is far from simple. Resources, clearly, are finite: the moment a mine opens, it begins to die; every ounce of gold mined is an ounce subtracted from the total stores. In its most recent report, Geoscience Australia estimates that stocks of five minerals – diamonds, gold, zinc, lead and manganese ore – will be exhausted within ten to forty years, at current production rates. Those figures could rise (or fall), however, depending on exploration, scientific advances and fluctuating prices; they are also based on identified resources, and it appears likely that Australia will yield more underground riches, even if they are hidden much deeper down. The Perth Mint's Edward Harbuz considers it 'perfectly feasible' that another Super Pit could be found in Western Australia. 'Much of the state is under sand and has never been explored properly,' he says. 'I think we've only just started to extract the minerals of Western Australia.'

Gavin Mudd, a civil-engineering lecturer at Melbourne's Monash University and the author of a study on the sustainability of mining, is convinced that very few commodities will run out in the conceivable future. Nevertheless, he argues: 'It's not how much you're got left; it's the environmental costs of getting it out of the ground and using it. Then you get to the heart of whether the industry is sustainable or not.' As ore grades decline, according to Mudd, increasing volumes of rock have to be moved, consuming ever more energy and water, and creating bigger waste dumps, tailings dams and carbon emissions. In Queensland, ten tonnes of dirt are excavated for every tonne of coal. At Boddington, Newmont is mining ore with less than a gram of gold (the size of a grain of rice) per tonne; a hundred thousand tonnes of rock will be dug up, processed and dumped daily when the site reaches full capacity later this year. Mudd says: 'The pattern of mining for the last hundred years has been bigger trucks, bigger shovels, bigger processing plants. We can't sustain that pattern for the next hundred years.'

Scandals over toxic emissions in towns such as Mount Isa hint at the underside of the mining boom. The Super Pit was one of Australia's largest emitters of cyanide in 2007–08, according to the National Pollutant Inventory, and it topped the league for mercury. Cyanide-laced dams have been blamed for the death of wildlife, including sixty thousand budgies in a single incident in the Eastern Goldfields in the 1980s. Waste rock contains sulphides which, when exposed to air and water, turn into sulphuric acid and drain heavy metals into waterways. The Mount Lyell copper mine in western Tasmania is a notorious example: there is no aquatic life in the nearby Queen and King rivers.

In Western Australia waste dumps are vulnerable to erosion by winds sweeping across an arid, mainly flat terrain, according to Robin Chapple, the Greens politician, while the open pits – apart from being eyesores – are a hazard for cattle. Disused pits fill up with groundwater, which can become hyper-saline, contaminating aquifers and killing vegetation. There is no legal requirement to fill in pits and, so far as the Eastern Goldfields are concerned, Chapple believes: 'It's a case of out of sight, out of mind. The perception is it's a desert and it doesn't really matter.' The Goldfields were once well forested, but they were clearfelled for sixty years to supply the mining industry with fuel.

On the other side of the equation, environmental standards, along with worker safety, have vastly improved – although some companies apply different benchmarks overseas; the infamous Ok Tedi mine in Papua New Guinea, for instance, was majority-owned by BHP until 2002. The Minerals Council of Australia says mining disturbs just 0.26 per cent of the landmass, and companies spend at least $200 million a year rehabilitating slag heaps and tailings dams. The new dam at Boddington, set amid incongruously bucolic scenery, is said to have been designed to world's best practice standards; Newmont is also part-funding a program to conserve endangered cockatoos in the surrounding jarrah forest. Some in the industry describe their interaction with the land in intriguingly positive terms. Campbell Baird, of Focus Minerals, calls mining 'creating something…building underground', while Silverlake's Chris Banasik speaks of the 'privilege' of observing a rock face before it is blasted. Banasik says: 'You've got to treat it with respect, because what you see will never be the same again, and because those rocks are giving you a sneak peek of processes you can't even imagine. Most ore deposits are formed at between six hundred and eleven hundred degrees Celsius. Most are formed under thousands of metres of rock. Most are made from fluids that have come from twenty-six kilometres down. They've tapped the mantle, the earth's molten core.'

FOR TWO WEEKS in 2006, Australians were transfixed by attempts to rescue Brant Webb and Todd Russell, trapped underground at the Beaconsfield goldmine in Tasmania. A century earlier, the nation had been equally gripped by the fate of Modesto Varischetti, an Italian miner who spent nine days in an air pocket in the flooded Westralia mine, near Coolgardie, before staggering out alive with the help of two divers. Fascination, fear, awe, revulsion: the mining business has always aroused strong emotions in people living in urban and coastal areas. It is viewed as dangerous, dirty, brave work; mining has a mystique, but it also has a poor image because of its effects on the environment, and its questionable ethics in some developing countries. John Bowler, the Independent state member for Kalgoorlie, says: 'A lot of people in the cities hate mining, and the industry doesn't sell itself very well; it just gets on with the job of creating wealth. People in the Middle East have a far more positive image, and greater knowledge, of the oil industry than Australians do of mining. The vast bulk wouldn't know and wouldn't care, and some would say: "Close it down; it's raping the landscape.'"

Unlike farming, mining is not part of the Australian psyche, nor is it a sacred cow. Competition for limited resources brings it into conflict with farming and with the wider community; in Orange, fruit growers fear the Cadia Valley expansion will jeopardise their water supplies – in 2007 the town had to donate 450 million litres of water to the mine after Newcrest warned that otherwise it would have to shut down. In Western Australia companies complain that the approvals process is slow and cumbersome, and environmentalists claim the industry almost always gets its own way eventually. Barrow Island, off the Pilbara coast, often called 'Australia's ark' because of its profusion of species that are extinct or endangered on the mainland, is to house a massive plant processing LNG from the Gorgon field, despite the state's Environmental Protection Agency expressing grave reservations. On the Pilbara's Burrup Peninsula, the home of Woodside Energy's Pluto gas scheme, ancient rock art remains at risk. On the Kimberley coast Aboriginal leaders are split over plans to build another LNG processing plant, north of Broome, for the Browse Basin field. At other locations around Australia the delicate balancing act between mining, the environment and the rights of communities, particularly Indigenous people, continues.

Meanwhile, the digging frenzy goes on, along with the debate about Australia's economic future and such issues as clean energy, water scarcity and a carbon tax. Robin Chapple, who has worked for both BHP and Western Australia's Mines Department, is one of many voices disputing the notion that the country's resources are infinite, or as good as. 'Our problem is that we actually believe mining will last forever,' he says. 'What are you going to be doing as a nation when you can't mine, or make mining equipment, or do all the other things associated with mining? Do we have a plan? We don't, because governments of the day can't think beyond the next election.'

The flipside of gold fever is greed, and in the nineteenth century some commentators were perturbed by the rampant materialism associated with the rushes. A letter to the Melbourne *Argus* in 1852, quoted by David Goodman in *Gold*, demanded: 'Should Gold, Gold, Gold, be our only desire? …Was man made merely to acquire glittering metal…Is there no higher object, no more noble aim?' In rather more sober language, the Minerals Policy Institute's

Charles Roche questions the philosophy behind modern mining practice, which he describes as 'ripping the minerals out of the ground as quickly as possible, without lasting benefit to local communities'. Roche suggests that deposits could be mined sequentially, rather than all at once, enabling people to move to a place and build lives, assured of long-term job prospects. He says: 'I believe that the minerals belong to all of us, current generations and future generations, rather than to a particular mining company. Often the benefits leave the site and the problems remain there.' A May 2009 report by the Australia Institute, a left-leaning think tank, reached a similar conclusion: 'Overall the mining boom seems to have had very little positive impact on the wellbeing of the majority of Australians other than those directly affected by the expansion in the mining industry.'

A few decades ago, Kalgoorlie was peppered with headframes, and the town consisted of separate neighbourhoods, each one centred on a mine. Over time they were all consolidated into what became Kalgoorlie-Boulder – except for one, Williamstown, which sits sandwiched between the Super Pit and Mount Charlotte, the sole surviving underground operation. A bleak, sunbaked spot, Williamstown is Kalgoorlie's other forgotten community – although, unlike Ninga Mia, it does appear on the map, and is even pointed out as a curiosity to visitors on bus tours.

Callers to KCGM's 'Public Interaction Line' are greeted by a recorded message advising them to 'please press 2…for today's blasting times'. In Williamstown, Keren Calder points to widening cracks in her living-room wall. 'When there's a big blast, the whole house shakes and it feels like the floor's going to cave in,' she says. 'All the pictures are at an angle, and I've had ornaments fall off the shelf and smash. Visitors get a hell of a fright. The dust is diabolical, too – if I don't sweep my floor every day, it's like someone has emptied a vacuum cleaner over it.' Cheri Raven hears drilling beneath her feet when she takes a shower. 'Sometimes it sounds so close you think a miner's going to pop up the plughole.' Like her neighbours, Raven is certain that KCGM – which has already bought and bulldozed houses in the suburb – would like Williamstown to fade into history. 'But I'm not moving; it doesn't matter how much money they offer me,' she vows. 'My grandparents lived here; my husband and I were both raised here; I've got history here.'

Tony Cooke, an adjunct professor at the John Curtin Institute for Public Policy in Perth, was commissioned by the Western Australian Government to report in 2004 on the gold industry's impact on Kalgoorlie. He says that valuable ore bodies lie beneath residential streets, and he predicts some households in Boulder will have to move as mining activity creeps closer. (KCGM denies it.) Cooke also maintains that the area is unstable because of decades of shaft mining: one person 'lost their washing and Hills Hoist into a hole that just opened up in the back garden', he says, and even cars have been gobbled up. Seismologists, meanwhile, blame mining activity for some of the tremors that periodically shake Kalgoorlie. 'It feels like the Super Pit is swallowing up the town,' says Steve Kean, a Williamstown resident.

Others, in Kalgoorlie and beyond, remain dazzled by gold and its seemingly limitless potential. Tyler Mahoney, Ted and Lecky's fourteen-year-old daughter, found a sliver lying in a puddle in Hannan Street recently, a few hundred metres from the site of Paddy Hannan's strike. In 1995, near Coolgardie, in ground that had been intensively worked for more than a century, the second-largest gold nugget in existence – the Normandy Nugget, weighing more than eight hundred ounces – was discovered. The mine at Gwalia, already reborn once in the 1980s, reopened in 2008, and historic mining towns such as Bendigo and Charters Towers are once again producing gold. Boom and bust, winners and losers, elation and heartbreak: Australia's love-hate relationship with the mining industry shows no sign of waning.

Kathy Marks grew up in Manchester and has been a journalist since 1984, working first for Reuters and then for national newspapers in Britain, including the *Daily Telegraph* and *The Independent*. Since 1999 she has been based in Sydney as *The Independent*'s Asia-Pacific correspondent. *Trouble in Paradise* (HarperCollins, 2009) is her account of the background to the Pitcairn Island sex-abuse trials.

Songlines and fault lines

A question of belonging I

Kim Mahood

K: *Kartiya*, desert term for white person
K: *Kumanjayi*, word that substitutes for a name that can't be spoken

WHEN K rang the station to see if they needed her to bring anything, the manager said, 'Yeah, good, can you pick up a couple of cartons of bread and two packets of .22 Magnum bullets. The TOs have used all my bullets shooting bush tucker. And, yeah,' he said, 'that old Jakamarra says he's going to shoot you when you get here.'

'Why would he want to do that?'

'He's got some idea in his head that you're coming back with a company to take his country away from him.'

'Where did he get that idea from?'

'You know these fellas – someone gets in their ear and winds them up. I told him it was just you coming out to do stories with them. But the old man's adamant. *I'll shoot that woman when she gets here*, he reckons.'

'As a matter of interest,' K asked the manager, 'if they've used all the bullets, what's he going to shoot me with?'

'Probably one of them you're bringing with you, unless he's saved one specially.'

K told him no one was getting any bullets, or bread either, until they'd convinced the old man she was no threat to him or his country.

The old man belonged to a family line she'd not had much to do with, though he'd been present the previous year when they had all discussed the project to record as much surviving traditional knowledge as possible through map-making and oral histories and stories.

The confusion about maps and stories stems from the association with land claimants and royalties accruing from the gold mines in the region. Every year when the royalties are handed out a feeding frenzy ensues, with endless arguments over who is or is not entitled by birth or tenure to claim traditional ownership to the gold-bearing quartzite ridges of the region. Light-skinned distant relatives turn up and are welcomed with open arms, until their claim of kinship entitles them to a chunk of royalty money, when relations turn sour and they beat a retreat with their booty.

K might well turn out to be one of these, given her childhood connection to the country, and the old man was taking no chances. His threat was not to be shrugged off. When he was little more than a boy he had murdered his brother with an axe.

EVERY YEAR SHE comes back; every year the questions resurface about why she does it; every year the first encounter with the light and colour of the desert presents her anew with the astonishing reach of the sky, the symmetries of termite mounds and spinifex, the subtlety that to the untrained eye looks like sameness, that is in fact a country on which the ancient story is written close to the surface.

Why does she come back? Guilt has never troubled her: it has always seemed rather useless. But she has always felt implicated in the Aboriginal story; she can't make sense of her country without its Aboriginal heart, which is neither as simple nor as welcoming as one might wish. Through some accident of association this part of Australia has come to represent something very particular for her. A little to the north is the Aboriginal community to which in the 1950s a young mother took her newborn daughter and joined her husband on what was then one of the remotest places on the continent. Maybe those first years of the child's life wired up the circuits of her brain in a way that left her half-tuned to a world that was always on the brink of audibility, its static interfering with her capacity to give her full attention to the world that she was by skin colour and education destined to inhabit.

Or maybe this is a romantic notion to make sense of the radical instability of her life in middle age, when the static is no longer the secret voice of the country but tinnitus, made more insistent in the night silences of the desert, though there have been nights when the chirrups and hums she thought were the product of her inner ear have proven to be the busy nocturnal conversations of scuttling, creeping desert creatures going about their business.

THE OLD MAN was duly placated, and K travelled with him and his family out to a part of the country where he'd walked as a boy, before he came into the mines and had his first encounter with white people. He was in pain, and grumpy, and continued to refer to K as 'that woman'. She was merely a vehicle to drive him back to his country and give him the opportunity to sing some of the songs he'd been taught, and to claim emphatically as his own a section of the sacred dreaming track that intersected with what K later learned was a possible site for a new gold mine. He had a young wife who kept him hopping. She was a tall, glossy, confident girl, and expensive to keep. The old man was short and froglike, with a vast mushroom of a nose that oozed sebum from its enlarged pores, and she had run away from him several times. He had hunted her down on each occasion with the connivance of her family, who did not want to lose access to his royalty money.

She wasn't impressed with the discomfort of the slow drive through the almost impenetrable wattle and over broken sandstone rubble; she wanted to be back home in the community, watching DVDs and hanging out with friends of her own age.

An account of the old man's early life records the way his people lived in the desert, and it is filled with a hard sexual jealousy that kept the young unmarried men segregated from the married couples and treated as potential predators.

K felt sorry for the old man, and there were moments when he spoke and sang of his country that were very moving. There was a rock hole he remembered, but it wasn't quite where he thought it was, and his pain and exhaustion defeated him. A wattle stake punctured a tyre on the vehicle, and while K changed it the old man and his young wife sat passive and indifferent in the fine winter sunlight. Later, when he had recovered, they sat by the freshwater claypan that marked the northern boundary of his track and K recorded his reedy voice reiterating his claim to that piece of country.

'Mine!' he said over and over. 'Only mine, and that other one Jakamarra. We two for this country, that's all.' He listed all the names of people who might dispute his claim, or make their own bid, and outlined the evidence against them. 'That old man Mosquito, father for that mob, he sat down here only once. That's a liar story they telling for this country.'

'When I was young boy anybody stranger came into our country we spear 'em, same like kangaroo.' He sounded regretful that things had changed.

Kim Mahood grew up on Tanami Downs station. Her memoir *Craft for a Dry Lake* (Anchor) won the 2001 New South Wales Premier's Award and *The Age* Non-Fiction Book of the Year. Her essays have been published in *Griffith REVIEW: Divided Nation, Re-imagining Australia* and *Essentially Creative*.

The resource curse

New outback principalities and the paradox of plenty

Marcia Langton

KARRATHA and Roeburne are neighbouring settlements, one a port and mining dormitory town on the coast of the southern Pilbara region of Western Australia; the other an old town, half an hour inland, where most people are Aboriginal. Karratha has new brick houses, tree-lined streets, substantial amenities, a motel, shopping centre, restaurants and tennis courts. Roeburne is old, dusty, and showing signs of years of neglect: broken fences, potholes, weeds and flaking paint. Here and there a well-kept house and garden appear incongruously among the other homes. A TAFE college, a few offices and a basketball court signal that someone decided to spend some state money in Roeburne, rather than concentrating all new investment in Karratha.

The disparity between these towns is accelerating, and it is driven by the mining boom. In Karratha, everyone who wants to work has a job. In Roeburne, few people have the skills and education to join the fast-paced industries transforming the area. It is not just Aboriginal people or the residents of Roeburne who are falling behind. Anyone who lives in a mining province but does not work for a mining company is disadvantaged in important ways: their income is much lower, yet they must pay the same exorbitant housing, food and services costs, thanks to the localised inflation brought about by the boom.

Not for the first time in Australian history, Aboriginal people and disadvantaged settlers are sharing the pain of the city–bush divide. Now, however, their shared disadvantage is a looming economic and national social policy problem that cuts across the conventional accounts of the 'tyranny of distance' and, in increasingly complex ways, the effects of the mining boom.

The largest escalation of mining and energy activity in Australian history is underway, led by the operations in the Pilbara feeding the astonishing Chinese industrial maw. A litany of new names from remote places has entered the national vocabulary: the Browse, Pluto and Gorgon Liquid Natural Gas Projects, North West Shelf, Barrow Island, Olympic Dam, the proposed Inpex projects and many more. Mining and chemical engineers, geologists and geophysicists are (once again) investment bankers' new best friends and the buzz about the scale of this new boom seems to know no limits.

Exploration expenditure topped $6 billion in 2008–09. In the six months to October 2009 fifteen projects with a capital expenditure of $3.9 billion

---

PREVIOUS PAGE: Fiona Foley, *Signpost II*, 2006. Image courtesy of the artist and Andrew Baker Art Dealer, Brisbane.

were completed. A further seventy-four projects were at an advanced stage with an estimated expenditure of $112.5 billion. The value of energy exports increased to $77.9 billion.

Australia is a rich first-world nation, largely because of this mineral wealth. Yet the wealth is not evenly distributed, and this has produced economic, social and political problems that are likely to become more acute. As always, these appear first along the traditional fault line of Australian politics: federal–state relations. The great wealth has led the federal Minister for Resources, Martin Ferguson, to push for the Commonwealth to be responsible for all resource sector approvals in Western Australia. The resource and energy companies operating in the state are outspoken about what they see as bureaucratic obstacles – legal and administrative hurdles – that engender high compliance costs and slow project timelines.

On the ground the most obvious problem is a growing disparity in income between resource sector workers and others; high salaries are the norm in mining provinces, essential to entice skilled labour to demanding work in remote sites and pegged to a highly profitable industry. It is scarcely surprising that workers are flocking to these new jobs. There is an income hierarchy, and the executive class of professionals, including engineers, are the most highly paid, yet even truck and haul pack drivers earn more than PhD graduates.

THE PERTH AIRPORT at 4 am on any weekday is a bracing experience, and this has nothing to do with the hour or the surly Federal Police and security guards. Upstairs, looking across the tarmac from the Qantas lounge, you can see aeroplanes stretching wing tip to wing tip along the tarmac. The check-in area bursts with workers heading to the mining towns in outback Western Australia. They are big men – there are very few women – and they have the right body mass index; they are fit and healthy. They wear bright orange safety clothes and there's a great deal of khaki and navy uniform-like clothing. Most wear steel-capped safety boots. These are the fly-in, fly-out workers who command high prices for their labour.

The crews fly into settlements that are under the control of the corporations that own the lease. When they are on the job they are billeted in the camps in temporary, mobile accommodation arranged in grids stretching in long lines in compounds surrounded by security fencing.

In the remote towns, local people – the residents of these areas – depend on infrastructure developed for mining operations: electricity, roads and rail, shops, fuel supplies, and even recreational facilities and activities are all provided by the companies. Some become regional hubs home to essential services but many are zones controlled by the companies. As the companies invest to provide normal facilities, the state governments cut back, investing the wealth from the resources boom in the cities. This problem of distribution caused by greedy state government rent-seeking behaviour disadvantages the local residents.

In the south-east corner of Australia, far away from the mines, we can be happily unaware of the new industrial landscapes sprawling across the outback, while benefitting in many indirect ways from the wealth they generate. We can also remain happily unaware of the threats to the Australian economy and social fabric that the non-stop industrial world in the outback might be creating.

The global financial crisis slowed the resources industry only briefly, and now the boom is gathering pace again. The difference between regions in income and investment will continue to grow, as will the other impacts of a two-phase economy, where even at the epicentre of the boom there are vast disparities.

In regions such as the Pilbara the boom has had a marked effect on costs, especially of food, services and housing. The last is a flashpoint: there is insufficient stock; increasing demand and slow building approvals, and inadequate public housing with long waiting lists, force up rents and prices, making housing less affordable. In 2008 Barry Haase, the federal Liberal Member for Kalgoorlie, told the House of Representatives: 'I have probably one of the greatest crises of accommodation of all time across the Pilbara region of my electorate. I know full well the problems. Recently I had a staff member in South Hedland move on from a $51,000-plus a year job. I am unable to replace that person because the person who replaces her needs to go to town and find accommodation that they can actually afford. What is available is going to cost somewhere between $850 and $2,500 a week. Do the math. It does not work.'

DURING THE PRE-GFC boom in 2005 I was invited by Michael Woodley, an Aboriginal resident of Roeburne, to visit the township with Don Voelte, the chief executive of Woodside ('Australia's largest publicly traded oil and gas exploration and production company with a market capitalisation of $13 billion,' according to its website), and several others concerned about how Indigenous people were falling behind while the mining workforce was getting richer. I knew about these problems only from a distance, through discussions with people who had been in mining for decades, people who had chosen the mining way of life. They spoke in worried tones about what was happening to the outback towns and those whose livelihoods now depended on the whim of a company executive on the other side of the planet – as the residents of Ravensthorpe found out in early 2009, when BHP Billiton decided to close the nickel-mining town.

We walked slowly down the street in Roeburne, a well-dressed group, shiny in our clean clothes and respectable shoes. I was becoming embarrassed, but need not have worried. It became clear that we were invited so that we could see first-hand the conditions and try to find some answers.

Michael took us to a particularly decrepit house. There were large holes in the wall, water seeping from broken drains, cracked concrete, and little time to look more closely – was that asbestos? – as we were introduced to the woman of the household. Don Voelte engaged her in conversation, and she waved us in and showed us through two rooms, explaining each problem and how many times she had complained to HomesWest, the state's public housing agency. She had telephoned and written, but no one came. Meanwhile, she paid an exorbitant rent. When we heard the amount, even Don Voelte sucked in his breath. Across the road, a freshly bulldozed site glowed red between two similarly decrepit houses. There had been a house only a few weeks before but it had been condemned, then bulldozed. 'Was a new house being built there?' I asked. 'No.' There was no intention to build on the block, despite the overcrowding in Roeburne.

As we walked around the town and talked to people I began to suspect that HomesWest, like government instrumentalities everywhere, was allow-ing the housing stock to run down in the hope that the federal government or the mining companies would build new houses for the Aboriginal residents, relieving it of maintenance and renewal costs. I had observed this trend before. If there is a single factor, apart from the burden of history and racism, contributing to Aboriginal mortality, ill health and disadvantage, it is the implicit refusal of state and territory government agencies to manage and maintain public housing in areas with high Aboriginal populations and on Aboriginal land tenures.

Settler-Australians not working in the resources sector and Aboriginal people in the mining provinces are at the mercy of economic and policy forces that lower their everyday living conditions, and limit their life chances and opportunities. This has the mark of the 'resource curse,' an economic condition that blights many mineral-dependent nations.

The phrases 'resource curse' and 'paradox of plenty' are used by Richard Auty, emeritus professor of geography at the University of Lancaster, to refer to the social and economic phenomenon in which many natural-resource-rich countries experience poor economic growth, conflict and declining standards of democracy. The Nobel Prize-winning economist Joseph Stiglitz has considered the curse through a development paradigm, based on the distinctive analysis of another Nobel Prize-winning economist, Amartya Sen. Stiglitz argues that the flawed distribution of resource-derived wealth causes poor social and economic activity in mineral-rich areas. In his view this can be overcome by partnering institutional quality and improved governance with sustainable wealth management. He emphasises the need for open and accountable institutions, which reduce the scope for corruption and improve the conditions for investment.

The costs borne by local communities are a concern for the Canadian mining engineer Jason Switzer, who draws attention to the gap between natural resource wealth and social prosperity as a source of conflict in mining regions, which he explains as a result of the inequitable 'distribution of impacts and benefits'. Citing a World Bank assessment of four projects in Columbia, Papua New Guinea and Venezuela, he notes that 'governments reap the most benefits from these projects, while social and environmental costs tend to be borne by local communities.' It is highly unlikely that Australia will suffer the effects of the resource curse at a national level and fail to benefit from a favourable endowment – in Auty's words, 'actually perform worse than less well-endowed countries'. All the indications are that the Australian economy is robust, well-managed and comparatively corruption-free.

The threat of the curse still lingers. It is likely that costs in the mining provinces will rise and cause problems for residents who are caught in highly localised impacts. In the Pilbara anger is mounting as the distress of the locals becomes more apparent. A caravan park berth now costs a thousand dollars per week.

In 2008, even before the most recent phase of the boom, Barry Haase told the parliamentary Housing Affordability Committee how severe the situation had become, painting a vivid picture of a housing crisis with all the hallmarks of the resource curse: 'I am afraid that, like the former state Labor government in WA, this federal government has no idea of what is happening out in regional Australia…The electorate of Kalgoorlie is a far cry from the comfortable metropolitan electorates. Years ago, if Australians talked about high rents, they may have, with bated breath, told each other stories of the unbelievable rental prices they heard of in Sydney, maybe even of the prices in some of the suburbs in the Housing Minister's electorate.

'That was before the mining boom. Now we hear stories about the unbelievable rental prices in mining towns, the seemingly ridiculous prices people will pay and the lengths they will go to just to secure a caravan site, a shipping container or a shed to live in. If you are lucky you will get a two-storey shipping container, and that is high living!

'Mining is a key industry in the Kalgoorlie electorate and it is not just my electorate but Western Australia at large and, indeed, nationally. The economy's big benefit from the boom, of course, has been national. Everyone is getting a slice of the Pilbara cake, but they do not suffer the pain would-be residents are suffering. There is a predictable effect when an industry that generally operates in remote areas increases exponentially almost overnight. The Pilbara has made its name in iron ore and, as iron ore boomed, the industry cried out for more workers and affordable accommodation became harder and harder to find.

'It is especially true for permanent affordable accommodation...a modest three-bedroom, one-bathroom house can set you back $1,500 a week in rent and a brand new four-bedroom, one-bathroom house will set you back more than $2,500 a week – that is, if you are lucky enough to get a rental. There is such a high demand that landlords can choose from the many applicants for each house, and I know that when a tenant moves on, often because of the absolutely unsustainable rental prices, the landlord has the opportunity to increase the rent. In the early days – and I am talking two years ago – rents were doubling from one tenant to the next. There is a very scary world out there if you have not been to the Pilbara and you lob in there expecting to find accommodation.

'It is common knowledge that our miners work hard in tough conditions and get paid well for it, but what about the rest of the community which supports those mine workers – government workers, nurses, teachers, et cetera?

'The whole GEHA [Government Employees' Housing Authority] housing system in Western Australian regional centres has virtually collapsed because the Labor government, over the last eight years, has not put money into it. Local government employees and small councils simply have to acquire land and build houses to try to accommodate their workers. Small service organisations cannot get staff simply because they cannot accommodate those staff. So the level of service for all industries in my Pilbara towns deteriorates.'

A YEAR BEFORE Barry Haase's impassioned plea the then Treasurer of Western Australia, Eric Ripper, had gone cap in hand for an increase in funding for Commonwealth Rental Assistance payments for the low-income earners in his state. The Department of Treasury and Finance had found that low-income earners in the private rental market have been hit hardest by strong house price growth. In Perth, where rents have increased by 83 per cent since 2001, rental assistance payments had increased by only 18 per cent. In December 2001 assistance covered a third of the median rental price for a three-bedroom house in Perth; five years later it covered just over a fifth. Ripper wanted more Commonwealth funding for the scheme, because this 'would provide an added incentive for people to live and work in areas such as the Pilbara'.

At the time that Haase and Ripper were complaining about a lack of Commonwealth assistance, Western Australia received astonishing mining royalties. The royalty income from iron ore alone in 2005–06 was $679,628,477 and by 2008–09 had jumped to almost three times that, at $1,946,717,875. In 2008–09 the total value of production of iron ore was $33.6 billion.

Western Australia's dependence on mining incomes is a particular feature of the national economy, accounting in 2006, before the GFC, for more than a quarter of Australia's royalty collection. The WA government expects to receive $2.6 billion this financial year from mineral royalties, thanks to increasing iron ore prices (which are predicted to make up 80 per cent of mineral royalties) and the depreciation of the dollar.

The scale of mining revenue elsewhere is equally remarkable. In 2008–09 Queensland received $3.3 billion in mineral revenue and New South Wales $1.28 billion. Mineral companies contributed more than $7 billion in royalties as a part of $18 billion in state and federal taxes in the 2008/09 financial year.

Forecasters are confident that China's economy will continue to grow. Some think it will continue to grow rapidly for a long time, while others predict that the rates will decline but remain above those of developed economies. China's rising incomes, extraordinarily high investment rates and increasing urbanisation are leading to almost exponential rises in demand for resources – and driving the Australian boom.

In 2008 Treasury officials considered that, while previous 'terms of trade' booms were short-lived, the current boom could be more enduring. Following the initial GFC-induced slowdown, this view is still strongly held. The prospect of 'Dutch disease' – whereby other traded parts of the economy shrink in real as well as relative terms, becoming less competitive as the resource sector surges ahead – was deemed to be less of a threat than expected. So far, Treasury officials say, 'The economy's reactions to the terms of trade boom have largely matched the predictions of economic theory: incomes have risen, as have employment and investment, in particular for the mining industry and regions where mining is concentrated.'

'Dutch disease' describes the 'economic distortion that export booms can induce in a mineral-dependent economy' as non-mining sectors suffer and other exports become 'less competitive and wages more expensive'. Political explanations of the failure of resource-rich countries generally point to mismanagement of the boom and identify 'policy failure as the prime cause of the underperformance'. This might include greater 'rent-seeking behaviour by individuals, sectors or interest groups, and the general weakening of state institutions, with less emphasis on accountable and transparent systems of governance'.

Before the GFC, the resources and energy companies were able to recruit workers in an economy with less than full employment without harming other sectors of the economy. When labour shortages became apparent, workers were imported on special visas from the Asia-Pacific region. It is clear that, as Treasury officials have noted, 'Going forward, expanding labour supply in the resource rich regions of the country will be a central policy challenge.' In other words, Dutch disease and perhaps highly localised resource curses could threaten the bright future where 'higher terms of trade presents an opportunity to raise Australian living standards.' Policy frameworks are being tested 'in ways they have not been tested before'.

The rapid rise of China and India as so-called emerging economies has proved wrong several predictions about the stability of the Australian economy. In the 2002–03 Budget Papers, Treasury described the diversification of Australia's trade, the 'improved insulation of the Australian economy from foreign economic events, and the generally more stable global economy'. Not long after, the terms of trade rose to their highest level in half a century as commodity prices soared. The impact of the rise of China and other emerging economies had been radically underestimated.

WE CAN FIND out easily enough what policy settings might be used to avoid Dutch disease, from Treasury papers online, but the approach to the welfare and living conditions of the residents of mining towns and other settlements in outback Australia, including the economic future of the growing Aboriginal proportion of that population, is almost impossible to discern. My question is this: *are* there any policies to counter the growing disparities in income, living conditions and opportunity in the mining provinces?

This question should be a high priority for the political class. The Australian Labor Party lost the last election in Western Australia, and the balance of power is held by an independent because of the failure to acknowledge the localised impacts in the Pilbara, Kalgoorlie and Kimberley.

The mining regions are the source of enormous revenue, yet their residents are disadvantaged and deprived of services. Because Australia is a wealthy, developed nation with a robust and well-managed economy, the policy problem has been disguised. Put bluntly, the state governments are rent-seekers, eager to extract benefit, slow to put anything back. Rent-seeking is one of the triggers of the resource curse, although it offers only short-term political benefits. As the resource economists from the Colorado School of Mines Graham Davis and John Tilton wrote in 2005: 'The mining rents captured by the state end up in government coffers, which often cater to the ruling elite. For this and other reasons, mining accentuates the income disparity between urban and rural areas and the poor are largely excluded from any benefits…Even worse, the presence of mining rents may lead to a decline in institutional quality…and in some instance to civil insurrection and war…Even when the rents are not squandered, but used by the government to promote economic development, the results are often disappointing, due to incompetence and poor planning.'

For these reasons, a widely supported view holds that the negative association between mining and economic development is not causal, yet the complexity of the problem works against universal policy solutions. The conventional view of mining is that good governance can 'ensure that mining rents are reinvested in human capital and other assets that promote economic development. As always, good governance requires adequate incentives, either by extensive property rights and a domestic political structure that constrains inappropriate public sector behaviour, or by international pressures to loan programmes.'

The Commonwealth Grants Commission calculates the federal redistribution of income according to levels of need in the states and territories. This money rarely finds its way back to the most disadvantaged communities. State governments that engage in a form of rent-seeking are more inclined to use the Commonwealth transfers to benefit the residents of capital cities and marginal seats. This further accelerates the disadvantage of those in mining regions, especially Aboriginal citizens.

Monash University's Professor John Nieuwenhuysen, the first economist to study mining and its impacts on Aborigines, wrote in 2009: 'After yet another major mineral boom in Australia, when in the five years to 2006 mining export revenues rose by over $100 billion (or around 70 per cent), Indigenous people still do not share equitably in the vast incomes which are generated from their lands in the remote regions of Australia.' The words of Minister Jenny Macklin in 2008 that the potential of 'millions of dollars to be harnessed for economic and social advancement of native title holders, claimants and their communities' remained to be realised are also a sorry reflection on events in the last twenty-five years. In this comment, Minister Macklin was echoing former Minister Amanda Vanstone, who asked why land-rich Indigenous people were 'dirt poor', and why the traditional owners of the land were the most disadvantaged living upon it.

The contrast of Aboriginal poverty on the edges of the mining towns with the wealth of the mining workforce, despite the increasing numbers of Aboriginal people entering that workforce, is stark.

WEIPA, NHULUNBUY, TOM Price and Jabiru are examples of the distinctive contribution of mining to life in remote areas, where corporation-run principalities dominate the new outback. These places are company towns in every sense: companies not only generate the work and develop the infrastructure, but their ethos shapes social relations, opportunities and expectations.

The Australian patchwork of mining principalities is a product of a distinctive legal framework. From the nineteenth century, mining towns were gazetted and acts of parliament framed mining leases and large-scale operations. Since then, and for much of the twentieth century, mine operators and governments ignored the detrimental effects of mining on traditional owners. Indeed, governments often removed Aboriginal people from mining areas to allow unimpeded development.

This began to change with the election of a Labor government in 1972. The Whitlam government recognised distinctive Aboriginal and Torres Strait Islander cultures, and the need for Aboriginal organisations to deliver services. The symbolism of this was captured when Whitlam gave the Gurindji people at Wattie Creek a lease over their traditional lands. Aboriginal land rights in the Northern Territory and national anti-discrimination laws soon followed. These policy changes have had a direct, if delayed, impact and helped create the new outback which is now underwriting the wealth of the country.

At first mining industry leaders were among the most outspoken opponents of land rights and native title. Many believed that Aboriginal responses to proposals for exploration and mining were unreasonable, largely because they were different to the conventional arrangements. Industry bodies argued that Aboriginal objection to the rapid expansion of mining was holding back economic development. Aboriginal people were demonised. Gloomy investor forecasts made matters worse. There was fear that open-ended land claims by Aboriginal people would limit expansion, and produce unsustainable legal and financial consequences.

It was widely held that Aboriginal people were making ambit claims to which they were not entitled. Many in the industry treated Aboriginal objections with contempt, and state governments inhibited constructive talks between mining companies and Aboriginal groups.

During this period interaction with mining companies increased and became more confrontational. In 1978 the Kimberley Land Council was formed to prevent mining companies from proceeding without the approval of traditional owners, and international campaigns protesting the desecration of Aboriginal sacred sites damaged the industry's reputation. Previously, few questions had been asked about the way the industry operated; governments had encouraged unfettered exploration and new operations because of their contribution to economic growth. By the 1980s concerns were raised and attracted public attention throughout the world – protests were delivered by critics at national and international forums.

There was scepticism in mining and government circles about what they saw as the 'politics of embarrassment', yet it provided a powerful incentive for the industry to build a new relationship with Indigenous people. When in the late 1980s mining companies began to explore the reasons for resistance to mining, they discovered that many Aboriginal groups were not opposed to mining but concerned about racist and inequitable practices being replicated in new ventures. What the groups wanted was guaranteed recognition of their inherent rights and interests, and acceptable terms for cultural, social and economic futures.

It became clear that while the mining industry was the target of criticism, governments were avoiding their responsibility to provide education, training and health services in the areas where mines were operating. At the time, the legislative framework that the mining industry now relies on for consulting with Aboriginal people about mining proposals did not exist in most states; in the Northern Territory the mining provisions of the land rights legislation had not been tested.

Mistrust and fear on both sides prevented clear communication. Indigenous people were poorly consulted about new proposals, and anxious that their cultural heritage would be destroyed, the environment irreversibly degraded, and their rights and interests as traditional owners lost to company leases. Aboriginal people had long been discriminated against in employment and training, and there was little evidence that companies would provide employment for local Indigenous people.

THE EFFECTS OF the current resource curse in the Pilbara are reminiscent of the mining boom in the 1960s. Aborigines were the intended losers then; now all locals, regardless of background, are losers if they do not work in the industry. In the 1960s government policies were raw and brutal, and companies took a bare-knuckled approach to securing resources. Bauxite was discovered near Weipa in 1955, Comalco was established in 1957 and the first commercial shipments of bauxite commenced in 1963. That year, at a tiny remote Aboriginal settlement on western Cape York, the state police burnt down the houses and church. The Aboriginal community living at the Mapoon Mission was forcibly relocated to New Mapoon, near the tip of Cape York. The official explanation referred to the rationalisation of missions, but many believe that the intention was to allow bauxite mining unimpeded.

This act had lasting implications for relations between the Indigenous people and miners, and sullied the reputation of the industry. A campaign by churches, unions and international groups protested the treatment of Aboriginal people, and Aboriginal land councils were formed to prevent recurrences and secure recognition of rights to traditional land.

In 1965 the Queensland Government granted a mining lease covering 5,500 square kilometres to Comalco, a lease area now reduced to 2,500 square kilometres until 2041, with the right of further extension for another twenty-one years. Weipa was built as a company town and is largely populated by non-Indigenous people who have relocated temporarily. It is connected by a daily jet service to Cairns (some seven hundred kilometres south-east) and by eleven hundred kilometres of unsealed road that is usually impassable from December to April. Bauxite is transported out of Weipa, and supplies come in to it, through the Gulf of Carpentaria.

In response to the common law recognition of native title, Comalco's parent company, Rio Tinto, developed a policy of active and formal engagement with Indigenous peoples. At Weipa it recognised that a sustainable long-term relationship with traditional owners and neighbouring communities was essential and, following the Wik judgment by the High Court in 1996, Comalco signed a Memorandum of Understanding with the Cape York Land Council and agreed to negotiate a comprehensive agreement. Comalco was not legally required to enter this agreement, but understood that reciprocal recognition of the interests was overdue. The negotiation of this agreement took six years, and the Western Cape Communities Coexistence Agreement was finally signed in early 2001.

The township of Weipa, with two thousand mainly non-Indigenous people, has a hospital, well-resourced schools and other essential amenities, and has become the regional centre. Seven kilometres south, Napranum is home to a thousand predominantly Indigenous people. Two hundred kilometres south by dirt road is Aurukun, another Indigenous town of a thousand. Eighty kilometres north of Weipa, on the site of the former mission, Mapoon (Marpuna) is a recently established township of 350 people.

Nhulunbuy, on the Gove Peninsula on the western shore of the Gulf of Carpentaria, is a mining town established by legislation in 1968 to enable the mining and treatment of bauxite. The leases were contested by traditional owners, and although the plaintiffs were ultimately unsuccessful the Northern Territory Supreme Court recognised that they had a system of traditional laws and rights.

Construction of Nhulunbuy commenced near Yirrkala, the Methodist mission where the court challenge originated. The town was established to service the mining operations throughout the region. In 1973 Nabalco, a Swiss–Australian consortium, started mining and processing the 250-million-tonne bauxite deposit – one of the largest in the world. Nhulunbuy, the fourth-largest town in the Northern Territory, is home to about four thousand people.

The traditional owner Galarrwuy Yunupingu has said, 'When we first responded to mining, we said, "No mining, no mining." When the mining companies came, they brought social change. There was walkabout land with food, a billabong. That land became the Woolworth's. Now everybody stands around the takeaway, the diet gives us diabetes…it is now no good thinking that mining can be stopped and will not continue. We have to work together with the mining companies to mitigate the socially damaging side of mining.'

Another Yolŋu man added, 'what is left is *not* his land.' Mining is by nature finite: the ore body is removed. In the process the land, rivers, underground water and vegetation are irreparably and irreversibly altered.

In the Pilbara, Aboriginal people were artisanal miners after World War II. They have lived on the margins of the large-scale mining operations that commenced in the 1960s. There are more than ten agreements in the region, including the Yandicoogina Regional Land Use Agreement, the first for a major resource project to be concluded after the High Court's Mabo decision. It covers an area of 26,000 square kilometres in the central Pilbara and was signed in 1997 between Hamersley Iron, a wholly owned subsidiary of Rio Tinto, and the Gumala Aboriginal Corporation, representing the native title claimants. It was negotiated to enable the development of the Yandicoogina iron ore mine and its associated infrastructure. It includes provision for long-term community benefits, such as employment and business development, and financial benefits of $60 million over the estimated twenty-year life of the mine, paid in annual instalments to a trust fund to support the community. For complex legal and political reasons these funds have not resulted in improved socioeconomic outcomes.

More mining towns were gazetted by legislation in the following decades. As the settlements become operational the companies running them have become surrogate governments, delivering services and ensuring law and order. State governments effectively delegated their powers and responsibilities – formally through legislation and informally through budget cuts – to the mining companies. The governments rely on the companies to provide the services that they fail to extend to remote area citizens.

Historically, local Aboriginal people were excluded from working in the industry. More recently, the corporate resolve to employ Indigenous workers has done little to improve conditions – economic growth for Aboriginal people is declining relative to the population, life expectancy is in the mid-fifties for men and early sixties for women, dependence on government support remains high, and the relative wellbeing of Indigenous people living adjacent to major long-life mines is similar to that elsewhere in regional and remote Australia.

While the regional Pilbara labour market has grown in size and complexity, Indigenous participation has remained marginal. Over the past thirty years there has been a shift from reliance on the pastoral industry for employment to dependence on government through work-for-the-dole. Over this time the trade skills of young people have not improved. This is conspicuously similar to resource curse conditions in the developing world. The low levels of Aboriginal education and skills, combined with racism, poverty, poor housing, and high levels of morbidity and mortality, have contributed to low levels of participation, far below parity, 'across the full range of activities associated with the region's key economic sectors'.

THESE LOCAL IMPACTS reveal some of the tensions in the Australian mining boom: the lack of coherent and consistent policy, and confusion about the economic future of the Aboriginal people living in the shadow of mining projects. While the right to negotiate provides significant new opportunities, low levels of education and work-readiness pose difficult challenges for those companies seeking to ensure measurable improvements in Indigenous wellbeing.

There are sufficient similarities with other resource-rich countries to highlight the need for more effective measures within regionally integrated strategies. The relative absence of federal investment in education, health and social infrastructure, compared with the funding for mining projects, has the potential to make this worse – both during the construction and operational phases, and when the projects eventually close. The 'poverty as capacity deprivation' analysis so persuasively argued by Amartya Sen is evident in the Pilbara: 'Despite unprecedented labour demand…the capacity of local Indigenous people to benefit remains substantially constrained by their limited human capital.'

The effects of the resource curse in regional Australia should be a greater policy concern for all governments. The demographic profile of regional and remote Aboriginal populations is overwhelmingly young: their future depends on their inclusion in the economy, through education and work.

Mining is the only significant industry in remote communities, and dependence on it may leave these communities in a precarious position when an operation closes. This is recognised by the Minerals Council of Australia, which has expressed the concern of its members that their reputations will suffer when closures affect Aboriginal communities. The council recommends establishing lasting relationships to enhance 'the industry's sustainable development credentials by contributing to the development of prosperous and sustainable regional communities'. Mining company representatives see the failure of governments to invest in mining regions, despite the resource industry's royalty payments, as a significant contributor to the problem.

At core is the issue that Richard Auty described: 'The sustainable development of mineral economies lies in the successful diversification into competitive non-mining tradeables. The mineral sector should not be regarded as the backbone of the economy; instead it should be viewed as a bonus with which to accelerate economic growth and healthy structural change.'

Developing economic diversity in Australia's mining provinces has significant challenges. We need adequate political, legal and accounting arrangements to make possible community and regional 'import substitution' and 'export promotion' strategies. This is beginning, as Aboriginal organisations established primarily for community development and maintenance, or natural resource management and environmental protection, secure contracts from governments, mining companies and others for goods and services.

The vital role of Aboriginal organisations and individuals in regional economies suggests that, in addition to the potential for regional co-operation to enhance the capacity of individuals and organisations, there are significant financial benefits that may result from efforts to realise Aboriginal 'economies of scale' and leverage. Yet the responsibility for encouraging and funding education, health services, housing and other basic infrastructure lies with state and territory governments – which have historically neglected, and continue to neglect, the citizens of remote Australia, especially the Aboriginal peoples. Until this is resolved, and the other inequities addressed, there is a ticking time bomb in the remote economic heart of the nation.

References available at www.griffithreview.com

Marcia Langton has held the foundation chair of Australian Indigenous Studies at the University of Melbourne since 2000. She has undertaken ARC-funded research on agreements with Indigenous people, especially involving resource companies, and consulted to mining and energy companies, including Rio Tinto, Woodside and Argyle, and Aboriginal people involved in negotiations, since 1995. Her essays in *Griffith REVIEW* include the winner of the 2008 Alfred Deakin Prize for Best Essay Advancing Public Debate, 'Trapped in the Aboriginal reality show', and 'The end of "big men" politics', which was shortlisted for the 2009 John Button Prize.

Julie Chevalier

Coffee at Coledale

you escape from home during a real estate inspection,

a table outside chedo's   *special: croatian spit roast.*

focused on perfection, you adjust chedo's doormats,

move the sea-blue dog bowl one-half centimetre to the right.

a white cab glides to a stop

a woman in slippers and a belted coat steps out

more skim, flat and white than your coffee –

no longer hot, her ends split and roasted.

you redraw the parting in her hair, correct two spelling errors

on the blackboard menu, adjust the waitress's apron

& straighten the cab's antenna.

the woman sidles out of the-shop-with-the-

heineken-sign   two shopping bags clink

into the ample storage space in the boot.

the woman stumbles into the back seat

(you iron the surf calm as a silk sarong –

white caps & whales have no place

at a real estate inspection)

the cab slides away on automatic.

We Know the Coal Coast claims the real estate billboard.

Julie Chevalier's poems and short stories have appeared in *Meanjin, Antipodes, Southerly, Island, Overland, Blue Dog* and *Overland*. 'Suite: FA' was published in *Griffith REVIEW 26: Stories for Today*.

The dirt game

VINCENT LONG

From dwarves to giants

In the valley of the coal corporations

Sharyn Munro

The Cough... stone dust   22/50   Noel Counihan 47

A summer evening on the veranda of the old Minmi pub, a cooling uphill breeze, the beers cold and poured with the perfect head by publican Bill. It's the early 1970s and I am here as half of a 'blow-in' couple, residents of only five years' standing in this ex-coalmining village: two hundred people, one pub, one post office, no shop.

Pete stops by our table, fresh schooner of Old in hand and fresh news to tell.

'Well, looks like me truckin' days are nearly over. Bob just told me he's got me in at his pit. I'll be laughin' all the way to the bank, with the money them miners get!'

'But Pete, won't you mind being underground for hours and hours?' I ask, shuddering at the prospect.

He plonks himself down on the chair opposite me and takes a long pull on his beer. I bet he's thinking, *Bloody woman, always askin' stuff out loud that's best left in ya head*, but Pete's a kind-hearted bloke; he knows that if I haven't got all the rules of village behaviour right yet, I am trying.

'Ter be honest, I dunno, but I reckon if other blokes can put up with it, I can.'

Pete's been doing the interstate Brisbane run for years, flying past mountains and moors, forests and farms, under sun and rain; now there would be only tunnels and artificial lights, deep underground. While the men talked wages and loadings and perks to scam, I tried to imagine Pete as a miner, working where fairytale dwarves, not men, belonged. It wasn't easy, as I'd hardly ever seen Pete wearing anything other than thongs and faded navy singlet and stubbies, and he couldn't wear those down the mine.

I knew miners had hot showers at the pits these days, but still my mind's eye insisted on the blackened face, neck and hands of 'The Collier', on the contrasting paleness of his naked torso above the dangling braces and sooty trousers as he washed himself in the tin dish in front of the fire. My collier was as out of date as the rest of DH Lawrence's world, yet as the nineteenth

---

PREVIOUS PAGE: Noel Counihan (1913–1986), *The cough...stone dust*, 1947. Courtesy of Counihan Artworks and the National Gallery of Australia.

century rolled into the twentieth, when Minmi was in its coal heyday, its miners would have been very like him.

Old Charlie, the bar elder I had befriended despite my double handicap of sheila and newcomer, had told me his dad used to come home 'lookin' like a blackfella, 'n' send me straight upter this very pub with the billy fer 'is beer, while 'e scrubbed up'.

Six days a week, from 6 am to 6 pm, the miners had worked at depths of a hundred feet, picking away at the coalface by candles or oil lamps, with inadequate air, and often in high temperatures. Ventilation had depended on draughts induced by furnaces at the top of the shafts, with boys as young as eight employed to sit in the dark for the twelve-hour shifts to operate the ventilation doors; for decades the miners had fought unsuccessfully for adequate ventilation. To make conditions more unpleasant, there was water in the Minmi workings.

They don't sound as claustrophobic as the mine in George Orwell's 1937 essay 'Down the Mine', but would we know about that had not a literate and literary outsider bothered to go down and experience it for himself? 'Most of the things one imagines in hell are there – heat, noise, confusion, darkness, foul air and, above all, unbearably cramped space.'

Those men had to stoop or crawl through miles of tunnels to reach the coalface, and then shovel the coal from a kneeling position! Orwell noted they were well-built, strong men – and short. Not enough dwarves about, for 1937 was also the year in which Tolkien published *The Hobbit*; dwarves would have been undergoing a resurgence in the popular imagination, where they were too busy having adventures to go mining – or not for coal, anyway.

NOBODY HAS LEFT us a graphic underground story of Minmi's miners.

Bill's pub was the sole survivor of a reputed fourteen watering holes – only about half of which would have been even half-reputable – which had eased the dusty throats and worried minds of the men living and working in what coal had made the third-largest town in the Hunter Valley by 1900, with five thousand residents.

His pub was all that kept the bonds of community from fraying apart, stretched as they were between the remaining scattered inhabitants. The pub and some of the houses lined the one tarred road that zipped through the village to the world beyond, and a single proper dirt road, once the main street, ran parallel along the ridge of the hill, with the two churches and our place – once the courthouse–jail–police station–residence – standing in grand brick isolation.

Most people lived down dirt tracks threading through the green tide of kikuyu grass that still vaguely delineated the paddocks and fences and chimney stumps it had swamped. These remaining miners' cottages were tiny weatherboard boxes: pitched tin roofs, front verandas, low back kitchen skillions, outdoor laundries and further outdoor dunnies. Of necessity, the latter were still in use. Those tracks had once been streets packed with rows of cottages, slowly cannibalised to keep the surviving buildings habitable.

All the old bustle of butcher and baker and candlestick maker – well, shoemaker, at least – of grocer and haberdasher, and even jeweller, was long stilled. The last general store had collapsed by the main road, left as it fell in its final sideways slump, faded blue Bushells Tea sign askew, for all to witness that it had died on the job.

Only the village post office remained unaccountably open. I stepped back in time when I entered to check for our mail, since the post office slumbered on in a building as imposing as our courthouse. In the 1890s, the easily worked red cedar *Toona australis* was still plentiful. As in other boom towns of the time, the government builders had used it lavishly here, on ceilings and partitions and the broad counters of single cedar slabs, their red gold disguised under the dark varnish of the past.

Being a teacher, I always went after school, so the western sun would be pouring in through the big semi-circular leadlight window opposite the counter. It turned the official notices yellow, curling them like scrolls around their drawing pins, then jumped the counter to highlight the emptiness of the dusty pigeonholes before striking a gleam off the black marble fireplace in the office behind – like a flash of the grand old days, I used to think.

I'd blended pub lore with what I'd read about those days. The town had flourished after J & A Brown bought the mine from John Eales in 1859, who had built it and the rail line to Hexham. The Browns' new large engineering, smith's and carpenter's workshops, coke ovens and quarry attracted workers to what was considered an isolated place, with the offer of cottages for rent at a shilling per week or land on which to build their own cottages, but without tenure. It was a private town, and hundreds of families were turned out of their homes in the strikes of 1860 and 1895, when the miners refused a pay reduction.

For as the coal prices dropped, so did the miners' hewing rates – and they were paid only for what they cut, which in turn happened only when the company had an order to fill, so they could go for weeks without any income.

Even the other employers, the shopkeepers, were company tenants; every family depended on the mine. When the company declared 'Close the pit!' in 1925, it meant 'Wither and die!' to the town. It is said to have been a punishment to the miners who had insisted on quitting work to attend a fellow miner's funeral, following refusal of their official request to do so. A good story for the bitter unemployed to pass on – but though productive Minmi had long been a troubled mine, with legal disputes, a flooding, deals back and forth, the miners owed wages and, once out of work, on charity for eighteen months.

The coal barons had always called the shots, above and below ground; they abandoned both mine and town, but refused to sell anything. Families moved away as soon as their men found employment. Only the unsuccessful few had stayed on as squatters in the cottages, free of rent only because they were forgotten. These dwellings were shored up and tacked on to and passed down to descendants, some of whom worked in other Hunter pits. By the 1970s the world mostly passed the village by, though sometimes I spotted small groups of earnest elderly ladies arriving in Mini-Minors to inspect what headstones in the cemetery were visible under the encroaching blackberries.

Whenever I could, I explored past the realm of kikuyu into the surrounding regrowth bush of spotted gums, ironbarks and wattles. The ghosts of the old town stretched far beyond the present one, hiding behind a solitary intact chimney, small piles of crumbling pinkish bricks or a few staggering runs of grey picket fence bearded with lichen. Tin bathtubs, buckets or cooking pots lay rusting into filigree beneath bushes of telltale foreign bright green. As I foraged among the ruins, collecting small bottles and broken willow plate, the bush was peopled with my imaginings of the past lives here, both the living and the dying dictated by coal, with the swift blow of the crash reminiscent – for fanciful me – of Pompeii or Atlantis.

I found the railway line which had taken the coal to Newcastle, and ventured a little way into the mouth of its dark and dripping long brick tunnel under the hill; I was shown broad pit entrances gaping in a hillside, where it was said pit ponies still lived, coming out to graze only at night because their eyes could not stand the sunlight; I saw, rusting red against the sky, soaring iron dinosaurs straddling stands of gums. The Browns had been famous for their machinery.

Wherever I walked, I was always aware of the parallel world beneath, the honeycomb maze of mine tunnels that ran from coast to country, as I had seen from the mines survey map when we bought the property here. Nowhere was really safe in the valley, but nobody seemed to bother about it – even though, sometimes, when the underworld reached up too far, backyards disappeared and cottages tipped on alarming angles.

The pub folk reckoned the bush round the village could not be sold because it was too undermined, too dangerous, so trail bikes scored it with tracks and the mines cut pit props from its young trees.

THEN A REVIVAL of sorts occurred and the underground awoke, with a new mine going in just over our hill. Large coal trucks now frequently and noisily ground up the hill and round our corner, keeping the house coated with pale dust. An ex-mining village was quaint; a current one was not.

We bought a bush property in the upper Hunter as a weekend retreat; talked about moving there one day, of building a cabin. The people at the pub thought we'd be mad to leave just as the village looked like picking up at last. Local aldermen were promising that soon there would be houses all the way from the nearest town, seven miles off through the bush, to our village, which would then be a suburb of Newcastle. Under that threat, in 1978 we decided to sell up.

A pit prop contractor had half a load of props that the mines had rejected as too short: 'Anyone wanta buy 'em cheap?' While we had plenty of trees on our new property, we preferred not to fell them, so we took him up on it; the slim but strong round posts would make good supports and railings for a cabin veranda.

Thirty years later those pit prop posts still stand, grey and lichened with age, framing landscapes of tall trees backed by the dense green convolutions of the ridges and gullies of the World Heritage Wilderness Area. I like this link to my past, but have been told that bringing them here was like 'cartin' coals to Newcastle'. I like this linking image too.

The coal is catching up. There are now eighteen coalmines close, too close, to my nearest town, seventy kilometres away. Over the past fifteen years, whenever I have left my bright sunlit mountain I have driven down into an increasingly milky-brown layer that fills the broad valley and blurs or even obliterates the edging mountains, as the dust from the open-cut mines blends with the coal-fired power stations' output. What was once like the Rhine, green pastures and vineyards and clear country skies, has become a clone of the old industrial Ruhr. The air in the adjoining shires of Single-ton and Muswellbrook carries one of the highest concentrations of fine dust particulates in Australia: 50,000 tonnes. My grandchildren live near Single-ton; they breathe that air.

'Why do you all put up with it?' I asked a shopkeeper. 'You hardly ever see blue sky or sun until this smog lifts around eleven – if at all – and you can't see the stars at night for the lights of the mines!'

'To be honest, I've forgotten what it was like before,' he replied, 'and when you're in it you don't know any better; it's just seen as the weather. I reckon if everyone else in town can stand it, I can. Well, it's Progress, isn't it?'

Men – and women – earn good money in these mines. This is called the 'golden handcuff', for the wages tie them to twelve-hour shifts where they rarely see their families and are too tired to function properly when they do. Involvement in community, social and sports events is fractured, and so are families, as wives discover that being able to afford the biggest plasma-screen TV doesn't compensate for bringing up a baby on their own.

I see the workers off-shift, on pub veranda smoke zones or in the shopping centres, in their scuffed steel-toed boots and grimy blue-and-orange work shirts and trousers, banded with silver reflective strips. All who go on site from the support industries dress like this, not just the miners, so the uniforms dominate, as do the grey-spattered double-cab white utes, with their safety flags a-flying, somehow defiantly gay, if grubby, in the car parks and streets. It feels like a coal company town, just as Minmi was — except the ownership is corporate and multiple, an industry takeover, with no single owner to beseech or blame.

These once-rural towns now run on 24-hour mine time; dogs bark and babies cry as lights go on and utes start up in the early morning dark. The highway takeaway joints open then, too, to feed breakfast steak sandwiches and hamburgers and coffee and Coke to the long line of commuters from lower down the valley, where there are no mines, where the air is cleaner and a house won't be unsaleable when the mines pull the pin on towns that depend too heavily on coal.

When I look at the mindlessly unsustainable housing estates creeping further across the hills around Singleton and Muswellbrook, I see the old maps of Minmi and the density and spread of that town in its coal days. Will my grandchildren be wandering around the skeletal perimeters of their town in fifty years' time, marvelling that it was ever so big, and what will be the archaeological finds then? Rusting air-conditioners?

Rents have soared as transient workers compete for them; homelessness is a growing problem, as is the divide between the haves on inflated mine wages and the have-nots on normal wages or pensions. Mines are moving to contract labour, so job security for miners is no greater than in the Minmi days — nor is housing security, with high mortgages dependent on those high wages.

Townspeople mutter to each other and shake their heads about the dust; they agree the mines should be made to clean up their act or replaced with cleaner industries, and that the power of mining is out of control. Such talk is mainly in private: handcuffed directly or indirectly to coal, it's easier to ignore the downside and head for the shopping centres.

In public forums the audiences contain a majority of retirees, with more bald pates and grey hair than at any lawn bowls function. We grandparents are deeply concerned about the future of those we will leave behind, and no one can sack us. At a recent meeting on air quality – or the lack of it – a rare younger man in his mine work clothes stood up and said that he had foolishly believed all the initial assurances by the mines that 'strict environmental guidelines' would be adhered to, that there would be no negative effects.

In one recent 'Hunter Valley Mining Industry' info-ad insert in a local paper, amid all the trumpet blowing I managed to find two tiny articles with hints about adverse effects, together totalling about a quarter of a page out of twenty-four pages: one on the recently announced air-quality monitoring network, omitting that it's long overdue, compromised and inadequate; and the other on local demands – denied – for a study into the health impacts of the dust particulates they inhale daily. This coverage is unusual, as environmental matters are generally restricted to a slim self-congratulatory piece about tree plantings.

Our disillusioned young miner now has mountains of dumped dirt looming over his village of Camberwell, some only several hundred metres away from homes. There are six mines close by, four of which have lodged applications to expand – and are expected to be approved. Yet the water in the village house tanks already contains nearly twenty times more lead than the Australian Drinking Water Guidelines consider safe; the levels of arsenic, mercury, nickel and zinc also exceed those guidelines. With the dust and constant lights and noise of trucks and machines, and the blasting, as a tenable habitation Camberwell is the walking wounded, a village dying on its feet.

The miner might have a job, but he fears for the health and future of his children, and he has learned that the mining companies agree to any condition and hold to none, with impunity; he no longer believes anything the companies or governments say.

People talk about the increasing asthma, the year-round 'hay fever', the heart attacks and strokes, the long-term effects on the brain and genetics from heavy metals, the cancer and motor-neurone disease clusters, and the depression, which the visiting coal pollution expert Dr Dick van Steenis considers may well be caused by the chemicals in our toxic air.

Beyond the physical, Glenn Albrecht – then of Newcastle University, now a professor of sustainability at Murdoch University and writer at healthearth.blogspot.com – coined a term, 'solastalgia', for the psychological damage he was observing: 'the pain or sickness caused by the loss or lack of solace and the sense of desolation connected to the present state of one's home and territory. It is the "lived experience" of negative environmental change. It is the homesickness you have when you are still at home. It is that feeling you have when your sense of place is under attack.'

Prosperity? Progress? Not for the people who live where a mine wants to be. When one threatens, locals' only choice is to sell to the coal company; no one else will buy, and if they happen to live just outside the designated affected area – a highly arbitrary line that must assume a permanent absence of wind – they don't even have that.

They wonder when Australia became the sort of country where one person, the Planning Minister, can ignore all protective legislation to fast-track a project for the sake of corporate profit. They no longer think they're lucky to live in a coal-rich region, not now that all sense of fair play and proportion in land and water use is so evidently as much a thing of the past as the horse and plough. If their families have been here for generations, staying may be untenable, but going is unthinkable, out of loyalty to old memories. They need the memories, because the landscape is unrecognisable.

At last they have twigged that it is the big boys like BHP Billiton, Xstrata, Centennial, Peabody, Felix Resources – now Yanzhou – who are the lucky ones with the ear of the decision-maker. They don't believe the government will say no to a resources project, no matter what or whom it destroys; the processes to approval are judged to be shams, the outcome inevitable. 'Money talks, and those guys have billions. So what's the point of objecting?'

FURTHER WEST, JUST north of Mudgee, is the new intensive area of coal devastation, with the expansion of the once-solitary Ulan mine, the nearby newish Wilpinjong mine and the multiple-mine complex at Moolarben. At Cobbora and Laheys Creek, near Dunedoo, $17 million has been spent in land buy-ups by the state-owned Macquarie Generation before any coal exploration licences have been issued, so confident is the company of getting mines approved where and when they want.

Most of this development is yet to come, and many in the Mudgee district have taken the bait: jobs and prosperity. Sadly, I see the region's future in the mid-upper Hunter's ruined present.

The majority of local people won't see the need to make a fuss until it's too late.

They'll listen when you say that already small schools near mines, like Wollar near Wilpinjong, have to be supplied with bottled water because the tank water now has such high concentrations of lead. They can see that's tacit government acknowledgment of a problem – but they can't quite believe the mines can be doing this when they have to meet all those 'strict environmental guidelines'.

I could tell them that these get altered after approval, to suit the mine's economic needs, not the environment's, that Moolarben was up to the fifth modification of its consent conditions for Stage One. But they'd think I was just a cynical greenie trying to stop progress.

It'll take a while for them to see that the jobs are mostly not for locals, that unemployment is still high, that twelve- to fourteen-hour shifts are no fun anyway, that the money's not near enough for that nor the fact that shiftwork miners lose touch with their families, often lose them altogether.

They'll grumble if they have no water irrigation allotment in the drought or they're not allowed to wash the car on town water, yet a mine like Moolarben uses millions of litres a day to wash the coal.

They might care when the deservedly famous sandstone cliff face at The Drip in the Goulburn River gorge collapses, or their favourite swimming and picnic spots nearby are polluted with mine discharge.

They will care if Uncle Joe's farm, in the family for generations, has to pack it in because the creek's too polluted or saline for pastures or for stock, or disappears entirely when the long-wall mine goes under it. As the Bowman family had to when Bowmans Creek in the Hunter did.

ONCE UPON A time I too believed that government was there for the good of the people. I abhorred politics, yet I was driven beyond minding my own business, writing and living sustainably in my solar-powered cabin, as I watched with disbelief while the excessive number and scale of open-cut coal mines devastated that part of the Hunter Valley.

In my naiveté, I wondered why the government was allowing it. They mustn't have realised the overall disaster they were creating as they approved each individual mine; someone should tell them it had gone way too far and had to stop. So, about eight years ago, not long after my first granddaughter was born, I began to do just that.

And as my file of patronising ministerial replies full of empty assurances grew, I realised the government didn't want to know about the effects of their resources policy – their 'quarry vision', as Guy Pearse so aptly said – on places and people, that they operated in a paper world; and against all my innate faith in humanity, I began to accept that some of the most important pieces of paper in politics were not research documents but cheques.

The advertising supplement for the 2008 Singleton Mining and Industry Expo proclaimed: 'Open-cut coalmining occupies much of the open space between Singleton and Muswellbrook.' These towns are about fifty kilometres apart, and the statement is correct, but it shocks me that the industry has no concept that this is not cause for pride but for shame, for admitting that the region has been so exploited by coalmining.

In old pre-mechanised days mining was a secret honeycombing, and men brought only the coal, not the entire underground, up to the light. Now even the underground mines are excessive, as long-wall continuous mining machines extract coal by cutting tunnels 250 to 300 metres wide, with the roof above collapsing into the void after the machine has moved on, frequently causing such surface subsidence that cliffs collapse and rocky riverbeds crack open and the water disappears or bubbles with noxious gases from below.

In the Hunter most mines are open-cut, each creating thousands of hectares of disturbance, with vast stepped holes, toxic lakes and mountains of grey chitter crawling with huge yellow dump trucks like Tonkas on steroids. Giant excavators scalp the valley of its biodiversity, turn it upside down and inside out to get the coal, spew up their leftovers as artificial hills when they have eaten their target prey, and move on to the next piece of pastoral innocence. Their underlings come behind and insult the great complexity of

Nature by seeding grass and planting rows of trees of several species – see, it's as good as new! But they only bother where passers-by can see. The view from a plane tells the real story.

Coal-affected communities know that the so-called luck flows only one way: out of their region, and mostly out of the country. They'd like to see a fraction of those much-mooted royalties spent locally to help them survive now and into the future, to coal-proof them. Yet our governments give coal companies far more than the companies give back; the diesel rebate alone exceeds the royalties. This is the same federal rebate that farmers get for off-road vehicles, but their machinery is not giant-sized and does not run night and day, and I have yet to hear a farmer announce billions of dollars in annual profit.

Our resources boom no longer depends on picks and shovels and manpower, but on fossil fuels. Just one of those dump trucks uses more than 2,500 litres of diesel every twenty-four hours. I don't hear locals saying about the coal companies, as they do about farmers, 'Ah well, poor buggers are doing it tough; they need all the help they can get.'

The joke is on the people of the Hunter, and eventually, on the governments who perpetuate it. The laughter is heard only in the boardrooms of those who benefit – and it's mostly far-off laughter, ever more so as China's interests here expand.

My whole family history since 1830 runs through the Hunter Valley; I belong here. But if the resources companies continue to run our governments' policies, I may have to give up on the Hunter, and find somewhere that is my kind of lucky: lucky enough to be left in its natural state, or with such low-scale, balanced development that humans – or even dwarves – can make a living, but with no possibility of billions for giants.

Sharyn Munro is a freelance non-fiction writer and award-winning short-story writer. Her two books, both published by Exisle, are *The Woman on the Mountain* (2007) and *Mountain Tails* (2009).

FICTION

THE ENDS OF THE EARTH

EMMA ASHMERE

LASTING a good part of a minute, the sound was akin to the roar of two hundred horse carriages furiously ridden over cobblestones, writes James Palmer, surveyor of the newest southern colony, in January 1839. *I made inquiries of one of the natives who indicated there have been previous earthquakes of similar nature in these parts. However, it was impossible to ascertain their frequency or severity, were I to believe him.*

I frown beneath the shuddering roof of the tent, wondering if the earthquake has struck the area my husband, the surveyor, and his men have been engaged to map. I remain pinned to the bed, blinking at the dark, listening. Dogs are barking. People call out. Some have lit lamps with which to inspect the tents, the provisions store and the newly laid foundations of the hospital. Slowly I reach for the Bible I keep wrapped in a white linen cloth with my diary. *And every island fled away, and the mountains were not found.*

I will myself to think of how best to instruct the cook to roast the spatchcock for Sunday dinner, when the Reverend Merton will read a prayer and eat a good portion of stuffing and most of the bird, before retiring to his tent with bottle and pen.

But this is something I cannot shut out. The sound of this strange country shrugging us off.

My thoughts rush far ahead. I think of my unborn child. Of my child's children and their children. Will they continue to take part in this extraordinary experiment and make their lives here? James would think me foolish but I can sense their little souls about me now, a long luminous stream of family threading down the years.

James? Can you hear it? The fluttering of hearts? The trembling breath?

MY HEART. MY breath. This trembling. For the past year, I've watched my illness circling. Now it has begun its approach, like a figure shambling across a paddock, almost recognisable in its shape and gait, the face remaining out of sight. Now it has lodged itself inside me.

My daughter took me to see a neurologist yesterday. He sat in his spotted bow tie, making pronouncements over steepled hands. My daughter promised wine and cake. In our family, wine and cake always means something's up.

To stop her pleading, I lied. Yes, I said, spilling a little rosé over the tablecloth. Yes, I will give up my final pleasure. The daily visits to the State Library, where I've been immersing myself in the accounts of my great-great-grandfather James Palmer and comparing these to the private diaries of my great-great-grandmother, kept in a Sandler shoebox beneath my bed.

I couldn't tell my daughter that it's impossible to surrender any more of myself. Too much has been taken. Too much has been lost.

All this has been building. An inventory of omissions and mistakes. The empty pantry. The odd vine snaking its way inside. The discovery of that wad of unpaid bills. Then last week's visit to the library, when I tried to bring Palmer's papers home to reunite them with the diaries of his wife, carefully tucking them inside my coat, feigning amnesia when the woman on the desk cheerfully pointed out my little oversight.

There's one of his entries I particularly like: he's wading eye-high through reeds along the River Torrens to the cries and grunts of water-fowl. He's been looking for a place for his men to cross. Two chains, he surmises, at its narrowest point. He wipes his face. Sweat has been creeping like a beetle across his brow. The ink in his notebook has begun to blur beneath his thumb. For a moment, the blinding sun is completely eclipsed by a deafening flock of parakeets.

Then he sees it. Black eyes in the grass, to the left on the rise. His breath pulls in sharp. His hand goes to the musket. But no. It's only the face of old man kangaroo, chest pushed out between the white curve of shoulders. The kangaroo stares, waits for Palmer's party to thrash on past.

I WONDER IF the land James is surveying has also settled back into silence with the coming of daylight. I rise from my bed and exchange pleasantries with Doctor Myles, who has weathered another busy night. I hesitate by the tent door, watching men mending canvas, attending to a broken cart wheel and severing the limbs of a leaning tree. I steel myself with my Bible: *The earth quaked and the rocks were split*. Then my diary: *Thursday evening, parakeet pie.* Followed by: *One of the foremen, Ambrose Asquith, cut his own throat on the Sabbath and was found by his son in a water-filled ditch. The wretched man was known to Doctor Myles who had ministered to him during previous bouts of falling sickness. There is unpleasant talk of drinking and debts and a wife with child.*

AS I TAKE out my great-great-grandmother's diary from beneath the bed, I notice my own handwriting scrawled across the shoebox lid: *For donation to the State Library in the event of my death.*

In the event of being old, infirm, an invalid, doctors speak through my daughter, rarely to me. It was suggested I take an assortment of pills. Do they think I don't realise I am old? I tried to tell the doctor it's not the pills or even forgetting which bus I might be on. I know I'm old, because I've been drawn rather urgently to try to know the lives of my ancestors. To find my place beside the river before wading in.

Who were these people who came to this place in slow, stinking ships with futures as large as the land they intended to open up, cutting and burning, digging and ploughing, sowing new worlds with the ideas of home?

Just when I think I've begun to know them, they become unfamiliar. Often I'm aware of their presence as I read their words. It makes me anxious but it's also comforting. I wonder if they're aware of me.

I may be here alone living in a tent oppressed by all sorts of hardships in this strange land, but when James returns I will place his hand across my growing belly and he will smile as he feels the future there.

When I still enjoyed a greater proportion of better days, nobody cared if I caught the bus to the library with a thermos of tea and a box of shortbread and sat at the whirring microfilm machine. Throughout my husband's busy academic life, then his illness and long, bitter death, everybody admired me. You're so capable, they said. Adaptive. Generous. But now I'm watched. Managed. Cajoled. I have to dart out early to hail a bus. And then I have to sit among the spiky grasses beside the State Library in the smell of urine and last night's drink, as homeless men roll up their plastic sheets and unzip their tattered bags full of nothing, full of everything, begging a few coins or cigarettes, to the stares of the early morning pageant of city workers marching past.

After half-past nine the once aloof and peaceful realms of the library fill with people cramming backpacks into lockers, rattling coins into slot machines, tapping away at miniature screens. Unlike the house, where the heavy furniture of my past life has begun to stifle me. I like the ever changing theatre here.

With no fixed goal, I always find what I need by padding along the shelves, opening random books, rifling through newspapers, leaflets and ships' logs, exclaiming and often weeping as my increasingly tremulous fingers move down columns of ant-sized font noting reports of people born, murdered, loved, feted, ridiculed or despised.

I have found from experience it's best to avoid Genealogy. There's always some talkative soul lying in wait, bursting with details of their family history, as if their family was the only one to exist. When you're old people assume you have plenty of time, when the point is that you don't.

I've been working hard on this final project, culminating in a substantial letter to the editor of a national newspaper, the finishing-off of an old argument batted back and forth between me and my late husband about the realisation that it is we humans who are to blame for the decline and ravaging of the natural world.

I can hear him now tut-tutting at my shoulder. See? I reply. See, dear? I understand the arguments more clearly now. Even though you are ever the professor and I am the wife, I've been at the library boning up. Take this 1850s edition of the *Gardeners' Gazette*, for instance. While some 'scientific men' still claim that rain follows the plough, others say no, not in these parts where summer is brown and the winters rarely green. More letters to the *Gazette*'s editor rail against the clearfelling of trees. *We must not allow men to make the same mistakes as in the Americas*, writes one Thos. Mitchell in July 1856. *We must make pains to heed the experience of the other colonies where the soil has suffered when the forests were cleared of all of her verdancy.* Again, in the *Herald*, July 1899, a letter warning against the *wanton deforestation of this great, fair land as a precautionary measure against the very probable diminution of natural rainfall.*

I construct and dismantle my arguments as I wait for sleep. I'm thirsty, itchy. My mouth feels stiff, as if I've made a rude face and the wind has changed.

Is it possible to know how it felt when those first white gentlewomen were brought out here, to the ends of the earth? Even with diaries and the occasional letter, can we understand what went through a gentlewoman's mind as she placed a slipper in the South Australian dust, a clutch of hot clothes at her waist?

Perhaps she smiled as the eyes of labouring men traversed the coastline of her summer dress. Men who'd been left dangerously long without adequate work, food or pay due to the ineptitudes of the British government. Was it a relief to know there were no convicts here – just a slice of so-called free society apparently devoid of religious persecution, imbued with new ideas of self-sufficiency, an open-ended gamble in a huge and ancient place?

'But the sky,' the gentlewoman might have gasped. How would she survive such bright, hard light?

WHILE IT IS true that James warned there would be few women of my kind in the colony, I had not quite understood he would vanish so regularly for weeks on end to survey the great beyond, compiling important field notes for the Surveyor General, studying the clay beds and pink quartzite cliffs, and perhaps finding pleasure and power in the warmth and sport of darker flesh.

James?

I am not ashamed to admit I often speak his name in his absence.

It was well over a hundred degrees, I write in my diary. It is far better to tell of simple, familiar things. *We hung the hams from our tents and the Reverend Merton read psalms, and we raised our make-believe glasses to King and Country, having lost most of the glassware when the trunk was dropped on disembarkation. James and I intended to mark the Christmas occasion with as much spirit as was possible.*

I AM ALSO lying in my bed with as much spirit as is possible, listening to the ship-like creaking of the house. For some hours I'd been trying to read one of my husband's favourite books, *The Myths of Greece and Rome*, but I became overpowered by the labyrinthine parables and their savage imagery.

Suddenly I hear it: a rumble. It begins as a whispering, a chattering. The fidgeting of furniture. Paintings rattling against the walls. Books jostling along the shelves. The bedside light flickering on and off. Is it an earthquake?

I stagger from the bed, perhaps to the appalling sound of Surveyor Palmer's two hundred horse carriages rocketing over cobblestones. Or is it Enceladus, the giant punished by Jupiter to lie beneath the weight of Mount Etna, bound forever with adamantine chains? Poor Enceladus, forever turning in his lair, sending up great shots of molten fire to shake the tender plates of the earth.

Adam-an-tine? I know the word – I have read it somewhere else recently.

I feel my way downstairs, trying not to trip over the things scattered across the floor. I prise open a kitchen cupboard to discover the cups and saucers have been dancing together and now lie intermingled in jagged heaps.

I light the gas, heat a little milk, then sit down on the cold, hard floor. What luck! A scrap of blank paper and a runaway pen. *James has given me the duty of arranging a reception in honour...* What is that appalling noise? Just the fire alarm again, screeching overhead. The milk pot is spuming, brown with fire.

JAMES HAS GIVEN me the duty of arranging a reception in honour of the arrival of the new Governor and his wife; hence I am in charge of the decorations, the supper provisions, the guest list, the musical entertainment. At last, more of life's necessities have arrived: another piano, kale and cabbage and river bean seeds, a selection of wines and, mercifully, letters and books; also, bolts of woollen cloth as the winter will arrive surprising chill, an oak dining table and chairs, herds of much needed cattle and flocks of sheep driven in from the east, and scores of impoverished married men and women, hungry for opportunity.

I venture a small smile at the sky. There is much to do. Doctor

Myles has asked me to visit a labouring man's wife, Mrs Ambrose Asquith, who has given birth to a girl a week after the poor husband extinguished himself.

I duck my hat as I enter the tent. I expect – but am still shocked by – the smell. I sit by the Asquith woman in the sorry little tent, watching the grey curves beneath her eyes, the red dots spreading and then receding across her face. I wipe her doughy wrist, then take up the baby and stare at its eyes. The child lies unmoving in the crook of my arm, its mouth separated from my swelling breast by three layers of damp cloth.

Eventually I hand the baby back, informing Mrs Asquith that I must see to the reception for the new Governor.

The evening air is still stifling. The sky remains orange behind black trees.

The reception must be a resounding success, so no one will remember that the previous Governor was recalled to Britain under a cloud. James has suggested that the new Governor's wife shall become a great friend, there still being a shortage of certain kinds of women in these parts.

The sky has been orange for at least an hour. How these southern sunsets scald and sear the night. At first there was no sign of the new Governor and his lady wife, but we soon learned they had been sighted.

We wait in the yellow square of light thrown out from the door of the makeshift hall. A note arrives. Regrettably, the Governor has been detained. Somebody stays the violins. Food has begun to wilt on plates.

When the Governor finally appears, he is red and swaying. One look at the Governor's wife and I know she and I will not be friends. Her china-doll face; her furious eyes.

'The heat,' the Governor's wife says at last.

'I trust your Excellency's belongings arrived in an agreeable state?'

No answer.

'I trust…'

Nothing. Stillness in every eye and mouth. Then a sigh, long and loud. The Governor's voice booms. He smells of rum. And still the bawdy dusk refuses to fall.

The airless dark brings no relief from the day's heat. I lie wrestling with my sinful conscience, especially the duty of looking in on the Asquith woman thrice daily. Of course I will go tomorrow, to pat a fresh cloth to her face and filthy hands, but I will not note it in my diary when she clutches at me and cries, 'It was like a thousand bees had stung my heart, missus, when my little boy found my husband face-down in the ditch.' Nor will I mention giving my agreement when she said the nights were so dark and the towpaths so wet. Down by the ditch where the cold water glitters and the winds sing out softly, calling you in.

I AM ALSO in bed wrestling with my conscience. I look over to see my late husband's book of myths on the floor. *Adam-an-tine*. No. That's not the word I've seen somewhere.

Look. Here, on the labels of my collection of unopened pills. *A-man-ta-dine*. I've been squirrelling them away with the diaries in the shoebox for 'the event'.

As I reach over for my glass and gulp down a handful of the pills, a trail of water rains down, darkening, expanding then disappearing like tiny footprints across the sheets.

Over there, the fat yellow envelope addressed to The Editor, *The Australian*.

Outside, another unrepentant morning sun. But if we lie here very quietly, we might see the sky blackening with flocks of parakeets. The gouged, parched hills might bristle with saplings. The great rivers might begin to run again, tumbling through the thirsty earth. And the cool wind will carry voices of loved ones long dead.

Emma Ashmere holds a PhD from La Trobe University. Her writing has appeared in *Kurungabaa*, *The Age* and the University of Canberra's *Monitor*.

More than a gift from the gods

Rethinking comparative advantage

Jonathan West

THE concept of comparative advantage is perhaps the single most powerful idea in economics. It is taught to every undergraduate and printed in every introductory textbook. It has all the hallmarks of a great theory: simple, non-obvious, logically irrefutable, with sweeping implications. And adherence to it promises a better world.

Never expressed better than by David Ricardo, its originator, the theory states that even if England is more efficient than Portugal at producing both textiles and wine, but Portugal is relatively better at producing wine than textiles, both countries would prosper if England produced all the textiles needed by the two countries and Portugal all the wine. The idea is to allow free markets to allocate resources to the sector(s) in which a nation has a relative productivity advantage and then trade freely to enjoy the benefits. In turn, free trade nudges the economy to concentrate on its comparative advantage.

Nowhere has this proposition had more impact than in Australia. Indeed, many would have it define the destiny of the nation. Comparative advantage stands today at the core of the free-trade ideology that dominates public discourse about the future. Applied to Australia, the theory proposes that this country stop trying to produce goods or services in which we lack a relative advantage – say, manufacturing and tradable services – and focus on exporting those in which we do, namely resources. And that's exactly what the Australian economy has been doing in recent years: narrowing, largely with the support of official policy.

Yet, in spite of its logical power and its promise of a painless path to superior economic performance, the idea of comparative advantage has always struggled for supremacy in Australia. Over the course of this country's economic development, comparative advantage has repeatedly been dethroned by another proposition: that, rather than narrow its focus to resources, Australia should broaden its economy, using its natural resource advantages as a platform from which to build other sectors.

Deliberate broadening appears to fly in the face of the prescriptions of comparative advantage and its companion, free trade. It implies protectionism

---

PREVIOUS PAGE: Christopher P Halloran, *Heavy burden*. A line of monster dump trucks carry loads of rock out of an open pit mine.

and deliberate, government-directed industry policy. Today, these notions are almost universally rejected by economists and are even out of favour among political leaders of all stripes. Nevertheless, the impetus to broaden seems not to die, and every few years it re-emerges to shape the nation's view of its future. Indeed, the history of Australian economic policy can be seen as a century-long battle between these two propositions.

Why cannot such a great idea as comparative advantage – logical, simple and with the power to make everyone better off – achieve lasting dominance, particularly in Australia, which seems so obviously to be blessed by a compelling comparative advantage? How does such a seemingly discredited idea as protectionism keep reappearing? Put simply, why should the Portuguese (or Australians) exert extra effort to turn out five metres of woven cloth when, for the same amount of work, they could take advantage of their blissful climate and rich soil to produce six barrels of wine, trade three with England for perhaps ten metres of cloth and keep three barrels for their own enjoyment?

The answer is that as a guide to the economic future, and policy-making to shape the future, comparative advantage turns out to be fatally flawed. While as a snapshot fixed in time, and limited to the economic sphere, it is beyond reproach, looked at over time it ignores three vital dimensions of economic development: differential industry growth, technological improvement and the divergent social consequences of concentration in different types of economic activity. In fact, the theory of comparative advantage ignores economic development entirely – including the vital issue of the origins of comparative advantage itself. And therein lies its downfall, both as a concept and as a guide to good policy-making.

LET'S CONSIDER EACH of these three problems for comparative advantage. First, industries tend to grow at very different rates as societies become richer. Demand for meat grows faster than for rice, for automobiles faster than for bicycles, for televisions faster than for radios. This has an important implication for nations specialising in their comparative advantage. In Ricardo's illustration, for example, history shows that as Europe emerged from the centuries-long grip of poverty, demand for England's textiles grew much faster – by up to five times – than did demand for Portugal's wine. Clothing is much more 'income elastic' than wine; as people break out of poverty they buy many more sets of clothes than they do casks of wine. The result was that by specialising in their respective comparative advantages, Portugal's economy stagnated, growing only as fast as population, but Britain's roared. It matters a great deal in which products your economy specialises and has comparative advantage. The East Asian nations that have improved so dramatically in recent decades have done so by specialising in fast-growing manufacturing sectors, not slow-growing traditional parts of the economy.

Second, as with growth rates, industries have very different technological potentials over time. England's textile producers spectacularly increased their output during the industrial revolution by introducing a string of new machines, driving productivity to hitherto unimagined heights; Portugal's wine makers, by contrast, were forced to continue growing grapes and pressing juice from them, with only marginal increases in output over time. This effect is even more marked today, with huge disparities among industries in average technology-driven productivity growth rates, particularly in the fields closest to the twin revolutions of computers and biotechnology.

Third, and perhaps most importantly, different industries have divergent social consequences. Which industries a society specialises in can exert important influence over the type of society that emerges: its relative equality, its social cohesion, its propensity to democracy, and even its sustenance or otherwise of such intangibles as personal self-respect and the arts. Some industries generate novel skills, and with them equality and self-reliance. The English textile industry created new classes of skilled workers, managers, fashion designers, equipment engineers and dye chemists, all of which were well rewarded for their skill and experience. The industry further supported a network of educational, technical and scientific institutions—which in turn spawned further technological advance. The textile industry also demanded increasingly sophisticated and complex machinery, which led to the birth of other industries, in a virtuous cycle. The Portuguese wine industry, with its time-honoured – and massively unequal – mix of peasants, winemakers and landowners, needed, and generated, little external support.

Indeed, it can be argued that the textile industry was important not only for creating the wealth that made England the richest country in the world in its day, but also for laying the foundations for the broadening of democracy to the majority of the population, and the flowering of science and the arts that was so apparent in eighteenth- and nineteenth-century Britain. Portugal's wine industry offered no such potential. In general, a society dominated by industries in which artisans and small enterprises are the natural form of economic organisation (textiles) can be expected to develop a very different character to one in which a single wealthy and powerful landowner employs the other members of society (Portuguese winemaking), or in which most people work for – or receive income without work from – the government.

Had the eighteenth-century Portuguese been able to divine the future, they would have been much better off ignoring Ricardo's advice and imposing a prohibitive tariff on English textile imports, giving their own textile industry a chance to survive and potentially even expand.

The proponents of comparative advantage and free trade would respond that Portugal's citizens would have seen their living standards lowered by any such decision, and that in any case England might retaliate with a tariff on wine. They would be right. Residents of Portugal would have had to put up with lower-quality and probably more expensive clothes, and would likely have sold less wine. But in Ricardo's example, there was no other way for Portugal to escape what became its fate over the next two centuries.

WITHOUT DELIBERATELY SETTING their sights on industries against their comparative advantage, Portugal could not develop. And indeed, no country has broken the grip of underdevelopment without ignoring the theory, at least as it is traditionally understood. The United States in the nineteenth century, Japan in the twentieth, Europe after World War II, East Asia in the 1980s and 1990s, and China today: all nations that have developed have done so contrary to the precepts of comparative advantage. Far from being a guide to good policy for aspiring nations, the theory has been a poverty trap.

In the principal industries that have driven economic development over the past two centuries – manufacturing and services – comparative advantage is not endowed by God but created, by human effort, ingenuity and organisation: comparative advantage can be brought into existence by deliberate investment and sustained commitment. This recognition makes all the difference. Because the theory is mute on the origins of comparative advantage and how it changes over time, it offers no guidance to how it can be constructed. Instead of insisting that nations stick to what they start with, we should ask how comparative advantage is created and what can be done to change a nation's destiny.

Actually, most economists, or at least those even slightly acquainted with history and the real economy, know this. They know that no nation has developed by applying the theory of comparative advantage, and they are aware that in the most important industries that advantage is deliberately created.

But they are reluctant to admit they know it. The real reason most economists espouse comparative advantage and free trade has nothing to do with economic theory. It stems from political judgement. Economists fear that conceding the possibility that comparative advantage might be created by the tools of government policy – tariffs, quotas, import prohibitions, low-interest loans, tax exemptions, subsidies, targeted education, government-funded research and development, military spin-offs, to name but a few – will open the floodgates to government-mandated protection for monopolies that have no hope of ever standing on their own feet. They worry that government will be captured by special interests, and industry policy will become merely a cloak for the kind of inefficient and expensive government-connected industries that are so common in the Third World. Economists commonly fear that democracies are especially prone to such capture, and that rather than building the industries of the future the slogans of 'nation-building' will merely shelter dinosaurs.

THE FEAR IS valid. It may well be true that modern western democracies are no longer capable of sustaining commitment to future-oriented industrial development strategies, and that they will inevitably lapse back into pork-barrelling and special-interest protection. As western nations fragment into squabbling tribes, rancorously fighting over ever more hardened ideologies, perhaps we have lost the cohesion required to deliberate and to act. Certainly, the contemporary world offers plenty of evidence for such concern.

But if we accept this pessimistic view, it is important to be aware of the consequences. With the exception of a lucky few who do enjoy an insurmountable God-given comparative advantage, such a failure will likely doom western democracies to long-term economic decline. Successive waves of technological development rapidly supersede today's comparative advantage. If nations allow markets to narrow their bets to today's advantage and industries built in prior eras, they risk their industries being replaced as rapidly as the products they once made.

In this sense, all industries today are infant industries, the one exception allowed by the free-trade theorists. Technological change and targeted support from rivals can render a once healthy, grown-up industry a helpless infant within a few years. And along with these industries goes the service infrastructure that is intimately connected to them: banking, insurance, financial services, advertising and consulting. If assistance is denied to these industries, due to a fear of protectionism and in the face of competition from nations deliberately building new comparative advantage with every tool at their disposal, the overtaken industries will wither.

The overwhelming majority of Australia's manufacturing industry has already suffered this fate; much of North America's has gone down the same path. Failure to commit decisively to an alternative comparative advantage will lead inevitably to further narrowing towards our natural endowment in resources.

THE CONSEQUENCES WILL be not only economic but social and, for many, personal. Loss of the non-resource industries will transform our culture in as yet unimagined ways. But before we admit defeat, it is worth considering very seriously whether any other future is possible. Might we not be able to build a new comparative advantage? And what would be required?

One set of answers might come from our own past. The character of contemporary Australia, especially of its economy but also many of its social values, was forged more than a hundred years ago. In the decade following Federation, Australia's political parties negotiated an economic consensus that aimed to create the future desired by the population of the time.

This consensus survived largely intact until the late 1970s, and still underlies public assumptions about and expectations of government. The strategy was to draw upon the nation's natural comparative advantage in farming and resources to finance a shift to manufacturing. Key planks in the platform were tariff barriers to protect and promote manufacturing, racial and workforce insulation (the White Australia policy and the protection of wage workers from foreign competition went hand in hand), needs-based wages and judicially determined industrial relations, equalisation of revenues among the states, and a growing welfare role for the federal government.

These commitments were funded directly, through taxes on the resource and farming exporters, and indirectly, through tariffs and restrictive immigration. This 'Federation settlement' took eight difficult years to agree upon, during which time Australia had three elections, nine minority governments and two failed efforts to fuse the non-Labor parties. Stability came only in 1909, with the merger of the non-Labor parties as a credible alternative to the Labor Party.

It was a deliberate, and successful, effort to build a particular type of economy that would shape a particular type of society – essentially, the one Australians live in today. The structure of the Australian economy was purposefully transformed, as investment and employment shifted from farming and mining into manufacturing. Farming and mining employment declined from 30 per cent of the workforce in 1901 to 12 per cent in 1968, while manufacturing employment rose over the same period from 12 per cent to 27 per cent. Services (termed 'Other' in the statistics) remained largely stable, shifting only from 58 per cent to 61 per cent. To reiterate, this transformation was not a 'natural' shift or a simple response to 'market forces', but a consciously targeted and implemented political and social vision.

To succeed in the transformation, Australia's leadership had to understand comparative advantage in a novel way: not as an imperative to narrow the economy to a few advantaged sectors, which would export while the rest of the things the nation wanted to consume were imported; rather, as a source of finance to build the kind of economy that would support the liberal-democratic, diversified, middle-class nation in which Australians aspired to live.

WHAT WAS NOT undertaken, though, was the construction of a new comparative advantage. Australia's economic vision throughout most of the twentieth century was to continue exporting resources, while diversifying its economy into sectors that remained largely domestically focused and sheltered behind tariff walls. Unlike in other nations, tariffs were not employed as a means to construct infant industries that would ultimately prove to be export-capable. As the domestic economy diversified, Australia's export portfolio remained relatively unchanged.

Consequently, as the burden of protection increased in the 1970s, with a long-term decline in resource and farm-based global commodity prices (relative to the price of imports), Australia's manufacturing and service industries were generally incapable of competing globally. They had not built a comparative advantage – unsurprisingly, since they were never intended to.

With the progressive removal of tariffs in the 1970s and 1980s, the trade-exposed portions of manufacturing and services shrank. Manufacturing declined as a share of gross domestic product, from a high of 28 per cent in 1956 to 11 per cent in 2007; and of employment, from a high in 1954 of 28 per cent to today's 10 per cent.

In recent years, the narrowing of Australia's economy, especially its export portfolio, has accelerated. Today the nation's exports are more dominated by resources than almost ever before. Minerals alone accounted for 59 per cent of merchandise exports in 2006 and 63 per cent in 2007, with iron ore and concentrates rising from $5.3 billion to $12.5 billion, and exports of coal from $10.9 billion to $24.4 billion. This concentration in resources is in marked contrast to any other developed country, even other resource-rich nations such as Canada that have broadened their economies and exports.

The implications of this narrowing focus, and the domination of public discussion of the nation's economic future by notions of nature-based comparative advantage and free trade, are likely to be profound. At the purely economic level, although primary production remains a small proportion of the overall economy (less than an eighth), the prosperity of the growing service sectors and of the remaining manufacturing sector – to say nothing of the finances of the Australian Government, which underwrites a substantial proportion of household income – depends greatly on the resource sector. Should that falter, for example due to a downturn in East Asia, Australia would rapidly encounter difficulty in servicing its mounting foreign debt. (Although there are frequent assertions to the contrary, Australia is one of the most foreign-indebted nations in the world, but the debt is private rather than government.)

OF PERHAPS EVEN greater concern are the long-term effects on the character of Australian society of an ever greater economic narrowing and resource focus. Resource-rich societies tend to come in two variants: either the resources are privately controlled, usually by a shrinking number of larger companies, or the government gains control, 'redistributing' the wealth more or less widely. In the long run, even if successful – and there are many examples of failed resource-exporting nations – neither offers an attractive future. While privately controlled resource-rich nations can have high average incomes, the average almost always disguises a bifurcated population: a few rich who own or are employed by the resource-extraction industries, alongside many poor who don't, and little in between. The all-important middle class is absent, and with it the economic and social bulwark of democracy and opportunity.

Government is usually captured by the resource owners. And resource industries have traditionally proven to be weak multipliers of income and opportunity across society. In particular, they provide few opportunities for education- and skill-based advancement, and almost none for entrepreneurial achievement (outside of a very few exploration and service companies, usually critically dependent on connections with government and the large companies).

It is not an attractive picture. Fortunately, however, this is the least likely scenario. Most Australians would strenuously resist such an outcome, and the long-term strength of democratic institutions in Australia would almost certainly prevent the nation evolving into a kind of Saudi Arabia Down Under.

Much more probable, given Australia's history and social expectations, is that government will incrementally expand its control over the resource industries, seizing an ever expanding share of the proceeds. Indeed, around the world, from Russia and Brazil, through Norway and the Middle East, this is the model towards which resource-rich nations are gravitating. It is the one that fits best with the long-term Australian commitment to government as a guarantor of living standards, welfare and economic risk-bearing. In early 2010 it was reflected in new tax proposals under consideration by the federal government and at least two states.

But with fewer of the well-paid, skill-intensive jobs in manufacturing and non-resource-oriented areas, what would such a government-dominated society look like? As government is able to provide for its citizens more and more directly, its share of national economic activity would inexorably expand, and with it the dependence of the citizenry on government for economic wellbeing. The result would be a society in which the ability to undertake a task effectively is less important than getting along well with government, a society in which politics dominates self-reliance. It's ultimately a society in which the citizens are infantilised, as they remain lifelong mendicants of government. This can occur directly, with a growing proportion of the population dependent on government payments (in my home state of Tasmania, 34 per cent of households now have as their sole or primary source of income a Commonwealth Government payment), or indirectly, with a rising proportion of the population employed by government or government-owned entities.

COULD AUSTRALIA USE its comparative advantage to avoid – rather than fall into – this fate? It did in the past, through tariffs and domestically focused manufacturing. But that will not work in the future. With vastly improved freight to reduce import costs, and dramatically cheaper manufacturing in China and elsewhere, the cost gap of any attempt to resurrect the Federation settlement and manufacture most items in Australia would be prohibitive. That path is, in practical terms, blocked. Any simple-minded reintroduction of tariff protection won't achieve the aim of building comparative advantage in desirable industries. It will breed non-capable industries, possessed of comparative disadvantage, sheltered behind ever more expensive walls.

Two other alternatives are possible. Both focus on building new human-derived comparative advantage on the back of natural advantage, and both test themselves in global competition. One looks to value-adding in resources, by employing the income flows from minerals and energy to support massive new infrastructure and capital equipment investment. The other seeks to build on traditional strengths in industries in which the product is low-technology, such as food, by adding science and know-how to provide safer, more environmentally sustainable solutions.

But neither will be achieved by market forces alone, or by following comparative advantage as conceived by the economists. Economics is the study of markets: interactions and transactions among individuals and organisations. Why some individuals, organisations, regions or nations come to be better than others at performing the tasks that matter in market transactions is seen by most economists as being outside the scope of economic theory, a matter for historians, business analysts or organisation theorists. Yet, at its heart, comparative advantage is about just such economic capability: the ability to meet human wants better than rivals can.

Unfortunately, media coverage of economic issues rarely focuses on capability. It tends to dwell instead on eye-catching stories of managerial blunders or power struggles, mergers, acquisitions, business cycles, currency exchange and interest rates, taxes, fluctuations in energy prices. But none of these is fundamental. They can at best be thought of as contributing to shallow capability: short-term pricing and cost issues. Shifts in exchange rates, tax levels and interest rates might buffet companies' business and financial performance, inflating or deflating earnings for a year or two, but they are surface phenomena. Underlying the dramas that surround these topics are the permanent or enduring factors that determine sustainable prosperity.

Because the media focuses on the shallow factors, so too often do political leaders, ignoring the deep capabilities that develop more gradually and last longer. These include accumulations of strategic resources and proprietary knowledge, which demand for their realisation organisational routines and employee commitment, and in turn enable superior problem-solving. Deep capabilities are thus those aspects of the economy that are difficult for others to emulate and that support ongoing gains in competitiveness. To develop new capabilities – comparative advantage – we need to move from a static to a dynamic perspective. In the contemporary economy, deep capabilities are created more by human effort, skill, and organisational and institutional effectiveness than gifted from God. In reality, countries mostly make their own 'luck'.

THREE CHARACTERISTICS OF economic capability are of particular interest when considering the construction of comparative advantage. First, in their traded sectors, economies tend to specialise according to their comparative advantage. That is, they concentrate in the fields in which they have acquired or built deep capability. Products and services from these sectors in a particular geography can generally out-compete those from others. While all developed economies include large and relatively similar proportions of largely non-trade-exposed sectors – health, education, community services, security, home-building, retail, personal services – in their traded sectors economies can be remarkably concentrated. And the traded sector is especially important for two reasons: first, non-traded sectors generally grow only roughly in line with population and per capita income, whereas traded sectors can generate far greater expansion as they tap distant and overseas markets. In a modern economy, especially a small one, many of the goods and services citizens want can be obtained only from afar; generating the income to pay for these imports depends on what the community can sell to the world. The economic fate of relatively small communities, such as Australia, can thus rest on a surprisingly narrow base of capability in very few fields. Ensuring the long-term strength of these sectors ought to be a high priority for any community and its government.

Capability is commonly geographically concentrated. Successful industries show a marked tendency to cluster in quite small regions. Such clusters include famous names like Silicon Valley in technology and the City of London and Manhattan in finance, but also such less-known locations as Aalsmeer, twenty kilometres south-west of Amsterdam, the global cut-flower trading capital (with 60 per cent of the global trade), and Surat, in the Indian state of Gujarat, which cuts 92 per cent of the world's diamonds. Capability concentrates regionally because much of the basis for capability within firms exists and is maintained outside firms, in educational and research institutions, finance, local industry and community bodies, support and allied service industries, and community memory. The combination of these elements can be thought of as the local capability platform, and the health of these platforms is of vital interest to the future of these communities.

Capability also assumes different forms, and is created by different processes, in different sectors. If capability can be thought of as the ability to perform tasks that matter in competition, what matters in competition varies industry by industry.

THESE THREE OBSERVATIONS lead to an important implication: the construction of comparative advantage implies geographic and sectoral decentralisation. To promote capability and comparative advantage effectively, government policy ought to focus on sectors in which the economy specialises, and be geographically specific. There can be no effective one-size-fits-all 'best' economic policy.

How, then, might we navigate between the twin – but opposite – evils of, on the one hand, undesirably narrowing and potentially atrophying comparative advantage; and, on the other, coddling long-term state mendicants? We must expose candidates for strengthened comparative advantage to competition, while improving their ability to survive in that competition.

Consider coal and iron ore, Australia's most important exports. While a necessary precondition for the nation's prominent position in international trade in these sectors is a surplus of raw materials over domestic needs, that alone does not create global comparative advantage. In commodity competition, it is not sufficient simply to have been endowed with a surplus of the material in the ground. The tasks that matter in such commodities are the ability to deliver the right product (that is, with precisely the right specifications), to the right customer, in the right place, in the right quantity, at the right time – and all at the right price.

Achieving that requires far more than a mere surplus endowment. Otherwise, Africa would dominate almost every commodity sector. To be successful in the coal and iron ore sectors, Australia has had to develop a wide capability that ultimately comprises its comparative advantage, and much of its has been supported or provided by government and other non-firm institutions. To begin with, these industries require effective systems for financing and performing mineral exploration and discovery. Australia has built these.

It possesses the world's foremost risk-capital market for financing early stage mineral-discovery, with highly sophisticated market rules and governance for ensuring that potential investors can properly compare claims and evaluate risk in exploration ventures. The Australian Stock Exchange has invested in this capability over many years, and Australia leads the world in the field, with the result that the nation possesses the world's broadest and deepest markets for financing mineral exploration. The ASX includes hundreds of firms active in these fields – firms that must be able to tap a body of geological expertise and methodologies for engaging knowledge to create efficient search systems. Again, the country has invested in these, and leads the world in this field.

The rules for controlling ownership and access to raw materials must be designed and enforced without corruption. Australian government bodies are ahead in this area. Beyond discovery, highly complex and scale-intensive development projects must be financed. Australia's banks, financial institutions and resource companies lead the world in large-scale project finance and management. Logistics systems of great complexity must be designed, constructed, maintained and operated. Australia has built these. (To understand the scale of these systems, it is necessary only to note that more than half of all world trade, by weight, is in a single product: iron ore.)

Comparative advantage stems from the combination of all these organisational, institutional and individual capabilities, which must be deliberately nurtured and sustained, including often through downturn periods when markets don't yet want to pay for them, and whose interaction must be co-ordinated.

Australia has built similar, if not yet so obvious, comparative advantage in other fields. Consider wheat, humanity's most important food source. Wheat is grown on 500 million acres worldwide, taking more space than any other crop. Australia produces a surplus over domestic needs, and while it is not a major grower of wheat, it is able to be a major trader. Its farmers produce high yields. But comparative advantage in this case comes also from superior genetics – Australia is pre-eminent in wheat genetics and genomics, an unsung national treasure – along with superior logistics and trading.

THESE EXAMPLES ILLUSTRATE not only that comparative advantage in the modern world must reach far beyond natural endowment, even in areas that would appear most dependent on nature, but also that comparative advantage is continuously dynamic, changing all the time. Possession of comparative advantage must be deliberately led, to ensure that it stays abreast of the future.

This is not a matter of government planning and control, but of strategic investment to create the capabilities, incentives and rules through which private industry can succeed in competition. A vital part of government economic policy must be to consider which forms of comparative advantage the nation wants to build and sustain, and to help construct them; for that will shape the future.

Jonathan West heads the Australian Innovation Research Centre at the University of Tasmania, and for nearly twenty years studied and taught at Harvard University. His essay 'A new globalisation' was published in *Griffith REVIEW 25: After the Crisis*.

Facsimile days

Recollections of a GFC jobseeker

Nick Marland

I took to running. I ran a lot – shaved nearly five minutes off my best time over seven kilometres. There was plenty of time to stride out on Sydney's Bay Run in the long winter of 2009. It was one of the things tenuously holding my days together. Each morning I waged an internal civil war just to get up. The tabs opened out across my web browser: news and email, and then the baton relay of Seek, MyCareer, CareerOne, JobSearch, JobsNSW and artsHub. I prodded the vacancy-page recesses of the ABC and SBS. It was less like a trawler dragging its net through a lonely sea than like visiting a row of mongers who sold only a few fresh fish every week, placed strategically atop the stinking pile they had spruiked for weeks. There you were, in a crush of five hundred people, all bidding for the same gleaming meagre catch.

After sending one or two applications – if I found something I was even remotely suited to – it was time to don my paint-speckled shorts and an old T-shirt, and do my stretches. Around lunchtime I hit the tarmac in my worn Dunlop Volleys, finding my gait and settling into a rhythm, managing my breathing and my mind, holding focus, running along the water's edge at Iron Cove. The tide was out, but I was sure it would eventually come back in.

Australia's unemployment rate hit 5.8 per cent in October 2009. I'd followed it up there with my own weary eyes the previous eight months, ever since I was made redundant from my job of five years at Media Monitors. The Rate only ever registered peripherally while I was on a payroll. It was a number heard half out of earshot on a radio bulletin, a page five item in the newspaper, a screen graphic during the post-workday, pre-dinner catatonia through which I viewed the evening news. I did spare thoughts and best wishes for those suffering joblessness, but it still seemed like a trifling figure, a blip in the midst of Howardian prosperity. (If I'd been paying closer attention as recently as eight years ago, I would have realised it was not unusual for The Rate to hover around the 7 per cent mark.) I'd never struggled to land work and while, like most people, I had the peculiar mixture of resentment for my job and a lack of desire to leave it, I felt that if I needed to find something it wouldn't be too hard.

I knew the tide was turning: I'd watched the financial meltdown and concomitant jobs crisis unfold on news bulletins from my office desk. The problems of the world seemed intangible, to be reported on but not experienced. That was until the state manager asked me along for a quick chat.

It sat there on the meeting-room table, stark and crisp like the wing of a waterbird: a large white envelope, addressed to me. The manager invited me to take a seat. 'How is everything?' he asked, closing the door.

Four weeks' notice. My body thrilled with conflicting emotions. I enjoyed the company of the people I worked with, but the work was unchallenging and had nothing in common with my life's aims. To be leaving was not the most awful thought. Perhaps I could finally pursue my writing career! Or at least shift to a new sector and meet head-on the challenges it offered. That I was servicing a mortgage on my own was perturbing: I would have to find a new job within weeks. But something would turn up. Surely.

The manager was talking, but I was in a swoon. His attempts to manage the fallout and offer me corporate counselling would have been funny if they weren't infuriating. When he showed me the payout figure, though, much of that fury evaporated. Walking out the door into the January sunshine, I was young, rich and free.

GALILEO PURPORTEDLY SAID that numbers are the language with which God has written the universe. In the months that followed, that January smile ebbing from my face, it was true that, at least in my universe, everything had devolved into numbers: a tumbling bank balance, and calculations as to how many months it could last; a credit card balance climbing in inverse proportion; mortgage repayments; bills and levies; deciding what meal to cook, based on how many servings I could wring from it; the frugal but very necessary pursuit of cleanskin wine in bulk at $2-per-bottle prices; kilometres over time; litres per kilometre. I came to know the true value of a dollar, the true length of an hour, a day, a week.

Among all these figures The Rate was the Number of the Beast. I paid it the hateful respect of an exorcist. I'd been initiated into this dark cult, and I wasn't alone. Several colleagues went out the door at the same time; since then, other friends have lost their jobs. They are all intelligent, literate people with training in such areas as computer technology, audiovisual editing and journalism. Some have picked up scraps of work, casual stints and contracts, while others have moved into new full-time roles after months of search-ing. One friend trained in architecture found a four-month stint as a postie; another, a writer and great wit, currently works in a factory.

I have valuable skills, qualifications and experience. But the value of something, my father told me as a child, is what somebody else is willing to pay for it. I revised my CV again and again; worked hard at cover letters I considered selling to literary journals, such was their spare lyricism. I read long hours of 'how to improve your application' literature. What was missing? I could blame the economic climate, but perhaps the fault was mine, a fault of poor salesman-ship. When it all seemed insoluble I could be found out on the running course, where everything was breath and heartbeat and the steady pounding of feet.

I never signed up for the dole. This was not a matter of pride so much as of hope, a belief that something was just around the corner. Nine months of corners later I was still jogging along with the same naive expectation.

AS WE TURNED into the home straight of 2009, the prevailing mood in Australia was of cautious optimism. Treasurer Wayne Swan spoke of the nation as an escapist of Houdini-like ability; we had 'dodged a bullet,' in the words of almost every Australian financial reporter and subeditor, due to sound fiscal policy (and, let's face it, China's appetite for resources). Pundits and Opposition politicians were going so far as to declare the Global Financial Crisis over.

Post-mortems proclaimed the so-called worst economic crisis since the Great Depression to be nothing of the sort. 'The economic downturn in Australia has been far less severe than in the early 1990s [and there is] evidence that the economy is already recovering,' then Opposition Leader Malcolm

Turnbull told the Menzies Lecture audience in October. The IMF concurred: Australia was on the up and up in its World Economic Outlook. Turnbull responded by calling for a reduction in government stimulus spending. The Rate hit that 5.8 per cent mark and flattened out, and there was much rejoicing in the streets – the Crisis was over!

Except that I – and many others – still could not get work. If the 'shitstorm' had passed, everything was still covered in shit. As David Hetherington, from the independent think tank Per Capita, noted in an August 2009 interview on Radio National, while the financial crisis seemed to be passing 'the problem is, the effects linger in the real economy for a very long time… the real danger is unemployment.'

Back in January, when news leaked around the office that my colleagues and I were dead people walking, there was much sympathy, some indignation and plenty of disbelief. We were consoled with the observation that 'at least you can get out and enjoy the beach.' By December people were saying, 'At least you can get out and enjoy the beach. After all, it's free.' They envied me still, these friends! They thought I had it made. A casual glance at their Facebook statuses: each Monday, they complained that it was Monday; each Wednesday, the end to this barbarism was in sight; each Friday, the celebrations began in earnest, fifty-one mini-New Year's Eves dotted across the calendar.

They didn't understand how much I envied them their moneyed and varied lives. It was too abstract for them to comprehend that days without routine and commitment are dull and fraught with worry. There is no spare money to do anything; free time is spent ridden with guilt that you're not job-hunting. This is no way to live. Their taking-for-granted got to me. 'Would you like to swap?' I joked, my bitterness hidden. My days were cut from the same mould, with the same repertory of behaviour, the same rhythms. They were facsimile days, freighted with ennui and empty of self-belief.

I WAS FLAT-OUT landing an interview. The rejection emails slunk into my inbox several days a week: *We thank you for your time in applying… We regret to inform you…* Friends and family offered to take a look at my CV, or overflowed with well-meaning suggestions: 'You should try being a lollipop man at work sites, just until things pick up'; or, 'You can make fifty dollars a time writing those little descriptions of homes in the windows of real estate agents.' What price dreams? I had loftier aims. I was still confident that dream opportunity was around the corner.

Finally: a real, live human being on the phone wanting to schedule an interview. An interview! It was a junior writer role with a Fairfax title in Sydney. This development seemed to vindicate the latest bold revision of my CV: switching around the Education and Employment History sections. It struck me that this might well be the light at the end of the tunnel. The period of doubt and despond would all be worth it to land such a lucrative post with potential for career progression.

Despite having no formal journalism training, and having been selected as 'wild card' on a shortlist of thirteen – from an applicant pool of 450 – I managed to progress to the final three. As strongly as I performed in the second interview, the outcome was inevitable; excitingly, though, the editors saw enough in me to offer some freelance work. I'd always wanted to work freelance, and had never had the gumption.

Let me state the obvious: freelance work can be sporadic. It's not a living, especially when you're just starting out. I knew this going in, and yet it was still a hard lesson to learn. I was determined not to let the opportunity slip, but I would have to find other work to supplement my writing.

In early December I began investigating how exactly you become a lollipop man, and worked on pitches for the lucrative real-estate-window-sales-blurbs market. At one interview, for a basic transcription role, the hirer said with genuine amazement that she just hadn't realised how bad it was out there for skilled workers. She'd received upwards of 150 expressions of interest for the two three-month typist roles she was seeking to fill. She was fielding enquiries from PhD holders, the young and the middle-aged, professionals, novelists, people with tertiary qualifications and the potential to be doing something lofty. We had come eagerly on a Saturday morning, a 40° early summer's day, in our jeans and dress shirts and long skirts, our hands slick with worry and heat. The hirer stressed to us all, caveat emptor, that it was 'just typing' and the roles were temporary. 'Sure, sure,' we all said, 'that's fine.'

JUST BEFORE CHRISTMAS, when I'd almost forgotten about it, I got the transcription job. It's extraordinary how nonplussed you can be at such momentous news when it's been so long coming. My overwhelming sense was of relief. The job was temporary, so perhaps it was temporary relief, but it was more than welcome. The starting date was late January, which meant a month or so more of leftovers and canned food.

Coming together with family and friends over the holiday, we were to a man and woman counting down the remaining days of a hard year. 2010 seemed to entice us all with its hopeful prospects. We projected onto it our dreams of recovery, our plans to develop our career, our yearning to travel when we had the means: unrealistic expectations, and unlikely to all be realised, but we felt we'd earned the right to have them.

Where would I have been without these people? I'm exceedingly fortunate to have their support, be it moral, emotional or financial. Yet not everyone has them. There are people I know, and others I will never meet, who are enduring the same travails right now, in the shadow of the Global Financial Crisis that commentators have consigned to history. To whom can they go, if not to people like mine?

My pride made it hard to accept assistance from my parents, but pride doesn't put food in your belly. My dearest friends, too, lit a path for me. Until The Envelope came, I don't know that I truly realised the abundance of love in my life. These friends shouted me drinks, dinners, nights out and weekends away. There was an element of shame and embarrassment when I accepted their gifts, but they spotted it and told me to stop being stupid. I can take a hint.

I KEEP RUNNING. Every second day I try to get out there. In winter the sun was aloof and I often ran through drizzle, but now the days are clear and I can feel the bright orb a little closer. Always, though, the winds off the water can hit hard. Run anti-clockwise around the circuit and the winds are at your back; the journey is easy. Run clockwise, though, and it's headlong into a gust, fighting all the way. It is the same as running an extra kilometre, and at your destination you feel exhausted yet fulfilled.

Nick Marland is a freelance writer of fiction and non-fiction, having appeared in the UTS Anthology 2010, the(sydney)magazine and Voiceworks. He holds a Master of Arts in Creative Writing from the University of Technology, Sydney.

ESSAY

The politics of prosperity

Vulnerability, luck and the lessons of history

Tom Conley

'Luck always seems to be against those who depend on it.'

THIS is a lucky country. The challenge is to keep it lucky, and the danger is that thinking we are fortunate may make us complacent about real and ever present vulnerabilities. Avoiding the worst of the global economic crisis of 2008–09 reinforced Australia's sense of providence – waiting for the recession, it turned out, was a bit like waiting for Godot. By early 2010 it appeared that unemployment had peaked and Australia had outperformed the rest of the developed world.

But things change. And then they change again. After a year of dealing with the politics of a booming economy, the Rudd Government had to shift rapidly to avoiding a recession. Kevin Rudd looked to have continued an unfortunate Labor tradition of coming into office at an extremely inopportune moment. James Scullin had to deal with the Great Depression; Gough Whitlam tried to spread the luck of the postwar boom just as that luck ran out; and Bob Hawke took over when it was increasingly obvious that Australia's economic problems went beyond recession, to the very basis of its long-term prosperity. Determined to replicate the excellent record of the Hawke government, rather than the ignominy of Scullin's or Whitlam's, Rudd Labor quickly embarked on a massive program of government spending to stimulate the economy. The Reserve Bank added monetary easing to the stimulus, cutting interest rates by 4.25 per cent between September 2008 and April 2009.

The prescient action of policymakers was in stark contrast to the Hawke and Keating governments' delayed reaction to the early 1990s recession and helped Australia to avoid a technical recession, two quarters of GDP contraction in a row. Australia also benefited from the Chinese Government's huge economic stimulus, which helped to underpin China's continuing demand for Australian resources. Indeed, government actions throughout the world stopped the slide into a global depression.

As the news from the rest of the world started to improve, some Australian policymakers and business figures argued that the real problem for

PREVIOUS PAGE: Tom Roberts (1856–1931), *Shearing the Rams*, 1890. Oil on canvas on composition board. Courtesy of the National Gallery of Victoria.

Australia's future would be dealing with the politics of prosperity caused by the rise and rise of Asia. Secretary to the Treasury Ken Henry observed, 'China and India are only in the early stages of catching up with the living standards of the developed world and this process could have a very long way to run.' On the same day the chair of BHP Billiton, Don Argus, said, 'I believe we stand at the threshold of an era of unprecedented growth due to demand generated by China and, in the future, India.'

Australians' perceptions of their position in the world have oscillated between optimism and pessimism. Today, they once again believe they are living in a lucky country. When Donald Horne wrote *The Lucky Country* in 1964, he could not have imagined how iconic the phrase would become, or how completely the ironic intent of his title would disappear. Nevertheless, his argument that Australia's success was not the result of industriousness or innovation did not deny that Australia was genuinely lucky. While an abundance of natural resources has been a curse for many countries, this has not been so for Australia.

But resource wealth has never been, nor will it ever be, enough. It has to be converted into widespread prosperity through political action and the construction of appropriate institutions. According to the economic historian Ian McLean, 'The institutional framework is seldom offered as a reason for our economic success because it is taken for granted. Yet many growth economists now believe that, perhaps more than any other factor, appropriate institutions are the key to explaining why some countries are rich and others poor.'

By 'institutional framework', McLean means things such as the form of land ownership in colonial Australia, such as the family farm, the development of education and research facilities, right through to the political system itself. Why did the fortunes of Australia and Argentina diverge so significantly over the twentieth century, given their similar positions in the 1890s? It is the political process in Australia, flawed as it has been and remains, that has helped to spread the benefits of growth across society. Horne may have been too harsh on Australia's politicians, but equally some new counsel might be necessary.

Australians need to be aware that this is a vulnerable country as well as a lucky one. The country's economic history shows that booms are followed by periods of gloom. Maybe this boom is the one that breaks the mould; but regardless, it will not solve the fundamental recurring problem of Australia in the world economy: our vulnerability to changes in international commodity demand and international financial supply. Reliance on resource wealth remains a precarious path for Australia's future, especially when coupled with an explosion of unproductive debt. Australia is more indebted than ever before. Rising concern about global warming makes it even more urgent that we further diversify Australia's productive capacity and export profile. If the more dire predictions of global warming are realised, Australia will need to adapt and reduce its reliance on resource exports.

To these global vulnerabilities we can add a third, domestic one: our vulnerability to rising inequality. Australia cannot control what happens in the rest of the world – it is a minor player in the global economy – but it can control the way we adapt to global events and developments. Embracing the outside world stimulates competition and underpins expansive growth, but it need not come at the expense of the weakest elements of society. Governments should foster a socially sustainable globalisation that allows Australia to ride out the problems caused by our historical vulnerabilities without creating negative reactions that could push us back into insularity and protectionism, which was white Australia's first reaction to vulnerability.

THE ESTABLISHMENT OF a resource-based economy in the first half of the nineteenth century, through the colonies' support for private initiative, set the scene for Australia's future economic development. While boom times between 1861 and 1891 disguised inequalities and vulnerabilities, the 1890s revealed how external developments could exacerbate domestic economic problems. When the British bank Barings nearly went bankrupt through bad deals in Argentina, its investors undertook the sort of wholesale reassessment of developing-country investments that has in recent years been common at times of crisis. The substantial decline in the demand and price of commodities, and the drying up of foreign sources of capital, intensified the problems caused by over-expansion in the wool industry, property speculation (especially in Melbourne), banking collapse and over-investment by colonial governments in infrastructure. The severe drought from 1895 to 1903 added to the colonies' woes and delayed recovery.

Despite the Depression the view remained that Australia was a 'fundamentally prosperous economy', and in their attempts to establish the policy principles for the new Federation, policymakers 'set out to defend the economic structure as it presently existed', according to the professor of public policy Francis Castles. Both boom and gloom, therefore, helped to create the conditions for protectionism. Castles suggests that there were four main components of the protectionist policy structure: protection of manufacturing industry, the conciliation and arbitration of industrial disputes, the control of immigration, and a residual system of income maintenance for those outside the labour market. In *The End of Certainty* Paul Kelly adds Imperial benevolence – Australia's reliance on 'great and powerful friends' – as an integral part of the structure.

Recovery from the Depression of the 1890s was not dependent on foreign investment and immigration; rather, it was bolstered by gold discoveries in Coolgardie and Kalgoorlie, and development in Western Australia generally. Governments were trying to diversify the economy, with shifts towards manufacturing, mining, services and non-pastoral land use dominating their efforts. The good times did not last, however, as the world descended into depression during the early 1930s, exposing yet again Australia's dependence on primary commodity exports and reliance on foreign capital.

Public debt during this period was high – about 128 per cent of gross domestic product – because of government efforts to develop the economy through the provision of infrastructure and support. Rolling over debt was no longer possible after the crash of 1929, and unemployment skyrocketed. While governments were unable to find a way out of the downward spiral, Australia's more diverse economy meant that it fared better than did other primary producers around the world.

War finally brought an end to the Depression and showed how state planning could deliver beneficial economic results: full employment with low inflation. It also provided an impetus to the development of the Australian manufacturing sector. By the late 1940s Australia was booming, with the Korean War sparking massive American demand for Australian wool. With the addition of increased demand for metals, exports reached 30 per cent of GDP (compared with a low of 12.2 per cent in 1969, and 21.5 per cent in September 2009). The fall, though, was just as spectacular and the subsequent recession severe.

Again the Australian economy recovered, and international demand and the inflow of labour and capital stimulated a 'long boom'. Protectionism provided an institutional strategy – political and economic – for distributing

Australia's resource wealth and developing a more diversified economy. Manufacturing became a significant export earner for the first time in Australian history, but from the 1960s a series of technological and competitive pressures undermined its postwar expansion. The growth of mineral exports helped reduce Australia's reliance on agricultural exports. Trade shifted away from Britain and Europe to Japan and the US, and by the early 1970s Asia accounted for half of Australia's exports.

Postwar prosperity meant that unemployment remained low and welfare remained minimal. While social conditions improved throughout the developed world, poverty did not disappear, as studies of poverty in the 1960s and 1970s revealed. Research by Ronald Henderson turned into a wide-ranging inquiry into the nature of poverty in Australia, and the findings of the Henderson Report shocked many. In Western Europe a philosophy of social compensation was providing high levels of social protection within efficient capitalist economies. Sustained growth encouraged policymakers here to believe that they could do even more. Such was the position of Whitlam Labor when it won government in 1972.

Regrettably, the 1970s was a time of turmoil for both Australian politics and the economy. Whitlam's ambitious social-democratic program assumed continuing prosperity, but as the mid-1970s mining boom waned and stagflation beset the global economy, conditions for social reform became less favourable. The world economic downturn would have made managing the economy difficult for even the most economically competent and politically united government.

Whitlam's Liberal successor, Malcolm Fraser, continued to believe that the rural and resources industries would provide for Australia's future. He and many others saw the resources boom of the late 1970s as the solution to Australia's economic woes. In the lead-up to the 1980 election, Fraser claimed: 'In my policy speech of 1977 I said Australia could look forward to $6,000 million in development. Some amazement was expressed in this – even disbelief…And now prospective development is $29,000 million. This development promises to be as important to Australia and individual Australians as anything in the last thirty-five years.'

Unfortunately, the mooted boom failed to bring the economic windfall that some believed would present Australian policymakers with the 'problem' of working out what to do with excessive trade surpluses. Optimism was not just home-grown, with the OECD arguing that Australia had the best prospects of all developed countries in 1981.

The recession of the early 1980s was a turning point. The Hawke government's decision to float the dollar and liberalise the financial sector was the beginning of the end of the old Australia. Donald Horne's famous phrase was trotted out, but this time in commemoration rather than celebration. Resource optimism turned into pessimism and the perception was that Australia had a 'third-world' economy.

Nothing illustrates this decline better than the terms of trade: the average price level of exports versus the average price level of imports. It fell significantly after the short-lived mineral booms of the mid-1970s and early 1980s. And after gradually climbing from late 1982, it plummeted during 1985 and early 1986. Another marker of decline was the current account deficit: the balance between exports and imports, and the flow of interest and dividend payments into and away from Australia. The already growing deficit substantially worsened in 1986.

The implications seemed clear: Australia was in terminal decline. Paul Keating's infamous 'banana republic' warning was the public manifestation of crisis. 'We took the view in the 1970s – it's the old cargo cult mentality of Australia that she'll be right,' he said. 'This is the lucky country, we can dig up another mound of rock and someone will buy it from us, or we can sell a bit of wheat and bit of wool and we will just sort of muddle through…In the 1970s… we became a third-world economy selling raw materials and food and we let the sophisticated industrial side fall apart…We must let Australians know truthfully, honestly, earnestly, just what sort of international hole Australia is in. It's the price of our commodities – they are as bad in real terms since the Depression… If this government cannot get the adjustment, get manufacturing going again and keep moderate wage outcomes and a sensible economic policy, then Australia is basically done for…If in the final analysis Australia is so undisciplined, so disinterested in its salvation and its economic well being, that it doesn't deal with these fundamental problems…you are gone. You are a banana republic.'

The severity of the early 1990s recession had much to do with the zealotry of Keating and his coterie of economic advisers. Keating made what was perhaps one of the stupidest remarks in Australian political history when he claimed it was the 'recession we had to have'. He said it because he meant it: Keating believed that a recession would be good for the economy, because it would 'fix' the current account deficit (CAD), lower inflation and set up Australia for long-term growth. There's no doubt that it helped to quell inflation, and since the recession Australia has not had two consecutive quarters of GDP contraction. But it certainly didn't fix the CAD. In the lead-up to the 1996 election, the Howard-led Opposition exploited the recession, the worsening CAD and the growing level of foreign debt, arguing that Labor had solved none of Australia's economic problems despite its long hold on power.

THE AUSTRALIAN ECONOMY performed poorly between the early 1970s and early 1990s. But since then, Australia has experienced a record eighteen years without a technical recession, its economy expanding by around 80 per cent. Failing to enter recession in the global crisis of 2008–09 meant that Australia avoided two international recessions in a row, which is unprecedented. Most of this growth occurred under Howard's watch, just as Keating had feared back in 1991, when he declared: 'frankly, the only difficulty for the government is being around long enough.'

John Howard may have taken office at the most opportune time in Australian history, but it wasn't all plain sailing. Howard faced the Asian crisis in the late 1990s. And in 2000 and 2001, at the height of the technology boom, many commentators, attempting to justify the collapse of the value of the dollar, derided Australia as an 'old' economy with an archaic economic structure. These statements were the residue of the mid-1980s anxiety about Australia's primary commodity dependency and were remarkably ill-timed, because commodity prices were at the beginning of a steep and sustained ascent.

Revenue from the mining sector rose from an average of 7 per cent of GDP for most of the 1980s and 1990s to 11 per cent in 2008. Royalties and taxes boomed as well; together they contributed more than 1 per cent of GDP in 2005–06 and undoubtedly more in following years. Despite this largesse, the percentage contribution of mining and, indeed, agriculture to GDP would probably surprise most Australians. Agriculture accounted for 2.5 per cent of GDP, down from 4.9 per cent in 1990, and mining accounted for 8.3 per cent of GDP in 2008, down from 4.9 per cent as well. Manufacturing declined from 15.8 per cent to 10.1 per cent over the same time.

The contribution of mining and agriculture, however, is vastly more important in exports. From the early 2000s Australia reinvigorated its dependence on commodity exports. Exports of primary commodities increased from 56.1 per cent of merchandise exports in 2003 to 68.5 per cent in 2008. Manufacturing exports declined from 31 per cent in 2003 to 21.2 per cent in 2008; elaborately transformed manufactures declined from 21.8 per cent to 13.9 per cent.

Considering the increase in export values for primary commodities, it is not surprising that concerns about resource dependence have almost disappeared. The best indicator of this change in fortunes is again the terms of trade, which increased by 88 per cent between the September quarter of 1999 and the same quarter in 2008. It then fell dramatically from late 2009, but it still remains more than 50 per cent higher than the average of the 1980s and 1990s. Peter Costello said in 2007: 'our terms of trade will moderate, but will not be in long-term decline, which was the story of the twentieth century.' This appears to be the new policy consensus, but it is a big call given Australia's history.

There is reason to be confident, given Australia's efficient mining operations. Because much of Asia is in developmental mode, the region will require considerable resource-intensive development. When starting from a low base, growth can be very rapid indeed: Asia's share of world GDP was only 7 per cent of GDP in 1990 (at market exchange rates), increasing to around 15 per cent by 2008. Growth in East Asia averaged 7 per cent a year during this period, compared with 2 per cent for the developed world. In industrial production Asia, especially China, has fared even better. In 1990, China's share of global industrial production was 2 per cent; in 2008, the figure was 13 per cent.

The major short-term issue is whether commodity prices will stay high or revert to the long-term trend decline. Even if Asia continues to expand, without major reversals or periods of stagnation, it's likely that resource prices will decline as their supply increases. The most important growing market for Australian resources, China, is actively seeking to diversify its sources of supply. It will also eventually reduce its resource-heavy manufacturing profile, and is already striving for greater industrial efficiency. Technological change could also undermine demand, as happened with Australian's pre-eminent export until the 1950s, wool, now the nation's twenty-sixth most important export.

Another significant policy concern of the late 1980s and early 1990s was debt. Australia's major problem is private debt, although public debt is also increasing due to government efforts to stimulate the economy. After reaching a high of 18.5 per cent of GDP in 1995–96, Australia's general government net debt fell markedly to a net surplus in 2005–06. Continuous growth and a sustained resources boom can do wonders for a government's fiscal position; but given the revenue created by the boom, greater efforts could have been made to accumulate a true counter-cyclical budget surplus that could be used in a sustained downturn. In 1990 Norway legislated for the creation of a sovereign wealth fund to invest surpluses from its resource earnings, so that when the oil revenue runs out Norwegians will continue to reap the benefits of resource abundance. Still, counter to the scare tactics of the current Opposition and economic liberals, Australia's public debt position is sounder than that of most developed countries.

However, that concern about foreign (private) debt has lessened the more the debt has risen. High levels of foreign borrowings are not new in Australia, although previously this has been associated with particularly bleak economic periods. Before the 1980s, the highest debt levels were recorded during the depressions of the 1890s (34 per cent of GDP) and 1930s (39 per cent of GDP). In 2008–09, foreign debt was 50.3 per cent of GDP.

There has also been a huge expansion in household debt, most of it in housing. This has helped to make Australia one of the dearest places in the world to buy a house. Household debt is now at unprecedented levels – about 160 per cent of disposable income (or more than 100 per cent of GDP). Now that interest rates are on the rise, interest payments as a percentage of income will increase. The sustainability of the debt will be affected by the economy's capacity to maintain high levels of employment over the next few years.

Both major political parties now appear to accept the 'consenting adults' view of foreign debt – that so long as debt is a matter between private businesses with the aim of creating economic activity, it should not be a concern of government policy. Those who are concerned worry that not enough money has gone into creating the productive capacity that will contribute to increased domestic savings and a lower level of foreign debt. The warning of some analysts that expanding debt leaves Australia vulnerable to a change in global financial sentiment will eventually be tested if the debt doesn't stabilise.

Worsening current account deficits are often the spark that ignites the concerns of investors and analysts. By far the largest component of the CAD is the net income deficit, which includes interest paid to foreign lenders and dividends paid to foreign shareholders. Running a long-term trade deficit hasn't helped either. Ultimately, CADs can only be lowered through increasing exports, decreasing imports, increasing saving or decreasing investment. Australia's CAD has risen significantly over the past thirty years. The thirty-year average is a deficit of 4.6 per cent of GDP, while the twentieth-century average is a deficit of 2.6 per cent.

Australia's two most important economic bureaucrats both argue that higher CADs will not be a problem. Treasury Secretary Ken Henry has said: 'Australia has a long history of CADs, reflecting the need to supplement the savings of a relatively small population to take advantage of an abundance of investment opportunities.' The CAD, as an accounting entity, represents the extent to which investment exceeds saving, meaning that it represents either a 'deficiency of national saving or an excess of national investment'. There are several ways that governments can increase national saving; forced superannuation is perhaps the most direct. Henry contends that the major cause of the CAD is Australia's high level of investment.

The Reserve Bank governor, Glenn Stevens, also thinks that larger CADs will not necessarily be a problem. Instead, the capital inflow will mean that the risks of investment in Australia's resource capacity will be shared between Australians and foreigners. As growing CADs have in the past worried international investors when they have gotten too large, Stevens believes that some persuasion of international financiers might be necessary.

Not everyone agrees. The economics commentator Ross Garnaut argues that the failure to deal with Australia's CAD problem has been one of the major shortfalls in economic policy over the past decade. Garnaut maintains that much of Australia's growth rate is unsustainable, because it is not possible to keep increasing foreign debt indefinitely. Australians, he says, have been living beyond their means, with living standards bolstered by unsustainable increases in debt.

YET NOT ALL Australians have been living beyond their means: as in the late 1960s, many Australians have not benefited from the good times. Doing well has led to less concern about those left behind – partly because there have been fewer of them in recent years, and partly because of the view that if most have been doing well, then why haven't these people?

The final vulnerability – the dangers of rising inequality – appears almost to have disappeared from public debate in Australia. Most commentary on social outcomes now centres on whether outcomes have worsened, not whether they have improved after eighteen years of continuous growth. Not only is it a poor outcome in itself if a wealthy country doesn't provide widespread opportunities across society; it is also unproductive to have sections of the population disengaged and reactionary. And it's definitely not productive to have poor health and education outcomes.

A reasonable test for social policy should be whether children can access health services (preventative and remedial) and an education system (pre-school to tertiary) that allows them the possibility of advancement, regardless of the socioeconomic status or predilections of their parents. While expanding the range of education and health choices may be desirable, it is not desirable if it is aimed at only one section of society at the expense of the rest, who don't get to choose.

Australians do not have to make a diabolical choice between growth and equality. Rising inequality is not inevitable, but egalitarianism requires a greater role for government – something that should be self-evident, yet has either been forgotten in the haze of economic transformation, liberalisation and globalisation, or is seen as anathema to it. A more determined egalitarian government requires, in turn, an electorate prepared to support increased social spending and fairer regulations. A widespread belief that fairer societies are not possible under economic globalisation is likely to be a self-fulfilling prophecy.

Social outlays have increased over the past twenty-five years, contrary to the argument that globalisation would force a decline in the welfare state. This is even true of the three supposedly neo-liberal countries in the OECD: the United States, the United Kingdom and Australia. Even Sweden, which commentators constantly argued needed to reduce its social outlays, ended up spending more in the 2000s than in the 1980s. While social spending has not been forced down, it is also evident that spending has not been comprehensive enough to stop poverty and inequality from rising in many countries. What matters is the composition of spending. While social outlays increased in Australia during the Howard years, there was also an increase in the percentage of non-cash benefits – government services, spending on health and education, and so on – directed to higher-income households.

Australia is a prosperous country today in large part because policy-makers have redistributed its resource wealth across society. Such redistribution should have been more extensive, and governments could have used it to underpin a more competitive, less insular, manufacturing sector. Even so, Australia's ability to adapt – though often imperfect – has enabled it to be in a position today to respond more effectively to new vulnerabilities. Central to this future adaptation is continued redistribution – a dirty word for many, but a concept essential to a sustainable approach to globalisation.

Allowing inequality to rise could have a detrimental effect on Austra-lians' receptivity to the very process that has contributed to our recent success, globalisation and engagement with Asia (which Donald Horne advocated all those years ago). While Australia should never go back to protectionism, it should retain some of that associated spirit of egalitarianism which meant that it remained a lucky country for many and not just a few.

It is worth remembering, too, that this is a wealthy and relatively equal country because of political interventions, not despite them, as many economists would have us believe. Australia must use its luck to lessen its vulnerabilities.

References available at www.griffithreview.com

Tom Conley is a senior lecturer in Australian foreign relations and globalisation in the Griffith Business School at Griffith University and the author of *The Vulnerable Country* (UNSW Press, 2009).

The endless seminar

Making of a public man

Glyn Davis

baham

'The only kind of revolution possible is a cultural one. Simply to change the people in control of parliament or of the means of production is no revolution. It's a *coup d'etat*.' – Dr Jim Cairns.

Discuss.

SO began a 1980 exam paper set by Donald Horne for a course on Australian political culture. Across barely a dozen questions Horne quotes Cairns, Murray Edelman, Antonio Gramsci, Robert Menzies, Sol Encel, Dennis Altman, Keith Hancock and Denis Kavanagh. In three hours political science undergraduates at the University of New South Wales were invited to consider the theory of hegemony, the distance between description and reality within political institutions, Australia as a home-owning democracy, the influence of middle-class affluence and Australia as a derivative culture.

The man who set this exam had no tertiary qualifications. Donald Horne (1921–2005) had spent much of his life as a journalist and editor working for Sir Frank Packer. He was once known for his fierce anti-communism, his co-editorship of *Quadrant*, his book *The Lucky Country* that damned the nation's elites as second-rate, and his love of food, wine and conversation.

For a long time Donald Horne suspected there could be no role for public thinkers in Australia. 'Intellectual' was a European term, seemingly ill-suited to an egalitarian nation. When it appeared in a publication Horne edited, 'intellectual' was always surrounded by quotation marks. Yet the Donald Horne, academic, who set this exam paper had learned from experience that ideas can travel if articulated clearly, and presented as part of a conversation – that intellectuals 'give shape to inchoate ideas already agitating the public mind'.

By 1980 Horne had become a familiar public intellectual in Australia, a man who helped the nation understand itself. His regular books and newspaper articles, his lectures and political activism, and roles such as chairing the Australia Council, ensured a wide audience. How did Donald Horne come to embrace – and help shape – the category of public intellectual in Australia?

This was only in later years a conscious effort; the young Donald imagined

---

PREVIOUS PAGE: Louis Kahan (1905–2002), Portrait of Donald Horne, 1970. Courtesy of the National Library of Australia.

his destiny as a poet or novelist, and his middle years were focused on journalism. It took the unexpected success of his first published book, written when he was forty-three, before Horne began to speak regularly in public about ideas. Even this public Donald Horne was rarely a systematic thinker, since his early training made him suspicious of epistemological claims, as of any attempt to influence the world. It was the late-blooming academic Donald Horne who strived to order a set of ideas that had preoccupied him for many years, shaped by the question of how culture is formed and sustained.

Horne's idea of a public intellectual developed as a response to experience – the thinking arose from the life. He observed his immediate world closely, and drew from this examination broader lessons about how to live and what to value.

The search for patterns, executed through a continued cycle of observation, speculation and writing, starts early. The method, as much as the content, marks his engagement with public issues. To capture his experiences, Horne kept diary notes, alongside the paraphernalia of a busy life. These Horne condensed into a series of popular autobiographical volumes, including *The Education of Young Donald* (1968), *Confessions of a New Boy* (1985), *Portrait of an Optimist* (1988) and *Into the Open* (2000). Each volume chronicles a phase of life, reading, conversations, friends, private and political passions. Perhaps it is this richness of primary material that has discouraged any detailed biography of Donald Horne to date, and yielded only a modest list of secondary works touching on his life and writing.

It is risky to rely closely on self-reporting. Horne began publishing his chronicles in middle age, and continued intermittently until his final years. We all hazard selective memory when recounting youth and early ambitions. Yet there is an appealing openness in Horne's account of failures and flaws, a coherence in his account of a shifting worldview nestled closely within the flow of his life. Taken together his writings offer the self-portrait of an intellectual who, as Horne observes, is at his worst when ideological and at his best when curiosity and scepticism make him question conventional wisdom.

It is instructive to trace the characteristic ideas and public arguments to emerge from each stage of a well-documented life. These suggest broadly four phases in the development of Horne's thinking: the early enthusiasms of student years under the influence of the philosopher John Anderson, a long period as a journalist and editor associated with causes of the political right, a shift in middle age to an interest in how culture is formed and sustained, and the final decades committed to political activism around issues of democracy and representation.

There are important continuities, notably Horne's libertarian beliefs and sceptical view of the state. There are also significant changes – not least, in recognising and promoting the possibility of public intellectuals in a culture that once seemed hostile to a public conversation. As a public intellectual, Horne believed in independence of judgement. Diana Gribble noted that Horne was capable of 'startling moments' in which he would be persuaded by someone else's point of view and 'completely change his mind'. This openness to new ideas makes it impossible to describe Donald Horne in conventional political terms. He was not simply a man of the right who moved to the left later in life, but someone who came slowly to a view about the role of ideas in society. The thinking and the journey are one.

DONALD HORNE WAS born in Sydney in 1921, the eldest child and only son of a schoolteacher shell-shocked by service in the Great War and a mother who put aside work for family. He could later recall his early years in astonishing detail: the buildings and families of his early home in Muswellbrook, the books on the shelves, the ten houses of his first sixteen years, the social structure of the town with its gradations of status and influence. When his father transferred to a new school in Sydney, the Horne family left the Hunter Valley for life in the suburbs during the Great Depression. It was a caring family, but a lonely life for a talkative boy with no siblings until a teenager and few opportunities to discuss the books he loved to read.

Young Donald found solace in the four volumes of *The History of the British Nation*, with their optimistic view of Empire and virtue. Yet he did not miss the subtext revealed amid glimpses of setback and defeat – the 'inhumanity, treachery, stupidity, and meaninglessness' of history. His father's later breakdown may have reinforced a disturbing realisation that life could be disconnected, discordant, irrational and unpredictable. During Horne's teenage years in

Sydney the family would move once again, this time to his grandmother's house, 'Denbigh', at 40 Arthur Street, Kogarah, to live on modest means.

Yet in retelling his time as a final-year student at Canterbury High – the same school attended two decades later by John Howard – Horne preferred not to dwell on family misfortunes. Instead, he recalled fondly the sympathetic worldview of a new newspaper, the *Daily Telegraph*, owned and run by Frank Packer – a very different paper from its present incarnation, with much serious writing and influence. The *Daily Telegraph* spoke to Horne's desire for modernity. Horne 'fell in love with it from the first issue' – its contemporary voice, the 'rebelliousness of spirit' in a newspaper of firm opinions. Through the *Daily Telegraph* Horne could take the 'side of Progress against Reaction or, perhaps more exactly, of Intelligence against Stupidity'. He became so immersed in the publication that one day while in the city he 'walked into the *Telegraph* building to see what it looked like'.

Horne would spend much of his professional life as a journalist and editor, working for Sir Frank Packer. He found in the *Daily Telegraph* a voice that matched his own character – optimistic, impatient with artifice, allied to the new and occasionally brash. In the magazines Horne would edit for the Packer family, he could reproduce his original enthusiasm for the *Daily Telegraph* formula – popularist, sometimes crusading, but always with an eye to sales and profit.

The transition from enthusiastic reader to writer was not immediate. On finishing school Horne enrolled in Arts at the University of Sydney on a Teachers College scholarship that would fund his studies and require him to follow his father's profession. Horne arrived on campus at the start of 1939, just seventeen and thrilled to be at university. Yet he felt quickly the gap between his background and that of the many privileged students. He found himself dissembling about his family origins. To modify his accent, Horne taught himself new diphthongs from an English textbook. He would reinvent himself in more important ways. Horne swiftly discovered talk in the Quad was more rewarding than time in the classroom. Like many students he was swept by each new discovery. He used campus to try on a rapid series of identities – as poet, follower of aesthetics, psychology and Freud, as scientist, artist and laconic conversationalist; 'young Donald, mumbler of witticisms', as he later observed ruefully.

Horne seemed determined to test himself with the challenging ideas of his time. He found these personified in the most famous man on campus, the Challis Professor of Philosophy, John Anderson. 'On the day I first arrived at the University I saw Anderson walking along the cloisters in the Quad: someone pointed him out as the Scottish radical who was the University's main rebel, a renowned atheist, not long ago a Communist, censured in the New South Wales Parliament and by the University Senate. Anderson seemed the most important person at the University...He was in his forties, very tall, stooped, gangling, striding loosely past in a brown suit and green hat with an upturned brim, usually sombre, with his pipe jutting out from between his teeth. He seemed an embodiment of what was grave and constant in human suffering, but sometimes he would wave an arm at a student, loosely, as if it were a puppet's, and smile, strong teeth bursting out beneath his full black moustache...Recognition. Sunshine...I was gripped by the need to know him.'

Horne began attending Literary Society meetings, with Anderson in the chair. The Professor's papers were heard in reverent silence. 'It took only an hour,' recalled Horne, but 'we felt that we had just witnessed an important new contribution to the theory of aesthetics.' In the Quad, Horne sought to master the argumentative style favoured by Anderson's many acolytes, with an emphasis on logic, grammatical integrity and precision. Horne found himself pounced on for many careless phrases – 'But what do you *mean* by that?' – and bewildered as his flights of fancy were critiqued by others more attuned to acceptable utterances.

That Horne struggled to capture the essence of Andersonian thought is not surprising, for the Challis Professor was reworking his philosophical position. During the 1930s John Anderson had been associated with the Communist Party, then briefly became a Trotskyite before breaking with organised Marxism to embrace a libertarian position. This pitted him against authoritarian states and institutions, including the formal requirements of university life; he led a campaign, for example, against the presence of a university regiment on campus. Anderson sometimes characterised his later views as anarchist, but eventually rejected political labels and any suggestion that meaningful change can be achieved through political action. He turned to exposing the illusions of progress and the need to promote freethinking in all spheres of life. Anderson's vehicle, in part, was the Sydney University Freethought Society, which for a while welcomed DR Horne as secretary.

It can be hard from a distance to grasp what makes a teacher charismatic. Anderson's striking influence on generations of students attest to his magnetism. When Anderson spoke 'in his urgent Glaswegian sing-song the room seemed stilled by significance,' Horne said. Anderson could project certainty – Horne was 'thrilled by his implacable lack of compromise and the way he argued stubbornly and passionately against almost everything said by anyone apart from the Freethinkers at Sydney University'. Anderson 'led the Freethought Society with the distant assuredness of a prophet on a faraway mountain'. He appeared to the admiring young student an 'intransigent believer in the exposure of all illusions and a prophet of the ideal of a life lived in permanent protest'. Anderson could seem entire and sufficient unto himself, a philosopher who had 'lost interest in the intellectual world outside Sydney, apart from sometimes sneering at what was going on in Melbourne'.

Anderson's influence on young Donald would be primarily political, and run counter to Horne's personality. As Horne later grasped, he was by temperament an optimist, but his intellectual training made him a pessimist. He took from Anderson an understanding that a freethinker should attack both right and left in politics, which Horne would do enthusiastically for decades to follow. But Anderson also reinforced an underlying conservatism in Horne's outlook – a sense that people cannot influence their surroundings, which are shaped by social forces rather than individual agency. Hence attempts to 'reform' society are doomed to failure – 'one must *account* for things, not try to *change* them. To plan for the future was sheer phantasy' – as Horne summarised a key learning from Quad discussions.

Above all, Horne was influenced by Anderson's article 'The Servile State', from which he derived an argument that 'the well-intentioned reformer always produces results which he did not anticipate.' Like Hayek in *The Road to Serfdom* Anderson resisted the claims of the state to order individual lives in the interest of better social outcomes. Anderson evoked the phenomenon of unintended consequences – the assertion that attempts at social amelioration produce results that undermine the intention. This insight justified Horne's rejection of Labor politics as 'meliorist' and misguided, preferring a view of himself as a 'radical conservative'. In the Andersonian spirit – 'the servile State is the unopposed State' – Horne did not register to vote and delighted in attacking 'welfare' and 'planning', as a student and later as a journalist.

Yet maintaining ironic detachment was never Donald Horne's most plausible persona. He was by instinct an activist. Even while professing Andersonian beliefs about the futility of individual agency, the undergraduate Horne embraced student and literary life with gusto. Student politics was unacceptable to the Freethinkers, but Horne launched an unsuccessful campaign against sex segregation in the university unions, before standing and failing to be elected to the student council. He eventually found a new home in the student newspaper, *Honi Soit*, and loved the immediacy of journalism – 'I could think of some new thing on the tram on the way to the university and, minutes later, I could hurry to the *Honi Soit* office and start doing it.'

Donald Horne found a sense of purpose and achievement through student politics. 'However trivial a source of power,' he decided later, 'it can provide the same pleasures as the greatest office…this was my education.' Finally, the activist Horne symbolically slayed the father – he organised enough votes to depose Anderson as president of the Literary Society and install himself as leader.

Still, for decades to follow Horne remained enthralled by Anderson's ideas, judging his own actions as inadequate against Anderson's more austere standards. As he worked as a journalist Horne 'could go on feeling that Anderson's sad, brown eyes were staring over my shoulder while I was writing a *Daily Telegraph* piece…' Horne sought guidance to life decisions in Andersonian terms, and worked much of his life, in journalism and later academia, with others trained by Anderson. These long years saw the natural optimist battle the learned pessimist, as the public Horne criticised planning and the illusions of reform while the private man wondered whether the world was quite as it had been presented in the lecture theatre.

In early 1942, Horne's university career was cut short by conscription. He found himself first in the regular army – ironically, given his Andersonian views, in the Sydney University Regiment – and then in the artillery. Horne was not a natural soldier, though his usual powers of observation produced a fine running commentary on the social structure and organisation of the Australian military, which he shared with his university friend the poet James McAuley, then a schoolteacher in Newcastle. Horne spent his spare time reading new British literary magazines such as *Horizon* and *Scrutiny*. He also discovered *The Economist*, which introduced him to the new genre of 'current affairs', his first encounter with 'serious journalism'.

During the war years Horne began reading about Asia, as he wondered about the postwar settlement to follow. In 1944 this interest was given practical expression when Horne was selected for the first intake of the new Australian Diplomatic Corps. Horne left the army with relief, and moved to the Canberra University College, then part of the University of Melbourne, to train for overseas service. Thus the opponent of planning found himself recruited to the public service as part of a new generation 'coming to power to modernise Australia'.

In the long college holidays, Horne headed home. He enjoyed the chance to read classics of political science and diplomacy as part of his course, but found Canberra 'offered nothing more than the stunted amenities of an Australian suburb or country town'. There were interesting encounters, such as meeting Lieutenant-Colonel John Kerr over drinks at the Hotel Canberra, but the escapes to Sydney became more lengthy. Horne supplemented his cadet pay by writing for the *Daily Telegraph*. This involved a memorable interview with legendary editor Brian Penton, who warned Horne: 'Just because you've got a university degree don't think you can walk in off the street and become a journalist!…Remember…your Returned Soldier's badge is worth more to you than your university degree.'

Since Horne had neither a degree nor had seen overseas military service and yet had just secured work as a *Daily Telegraph* casual reporter, he delighted in Penton's supremely confident, though wholly inaccurate, advice. He relished too the world of reporters – his successor as *Honi Soit* editor, Murray Sayle, taught him the house style, the art of journalism in which 'the mysteries of existence would freeze into a few short, sharp and solid sentences'. Journalism meant making the world understandable for readers. It was teaching of a sort, a way to communicate with an imagined audience.

Horne had been plagued with doubt about the prospect of becoming a diplomat. How could he speak for an Australian national interest when he had learned that 'society was simply an arena of conflicting forces?' He imagined 'John Anderson standing up at his rostrum in the Philosophy Room: in his most urgent whine, he was exposing me as mere "solidarist" who believed there was a common good.'

SO IN 1945 Donald Horne quit public service for journalism, an apartment in Kings Cross and the 'general detachment from everyone's sense of reality' that defined the *Daily Telegraph* newsroom. He covered politics and city news and occasionally wrote features, including a two-page profile on John Anderson. He met legendary newspaper men in Sydney hotels, shared a Potts Point apartment with a fellow journalist, was excited and disappointed in love, and developed an enduring fascination with the court politics surrounding his employer, Frank Packer. He lived, in short, the life of a journalist engrossed in his work, skilled at his craft, at home in the heavy-drinking culture of newspapers, spending his income on books, hotels, taxis and restaurants.

Many of his memorable anecdotes from this period revolve around political argument at parties. Like his fellow student and lifelong friend Doug McCallum, Horne found himself a conservative in a profession more often peopled by the left. Horne was out of sympathy with the era of postwar reconstruction, quoting Hayek or *The Economist* to fellow journalists. 'To be an anti-Stalinist intellectual as late in history as 1947,' he recalled, 'seemed a gallant and lonely stand.' It did not help that fellow Andersonians had split into rival camps, with some upholding the writings of the present John Anderson and others denouncing the current philosopher as 'reactionary', preferring an 'earlier and truer Andersonianism'. Horne found this disconcerting, particularly when he came under attack from former allies – 'here were Andersonians attacking me. Andersonians were not supposed to attack each other. They were expected to unite against the illusions of the rest of the world.'

But Horne's thoughts were turning elsewhere. In 1948 he married Ethel, an Englishwoman living in Sydney. He was keen to pursue his literary ambitions – 'reminders that I was now aged twenty-seven and had not yet written even one novel could strike me momentarily senseless with disbelief.' Within a year he and Ethel had abandoned life in Sydney for the slow voyage to the United Kingdom and a new life as a novelist. Horne settled into an English village, became active in the local Conservative Party and began work on a novel. When publication proved elusive he began a second novel, along with occasional journalism as funds ran short.

Eventually Horne could no longer live a financially haphazard existence. He moved to London, there to work with fellow Australian novelist George Johnson in the Fleet Street bureau of the *Sydney Sun*, before shifting to the *Daily Telegraph*. He worked first in London, then as an international corre- spondent. Finally he was recalled to Sydney by Frank Packer to establish a new newspaper closely modelled on a successful British publication of little repute. He returned to Sydney without Ethel and the marriage, already failing, fell apart 'in an unexpected exchange of letters'.

Arriving home in Australia was a shock. 'All of Sydney seemed second- rate and run-down: I saw myself as an exile from the old world – itself shabby, but with a shabbiness rich in meaning. Australia was mindless, I would say to myself. Where were the art museums and theatres, the intellectual debate?'

Horne resolved to start a journal of ideas, to create in Australia the sort of reading he had enjoyed in Britain. But first he must learn to be an editor, leading a new publication with the less than promising title *Weekend: Austra- lia's brightest newspaper*. A quick study, Horne grasped the essentials of working in the Packer empire, in the newsroom and executive offices overlooking Sydney's Hyde Park – the need to generate profits, anticipate the whims of the boss and manage relations with current Packer favourites. Horne learned how to control costs and when to hire journalists.

It took longer to master managing a team. Horne's behaviour as editor could be 'monstrous'. Unhappy with the quality of one article produced for *Weekend* he tore up the typed copy and threw it out the window. His editor- ship was marked by bursts of rage, and he became notorious for his technique in sacking people, when he would lose his temper to give himself courage. The very male and alcohol-fuelled culture of journalism made such incidents the stuff of barroom legend – the brother of one sacked employee poured a glass of beer over the *Weekend* editor in a local hotel. Horne would look back on these incidents with embarrassment, and later change his approach to working with a team.

Professional success did not mean personal happiness. Now in his mid-thirties, and still with no published novel, Horne worried about his life editing Australia's brightest newspaper and acting as court jester to Packer. There were periods of depression and doubt for DR Horne the 'angry, ill-informed shouter', a failed novelist consumed by 'alcohol, rage and self-pity'.

It also proved a time of political uncertainty. In the 1950s communism became the defining issue, particularly following Khrushchev's denunciation of Stalin and the Hungarian uprising. Old friends, such as James McAuley, began to define themselves as anti-communists and established the Australian Committee for Cultural Freedom to publish a new journal, *Quadrant*, and build links with international anti-communist movements. Some fellow Andersonians followed McAuley into the committee. Others shared his opposition to repressive states but preferred to explore the 'anarchist potential of being'. They declared themselves 'libertarians' and became, in time, the Sydney Push, a subculture that lasted a generation.

Horne could not empathise with the Sydney Push — he disliked its masculine and often anti-intellectual culture, and its 'romantic playing with anarchism'. John Anderson could no longer provide reliable guidance — in his final years as Challis Professor the philosopher had 'now assumed a position so inherently contradictory that it was no longer available for imitation'.

As Horne pondered his political stance in his middle thirties, two important changes in his life would define the path ahead. The first was personal — he met Myfanwy Gollan, a journalist with the *Sydney Morning Herald* twelve years his junior, who like Horne learned her craft on *Honi Soit*. They married in 1960. Family life became central to Donald Horne and a source of great joy. Their close partnership would endure until Horne's death, forty-five years later. Myfanwy would recount at the memorial service: 'We were very lucky that we were able to make such a life together. He was my companion and our companionship grew richer over the years.'

The second change was an opportunity at last to edit an intellectual journal. Horne had long believed an audience for ideas existed in Australia, despite the paucity of serious books and journals about Australian life (as he noted, in 1950s Australia the number of foreign books banned each year was greater than the number of books published). With Packer underwriting publication, from 1958 Australians could read *The Observer* fortnightly, with commentary on local and international affairs, and regular writing from academics such as Henry Mayer, and writers such as Michael Baume, Robert Hughes, Bob Raymond, Bruce Beresford, Les Tanner and Desmond O'Grady. *The Observer* challenged the notion that 'Australia' has 'long since been reduced to an essence, bottled and labelled'. Through the pages of a journal he described as 'intelligently conservative', Horne developed topics and themes he would publish in 1964 as *The Lucky Country*.

To assist with the new journal Horne hired Peter Coleman, a student of both Anderson and the English philosopher Michael Oakeshott. Coleman and Horne would work together on a number of Packer projects, providing space at times for fellow anti-communists.

The Observer encouraged frequent parties and dinners at the houses of contributors and friends, often including visiting British or American participants. These stimulating symposia were arranged by a new friend, Richard Krygier, the founder of the Australian Association for Cultural Freedom, which published *Quadrant*.

Horne, ever social and interested in new ideas, sought possible *Observer* contributors among a lively group of political scientists and sociologists – his old friend Doug McCallum, now at the University of New South Wales, Brian Beddie, Arthur Burns, Sol Encel, Dick Spann and Hugo Wolfsohn, along with Henry Mayer. He was invited back to Sydney University to defend *Weekend* and found himself 'addressing an overflow lecture theatre in the same room in which I had made my first public appearance as a student, seventeen years ago, defending (as a poet) good verse against bad'.

A further significant change would take some years to play out, but went to the core of Horne's long-standing political beliefs. As a good Andersonian, Horne remained sceptical about the prospects for meaningful reform through the political process. So despite his personal misgivings, Horne judged it pointless to attack too vigorously the White Australia policy. Australian folk roots, he observed, 'are in many ways among the most reactionary and racially bigoted in the world'. The prevailing political culture argued for a 'realist' approach; 'there was not yet a chance of surmounting the prejudices of the Australian people.' The editor decided that *The Observer* would not press the issue of institutionalised racism in Australian migration policy.

He was to be convinced otherwise about the limits of political action. As he later observed, 'a year after *The Observer* got going, twenty or so young intellectuals, mostly from the University of Melbourne, began meeting in a suburban house in Camberwell to discuss the practicalities of reforming the White Australia immigration policy. In the liberal intellectual tradition they decided to publish a pamphlet...it was expressed conservatively, but it was a new way of looking at the practical chances of amending what was seen as one of the foundations of both the Australian state and Australian society and in only a few years it had practical effects, much bigger than those expected. As good intellectuals, they were negotiating part of the new sense of the possible in Australia.'

The campaign proved influential. By 1966 the Commonwealth Government announced it would assess potential migrants on skills and suitability rather than race. Horne recognised the Melbourne campaign called into question his assumption that social progress is an illusion. Further, it suggested that intellectuals could organise campaigns and challenge foundational tenets of the Australian settlement. Donald Horne the pessimist, carefully schooled in 'realism' by 'Anderson and a host of books', glimpsed the possibility of Donald Horne the optimist, who saw that culture was not immutable, nor government necessarily no more than a reflection of prevailing attitudes. Horne had always held as true that reform is overwhelmed by unintended consequences. Now he grasped the risk of inaction – failing to change might also be harmful.

Marrying, beginning what would prove a happy and stable family life, editing *The Observer* and watching a successful political campaign all encouraged Horne to reassess his assumptions about the world. As a social commentator in the pages of an influential national opinion journal, he discovered a 'new sense of the possible'. Ideas could matter; change was possible. And this could be led by people 'doing one of the things only intellectuals can do: good, bad or indifferent, they were providing new concepts of what was going on and new concepts of what could go on. Despite myself, I was an intellectual, if not in quotation marks.'

IN 1960 FRANK Packer acquired a venerable, if moribund, Australian institution, *The Bulletin*, in a deal designed principally to block the young Rupert Murdoch. *The Bulletin*, with its famous pink covers and proud slogan under the masthead, 'Australia for the White Man', had a reputation for 'diehard reactionaryism, even among the conservatives'. Packer gave Donald Horne a choice: he could fold either *The Observer* or *The Bulletin*, and edit the remaining publication. Horne chose to reinvent *The Bulletin*, and set out to confound. He hired new writers, dropped the pink paper and slogan, removed the tired cartoons about Aboriginal Australians. He was determined to produce a *Bulletin* that included 'as fellow Australians women, city dwellers, young people, New Australians, Catholics, Aborigines, scientists, intellectuals, executives and dozens of other previously forgotten species; and that now accepted that Australia adjoined South-East Asia and that we lived in changing times'.

Bulletin readers professed outrage, but for Horne it was 'one further step from pessimism'. In transforming *The Bulletin*, he was also rethinking his own views. When transferred to other projects, Horne decided to leave the Packer empire. He spent some time contemplating other careers – one colleague suggested he become a state Liberal MP – before settling for financial security in advertising. In quiet moments at Australia's third-largest advertising agency, Jackson Wain, he began what would become his first published book, with a sustained look at contemporary Australian life.

As young journalist Horne had in 1946 sketched out a book about Australia, to be written with Bruce Miller. He did not hold back – the book would show 'that the theory of democracy as representative government was a swindle; that Canberra had the mentality of a small frontier settlement; that Australian nationalism was arrogant pep talk; that parliament provided a living exhibition of semi-literates; that the most serious distortion of newspaper reporting of parliament was to make politicians seem better than they were; that John Curtin had not been a great man; that politics was marked by tedium, stupidity and vulgarity; that most politicians were too old;

that too few were university graduates, too few had been abroad, and most showed narrow prejudices against the "un-Australian"; that many politicians were openly prejudiced against modern trends towards sex equality and saw women as wives and mothers but not as citizens; and not one of them could be described as liberal. They were all book-banners and intolerant bourgeois moralists.' And all of this before he warmed to his theme about the poverty of Australian elites – the Labor Party as a movement of prejudices dominated by Catholics and unionists, with no room for intellectuals, while the conservatives remained secretive and Australia a 'desert of reaction'.

Horne did not get much further than a fifteen-page outline, but the idea of writing about Australia persisted. He noted the paucity of books about the nation, with the architect Robin Boyd's *Australia's Home* and *The Australian Ugliness* and the historian Manning Clark's three selections of Australian historical documents among the few exceptions. Beyond a few periodicals, such as the *Australian Quarterly,* he found nothing worth reading from the universities. So, drawing on his articles for *The Observer*, feature ideas for *The Bulletin* and the editorials he had been writing in his head since his teenage years, Donald Horne sat in a backyard deckchair on a Sunday afternoon after lunch in December 1963, next to his wife and sleeping baby daughter, and 'began writing a book about Australia'.

This was not a scholarly work. Horne did little original research, and relied instead on old clippings and some fieldwork, such as the visit to South Sydney Junior Leagues Club that opens the original edition. He had in mind a transient book, a collection of snapshots of Australia in 'The Age of Menzies'. The book would trace the 'innocent happiness' of Australians, the sense of national identity, the groups excluded from national conversation, 'government by imitation' and 'politics without ideas' in a 'second-hand culture'. Horne wanted a book that was realistic about contemporary suburban living, avoiding the idealised landscape of Russell Ward's *The Australian Legend*. As his key theme, Horne developed the argument that Australia was fortunate rather than clever or innovative. It was Geoffrey Dutton, editor of the newly established Australian Penguin imprint, who suggested the title, drawing on the title of the final chapter and, subsequently, the most famous sentence in the book: 'Australia is a lucky country run mainly by second-rate people who share its luck.' When the draft was complete Myfanwy 'went through the typed copy, nipped out unnecessary words and sorted out word jams – in a way that became characteristic of what, in the old-fashioned sense, is our partnership.'

Published late in 1964 as a Penguin paperback costing eight shillings and sixpence, *The Lucky Country* was serialised in *The Australian* and sold its original print run in just nine days. Through multiple editions it would eventually sell more than 260,000 copies, and inspire television documentaries, school exams and a national slogan that profoundly misunderstood the irony of the title. Meaghan Morris would recall reading the book in one sitting: 'I had never struck anything like it; we had old Australian novels and a history or two around, but I did not know that you could write like *that* about our way of life.' Donald Horne found himself modestly famous, a public intellectual who spoke to, and about, Australia.

The Lucky Country was both description and program, with Horne calling for government to encourage the innovation missing from public and business life. He urged Australians to think about Asia and to embrace diversity – the word 'multicultural' was not yet in wide use. As Horne observed later, he had become 'unconservative' in deciding that progressive state action was possible.

Yet if Donald Horne was reassessing his view of politics, neither he nor his friends perceived the shift at the time. Horne remained close to many in Coalition politics. As an advertising man he was engaged by the Liberal Opposition Leader, Robin Askin, for the 1965 New South Wales election. Horne helped design the campaign 'With Askin You'll Get Action!' In the closing days of the race, Askin put his arm around a staffer and said: 'I think we're going to win'. Then, with a laugh: 'And think of the money we'll make.'

As Horne said, 'I thought he was joking.'

In 1964, Horne agreed to become co-editor of *Quadrant* with James McAuley. The following year, he was also invited to return as editor of *The Bulletin*. At this time Horne was closely involved in the Association for Cultural Freedom, working with Sydney colleagues such as Richard Krygier, David Armstrong, Leonie Kramer, Jim McClelland and Laurie Short, and new Melbourne contacts such as Frank Knopfelmacher and Bob Santamaria. In their company Horne embraced a fervent anti-communism that, for a season, marked his thinking and writing.

Of his career as an anti-communist, Horne later observed: 'I did fall into folly for something like a year and a half, mainly from ignoring one of the key maxims of sceptical conservatism, *pas trop de zèle*' – no excessive zeal. He believed that no foolishness by himself or his friends 'matched the errors of those who saw in Stalin and then Mao Zedong liberators of humankind'. Still, Horne concluded that a too-passionate rhetoric had sacrificed the civil tone that characterised his earlier writing.

As co-editor of *Quadrant* Horne was an advocate of the war in Vietnam, of close ties with America, and was a familiar voice in the causes of the right. *Tribune*, the Communist Party newspaper, dismissed *The Lucky Country* as 'right-wing extremism'. Horne used his editorships to pursue alleged communists – a 1961 *Bulletin* story included sensational, but little substantiated, claims of red influence in the Faculty of Arts at the University of Melbourne.

Though Horne would later regret a failure to manage his enthusiasm, his anti-communism was shared by many former Andersonians within the Association of Cultural Freedom. As an editor, said Horne, 'I was the full Andersonian ticket: I believed that liberty was the active part of democracy (flourishing most in opposition); that people should be allowed to pursue their own ways of life in all their diversity; that all censorship should be abolished; that homosexuality and abortion should be made legal; that restrictions on drinking, betting and other forms of amusement should be taken off the books; and that the state could be a particular enemy of freedom.'

Horne retained these libertarian values through this life. By the later 1960s, though, he found himself at odds with aspects of the outlook reflected in *Quadrant*, which he found conservative rather than libertarian. Horne was criticised by Leonie Kramer and Peter Coleman for advocating Australian republicanism in *The Lucky Country*. Richard Krygier took Horne to task for his regular lunches with the avowedly communist author Frank Hardy. A rift occurred within the Association of Cultural Freedom following revelations of funding by the Central Intelligence Agency through dummy foundations. Horne argued that while CIA money did not influence the content of *Quadrant,* secrecy about the donations fostered 'image problems' for the association and raised questions of trust in its leadership.

Still, it was some years before Horne and his long-time political allies parted ways. In 1967 he handed the *Quadrant* editorship to Peter Coleman, though he remained on the management committee for some time. Horne attended occasional seminars until the 1970s, by which time he found the Association of Cultural Freedom 'a fortress defending cultural freedom against the threats of Whitlamism'. When Horne published *Death of the Lucky Country* following the 1975 Dismissal, relations cooled sharply with friends of decades' standing. Donald Horne was not mentioned at celebrations in 1981 for *Quadrant*'s first twenty-five years. James McAuley, a friend since 1939, did not speak with him again. In his final public speech, the poet condemned the works of Gough Whitlam and his four beasts: Germaine Greer, Manning Clark, Patrick White and Donald Horne.

Horne had formed his political identity as a student, and contributed to public debate as journalist, editor and author. He joined those former Andersonians who viewed communism as the larger threat to human liberty, and promoted their arguments with characteristic vigour and enthusiasm. This was a cause shared for decades with prominent and engaging Sydney intellectuals. To break with such company must have been distressing, but Horne published little about his personal response. His new political opponents, though, made clear their views. In a review published in *Quadrant* in 1998 the Melbourne University Press publisher Peter Ryan criticised Horne as 'the national know-all', a narcissist and showman. Horne would later reconnect with some old friends, but for many the rift was permanent and bitter.

THE LUCKY COUNTRY proved the first of numerous books by Donald Horne. Its success enticed many offers from publishers, and Horne used the opportunity to rework with Myfanwy an early unpublished novel as *The Permit* in 1965. Volumes of social commentary followed, along with a series of autobiographical books, beginning in 1967 with *The Education of Young Donald*. As Horne observed with pride, he had 'become "a writer" – average one book a year – our household had become, among other things, a workshop in which I had the physical pleasure of feeling all those words come out of my felt pen onto a long, lined foolscap writing pad, then of feeling them come onto the page through a typewriter and of writing revisions all over the typescript, then seeing a new, clean draft – a process that went on until there was something new and clean enough to give to Myfanwy for reactions.'

For some years, Horne combined this writing with editing *The Bulletin*. Through the final years of the long Liberal postwar incumbency, *The Bulletin* traced shifting preoccupations for Australian politics: the new priorities of Harold Holt, including the referendum to include Indigenous Australians in the national census, John Gorton and his interest in a local film industry, the emerging nationalism Horne had anticipated in *The Lucky Country*. He used *The Bulletin* to press causes such as republicanism, with the poet Les Murray designing a new national flag. As Elaine Thompson suggests, Horne's 'belief that you could energise people intellectually was obviously there'.

Horne recognised the emergence of the arts as definers of national identity, hiring younger writers such as Sandra Hall and Sandra Forbes to cover film and books. When the emerging novelist Frank Moorhouse failed to secure a Commonwealth Literary Fund Fellowship, Horne offered him a weekly grant through the *Bulletin* payroll to pursue his writing. 'It's a Frank Packer Fellowship,' explained Horne, 'but don't ever tell Frank Packer!'

Moorhouse in turn would encourage contact with a younger Sydney literary life. He and Horne became friends as they participated in the many seminars, workshops and symposia of the period. *Conference-ville*, a Moorhouse novella from 1976, includes a character named Horne, whose first rule of conference diligence is 'miss nothing and take one of everything' – that is, be committed to the whole experience.

Through these final years in journalism, Horne continued a long-established habit of long lunches and dinners with a shifting cast – his way to keep in touch with numerous worlds and associates. He enjoyed the company of fellow editors: Adrian Deamer of *The Australian*, Graham Perkin of *The Age*, John Pringle of the *Sydney Morning Herald*, Vic Carroll of the *Australian Financial Review*, Bob Raymond of *Four Corners* and Richard Walsh of *Nation Review*. There were new associations with publishers, political friends such as Jim McClelland and Neville Wran, longstanding fellow journalists such as Patricia Rolfe, old Andersonian friends until the 1970s, and thereafter a number of younger women writers and academics, as Horne began to 're-set' his 'personal compass' after reading Betty Friedan's *The Feminine Mystique*. Meaghan Morris remembers Horne as 'one of the great, old-school Sydney lunchers who could eat and drink for hours and go home clear-headed for work'. These conversations and a regular supply of new reading from Sydney's Pocket Bookshop shaped *The Bulletin* and his own writing.

Going to lunch with Donald Horne, recalled Frank Moorhouse, 'was like being part of an endless seminar'. Max Bourke noted that in speaking over lunch, as in his writing (in parentheses) somewhere into the third bottle of red Donald Horne would pause and say, 'I wonder what I meant by that?'

Yet amid the conviviality, Horne sensed his time with *The Bulletin* drawing to a close. He found the editing task 'tiresome' and felt out of place in the commercial machinations of the Packer empire. During a long walk through the city to think about the future, he decided to resign. Soon after the 1972 federal election, aged fifty-two, Donald Horne left the Packer building unsure what to do next.

The choice of academia was unlikely and unplanned; the suggestion came in a telephone call from Owen Harries after a newspaper column suggested erroneously that Horne had been fired from *The Bulletin*. Horne had no academic qualifications, and the research fellowship he was offered in the Faculty of Arts at the University of New South Wales paid less than half his income at *The Bulletin*. But Horne welcomed the opportunity to think and write, and could supplement his pay by acting as a contributing editor to *Newsweek*. He was invited to UNSW by the historian and dean Frank Crowley, who at a time of 'flourishing confidence and expanding budgets' could act as a 'spirited academic entrepreneur, enthusiastically appointing professors and creating schools like a good farmer trying out new crops'. Though a grateful beneficiary of this largesse, Horne would later head a faculty committee to trim an over-stretched Arts budget, a role he inherited from the historian Alan Gilbert.

WHEN HORNE JOINED the Department of Political Science, led by his friend from student days Doug McCallum, he had no experience as a university teacher. 'I had given less than a dozen lectures in my life; they had all been to small intellectual audiences and they had all ruthlessly exposed some form of intellectual folly. What was I going to do in preparing a lecture for an audience of "real people"? I recognised that I must avoid gabbling into the maze of unfinished sentences, switches in theme, illustrative anecdotes, even doing imitations, that sometimes made up the way I talked, so I fenced myself in with notes set out in simple, overall structure that I would be able to read easily with my bifocals. *Notes*, not a full text. Notes would give me a chance to seem natural and look the audience in the eyes, if there *was* an audience.'

Horne proved a talented educator, and would present 1,500 or so university lectures over the next fourteen years. He could stand at the podium and transform the apparently dull – constitutional arrangements, the work routines of journalism – into keys to the wider workings of politics and the media. He kept students engaged through striking assertions, rhetorical questions, amusing asides, always remembering to restate and reinforce his central points. When all else failed, a supply of anecdotes – and the occasional impersonation of political figures – carried him through until five minutes before the hour.

Students would seek some sense of the man behind the podium, and scan the books – *The Lucky Country*, now in many editions, the novels, the discussion of Britain in *God Is an Englishman*, the polemics – in search of clues. The later autobiographies were not published until the career in academia was all but complete, though students sometimes received essay comments scrawled on the back of rejected manuscript paper. 'He's describing a girl with blond hair. There's a line through the page. Perhaps she rejected him,' suggested Joanne Pemberton.

In his first years at UNSW, Horne sought to master academic research. He abandoned long notepads for neat little index cards that could be arranged or rearranged, though he was never an enthusiast for the apparatus of footnotes and detailed references, or for learned journals over books. His writing would be criticised for relying too heavily on the telling story, though his apparent fluent and accessible style often disguised considerable reading and careful construction. Horne spent time working in the Mitchell Library in Sydney, and established a friendship with Manning Clark when they ate pink iced cake together in the upstairs café during breaks from writing. On campus he watched with amusement the petty politics of academic departments: the corridor of closed doors; office space allocated according to academic rank; the empty common room and colleagues who never appeared, preferring to eat lunch alone at their desk.

As a new academic, Horne explored various intellectual approaches – 'behaviouralism', 'elite theory' and recent German writing in political sociology – before settling on 'political culture' as his research topic of choice. 'Even if I hadn't known it,' he observed later, 'ever since *The Lucky Country* "culture" was what I had been talking all the time.' The concept of political culture reminded Horne of John Anderson's phrase 'ways of life', understanding culture as 'a repertoire of habits of thinking and acting that give particular meanings to existence'. In an Australian context this meant the values, mythologies and shared assumptions that supported local social and political life.

Though appointed as a research fellow, from 1974 Horne began to lecture in first-year Australian politics. His staff seminars on contemporary issues drew interest across the campus, while his undergraduate courses included lectures with titles such as 'the coercive and conspiratorial apparatus of the state'. Some years before the rise of cultural studies in universities, Horne developed semester-long courses on 'Power and Democracy in Australia', 'Politics and Mass Culture' and 'Dominant Culture in Australia'. He could find few textbooks to cover the content, so he included in course guides the readings he discovered at the Pocket Bookshop and his own writing.

Horne looked for scholars interested in the same subjects. He found some in nearby departments such as History, others away from campus through his friendship with the film critic and later academic Meaghan Morris, who recounted how she was 'impressed by his natural energy'. An important friendship began when Political Science hired a new doctoral graduate, Elaine Thompson. She and Horne turned up to a departmental meeting with rival proposals for a new course, only to discover each had independently designed much the same curriculum. They would team-teach for years to follow, and publish together on shared projects after 1976.

When Horne began teaching a popular course on 'Politics and the Media' – then still a novelty in universities – he was made a senior lecturer with tenure. He would stay for the rest of his professional career, promoted first to associate professor and then to a personal chair, rising to be chairman of the faculty and a member of the UNSW Council before retiring as professor emeritus, aged sixty-five, at the close of 1986.

Teachers illuminate a subject but provide only partial glimpses of themselves. The pathway of his thinking was not immediately apparent to students who knew little of the earlier Donald Horne, the radical conservative. We could discern only someone discovering new fields rapidly, and communicating his enjoyment at the journey. There were gatherings for honours students at the family's terrace house in Woollahra, and occasional restaurant outings to welcome visitors or celebrate the safe delivery of a thesis. In the classroom we noted an optimistic reading of Gramsci (prevailing values can be subverted), harnessed to an interest in the concept of a national culture. In *Money Made Us*, published in 1976, Horne argued that by 'nation-building', he did not mean discovering rivers or building powerlines 'but only the true nation-building: the ways people see themselves as a nation. Nations exist in the mind.'

In the courses he offered by the start of the 1980s, Horne focused on the mechanisms which build a culture. Whether discussing political parties or the mass media, he proved less interested in institutions than in the technology and operation of hegemony. He wanted to understand how ideas, conscious and unexamined alike, work through language to shape our view of the world. Often a new course was the first indication of a book project about to begin; themes and arguments would be developed in seminars and lectures, then flow through to his writing. Like many academics Horne used teaching to think through new concepts, explore examples for argument and develop a structure for the text to follow.

Books from his UNSW years, such as *Time of Hope,* published in 1980, describe social change in Australia through the popular media. A reflection on William Morris Hughes was written for a wide audience, as were the autobiographical volumes. Others books, such as the internationally acclaimed *The Great Museum* (1984) and, even more so, *The Public Culture* (1986), were rendered in formal academic style.

YET SOCIAL OBSERVATION was not enough after the events of 11 November 1975, which became a central concern for Horne, who had known Whitlam distantly at Sydney University. Horne welcomed many Whitlam government initiatives, though neither aligned to the Labor Party nor unwilling to criticise specific government actions; the old suspicion of the state ran deep. But Horne was profoundly angered by Sir John Kerr's decision to dismiss a democratically elected government that had done nothing illegal. His opposition to the Governor-General, and to the subsequent Fraser government, inspired some of his most popular polemics.

On the day of the Dismissal, Horne was lunching with Frank Moorhouse and a number of political scientists at the UNSW staff club. A young woman waiting on the table, and listening to ABC Radio in the kitchen, relayed reports that the Governor-General had sacked the Prime Minister. The political scientists at the table carefully pointed out that such things could not happen in this nation – the ABC must have 'got it wrong'.

When the truth of the matter became clear, Horne the lifelong republican sent a telegram to the Governor-General at Yarralumla, caustically welcoming the Dismissal as the end of the Australian monarch; Horne later learned it was placed in the pile marked 'congratulations'. Kerr's decision became the core of Horne's critique of contemporary Australia, and the basis for a burst of political activism – Australia must be a republic, with a constitution to express the basic principles of democracy. In the weeks after 11 November, Horne spoke at rallies in support of Whitlam, wrote letters of protest and appeared in a television commercial with Patrick White. As Frank Moorhouse recounts, 'he discovered something else there and that was himself as an orator.' Until 1975 Horne had prided himself on being a professional 'independent', neither Liberal nor Labor, but he surrendered this identity in his passionate response to the Dismissal.

After Labor's resounding defeat on 10 December, Horne sought to keep alive the issue of constitutional change. Working with Myfanwy, academic colleagues, friends and supporters, Horne was part of public meetings throughout 1976, culminating in a 'Citizens for Democracy' rally at the Sydney Town Hall and the creation of a new movement to press for a democratic, republican constitution. Alongside his speeches Horne contributed a short polemic, *Death of a Lucky Country*, a satirical novel, *His Excellency's Pleasure,* and, with Sol Encel and Elaine Thompson, an edited volume titled *Change the Rules! Towards a Democratic Constitution.*

Through Citizens for Democracy, Horne enjoyed a new kind of political engagement: town hall meetings, pamphlets, banners, resolutions and, most importantly, people. The campaign allowed Horne to draw on contacts from his long life in Sydney – fellow republicans such as Warren Fahey, Faith Bandler, Les Murray, Fred Daly, Eva Cox and Don Chipp. Yet the moment passed swiftly. Horne found himself, by default, the 'principal media face of republicanism…while the idea of a new Constitution faded like invisible ink'.

Horne would be similarly disappointed in his involvement with the Australian Republican Movement from 1991, under the leadership of first Thomas Keneally and then Malcolm Turnbull. He found the committee frustrating, with an 'almost pathological sense of confusion and detachment'. So, apparently, did the second leader – arriving for one meeting, Horne found Turnbull 'sitting despondently in an armchair, hands hanging down listlessly, brow furrowed with care'. The campaign ended in defeat at a referendum in November 1999.

Despite the failure to secure a republican Australia, this period of intense involvement in constitutional debate led Horne to see possibilities for public intellectuals in Australian life. Community-based politics showed that Horne could be a talented public orator, speaking in compelling phrases and commanding a large audience; the *National Times* even praised his 'pleasing baritone' when leading the national anthem at the Sydney Town Hall. Horne, in turn, discovered a love of neighbourhood discussion. For decades to follow he would accept invitations to speak at clubs and societies, Rotary gatherings, Liberal and Labor party branch meetings, and other opportunities for civic debate. His later writing emphasised the importance of conversation and the necessity for democracy to be grounded in local, autonomous groups.

More broadly, the campaigns for constitutional reform affirmed in Horne an understanding of how to be a public intellectual in Australia. In his early years at UNSW, Horne had worried about whether his books were 'academic' or 'intellectual' – as though the only choice was to talk to other scholars or a popular audience. Involvement in public debate convinced Horne about the value of addressing both simultaneously. Donald Horne wrote admiringly of the 'high popularisation' favoured in France, where new ideas are made accessible by talented writers who together create a shared intellectual life.

A public intellectual, by definition, requires an audience. To sustain a viable intellectual life needs an informed community, supported by numerous publications, essays and critics. Horne concluded that sustaining intellectual life requires 'tens of thousands' of interested people, and a commitment by those in privileged places, such as universities and media, to be inclusive. Above all, intellectual life needs books that address contemporary issues for local audiences: such writing gives people 'new things to think about – or new approaches to old ways'. Without such writing about Australian topics, Horne asked, 'in what sense, as Australians, would we exist at all?'

Horne would pursue his vision of a public conversation, conveyed through accessible writing, during the balance of a long and productive life. His search for a more inclusive agenda would find expression in a new role as chair of the Australia Council from January 1985. Horne championed supporting people to create their own art, and promoted the arts as a necessary broadening of a political culture relentlessly focused on economic questions.

The new Australia Council chair took particular pleasure in stressing his independence from government. When pressured by one government MP about disappointed grant applicants from his electorate, Horne responded, 'Well, Minister, thank you for exercising your democratic right as a citizen to tell me your views.' He delighted in the work of the council and of its talented staff such as Andrea Hull, the director of Policy and Planning, though his impatience with 'bureaucratese' was widely understood. Many colleagues in the Australia Council appreciated the 'plurality, eclecticism and boundless curiosity' of their chair. They found him the 'ultimate humanist, with a fierce sense of nationalism', who championed the idea that 'all Australians should have cultural rights.'

While at the Australia Council, Horne commissioned events such as the National Summit of Ideas at Old Parliament House in 1990 and encouraged the creation of a National Council for the Humanities. On stepping down as chair in 1991, aged seventy, Horne continued the conversation through his involvement in Ideas for Australia, Arts Action and programs for the Centenary of Federation. He remained, as Andrea Hull recalls, 'intellectually curious, pixelated, curmudgeonly, charming, quick to laugh, and glorious luncheon company'.

Horne had established a role for himself as a public intellectual, and believed the model could work for others. The skill, he believed, is to influence debate 'through language and discussion', alongside the quotidian tasks of writing and editing, sitting on committees and accepting invitations to converse, no matter how modest the occasion. A public intellectual, he observed, should coin a new phrase, set out the argument for change, develop rhetoric to support the ides, and create events and opportunities for conversation.

Though now a prominent advocate of government support for the arts, Horne was no fan of the major statement of cultural policy during the Keating era, Creative Nation. He saw the conceptual underpinnings as flawed, and it was the old Andersonian who raised his voice to 'scorn not just the policy, but also its consequences – both intended and unintended – that affects arts, culture, politics, discourse and infrastructure'. He appeared ambivalent about the fall of Prime Minister Paul Keating in 1996, though he soon despaired of the Howard government.

IN 1997, HORNE published his most ambitious book, *The Avenue of the Fair Go*. He would explain core political concepts to ordinary Australians through an imaginary theme park of ideas 'visited by a small group tour seeking new ideals of public virtue'. *The Avenue of the Fair Go* employed the language of everyday life, and allowed Horne to distil a lifetime of thinking about Australian political culture.

Unfortunately, as John Button argued in his review, the 'persistent, seemingly tireless' Donald Horne, successful polemicist and public intellectual of 'a rare kind', struggled to capture the essence of an Australian identity. Instead, concluded Button, *The Avenue of the Fair Go* is 'an omnibus of the things that Horne has believed in, and the things which he dislikes'. The presentation of the argument as a series of conversations undercut the serious attempt to 'define and celebrate what makes Australia different'.

Button's assessment proved a reliable guide to the wider reception. The book has its supporters, and attracted some warm notices, but most reviewers were puzzled or hostile, and *The Avenue of the Fair Go* sold less than any of Horne's previous volumes. The aftermath of a particularly hostile assessment by Peter Coleman ended his friendship with the Hornes.

There were further publications after *The Avenue of the Fair Go*, but Horne was now speaking to a very different political moment. His themes of constitutional change, fairness and Australian character struggled to find an audience in the age of John Howard. As his public roles concluded, Horne had fewer opportunities to engage a wider audience. He remained an occasional columnist and opinion writer, and books such as *Looking for Leadership*, published in 2001, saw Horne still focused on contemporary issues, now seriously disturbed by the state of Australia during the Howard years.

Horne remained an optimist amid the challenges of old age. He completed his series of autobiographical books and enjoyed some recognition: an Order of Australia, inclusion in the National Trust's inaugural list of Living National Treasures and a Sydney book launch at which Noel Pearson acknowledged Horne as an 'elder'. Encouraged by Julianne Schultz, editor of the *Griffith REVIEW*, Horne began a new project writing about infirmity. Earlier work had described difficult operations on his eyes; now, in the remarkable essay 'Mind, Body and Age', Horne described illness and decay with the same detachment he earlier reviewed his childhood homes or years as a student. Horne would chronicle his decline and terminal illness in *Dying: A Memoir* (2007), a work completed by his widow, Myfanwy.

THE *GRIFFITH REVIEW* essay was launched at the 2004 Sydney Writers' Festival. It was the first time this prolific author had been invited to speak at this festival in his home town, and he appeared deeply moved by the affection of the hundreds of people who packed the Sydney Dance Theatre rehearsal studio.

Before he spoke, a small group of us took Donald and Myfanwy to lunch next door at Walsh Bay, with Sydney Harbour lapping below the window. Despite his frailty and failing voice, the 82-year-old Donald was sharp and engaged as he speculated on changes to the word 'culture' in recent years, the need for more civic identity, prospects for the forthcoming federal election and the foibles of former academic colleagues. It was the last time I saw Donald Horne, this engaging companion who entertained thousands of tables through decades in journalism and academia, the historian, gossip, chronicler and speculator, the writer who asked endless questions and turned answers into the next stage of an endless conversation.

In late April 2005 Donald Horne, complete with oxygen mask, finally received a degree from the University of Sydney – not his abandoned Bachelor of Arts but an Honorary Doctor of Letters. His moving graduation speech praised the 'marvels of the intellectual life', with its opportunities for imagination, wonder, inquiry and criticism. He recalled his training under John Anderson, who emphasised the 'rich variety of approaches to ways of being human'.

Donald Horne died some months later, in September 2005. To celebrate his life, Myfanwy Horne organised a memorial service at the State Library of New South Wales. Family and friends shared memories and reflections. In the spirit of the man, spontaneous contributions were encouraged. Frank Moorhouse recalled the aphorisms of Donald Horne. Deborah Mills remembered the 'cultural visionary, intellectual and enthusiast' who recognised the 'importance of culture in the lives of ordinary people'. Diana Gribble evoked the image of the 'clever little kid from Muswellbrook, the *enfant terrible* of Sydney University, the advertising man', and Chairman Donald of the Australia Council. Peter Manning spoke of Donald Horne as a fixture at the New Hellas restaurant beside Hyde Park, and Helen Irving later wrote of the man always interested in new ideas. Elaine Thompson remembered her university colleague with 'no degree, nor formal background, no "academic" publications', whose 'continued popular success and absolute refusal to use footnotes infuriated many academic colleagues'.

And Owen Harries, a friend of forty-eight years, observed: 'Looking back, it seems to me that the strongest impulse in Donald's life was the impulse, indeed the compulsion, to inform, explain, persuade, convince, and, certainly not least, to correct and refute. In short, to teach…Donald had the qualities that make for a very good teacher: enthusiasm, intellectual energy, wide-ranging knowledge, presence, a mastery of language and presentation. But he also had some extra qualities that made him a great teacher: a strong sense of the dramatic; a sense of fun and a marvellous eye for the absurd; a creative imagination; and – perhaps most important of all – a capacity to convey a sense of the cosmic importance of whatever happened to be occupying his attention at the time.'

Donald Horne's intellectual curiosity ensured he engaged with most of the great questions facing Australia through the twentieth century: identity, character, values and place in the world. He explored these issues with same drive whether a student, soldier, diplomatic cadet, young journalist, editor, advertising executive or academic. He believed that life has no objective meaning, only the purpose we give our existence. This meant interrogating the moment – understanding the contemporary, and through it the broader patterns of history and culture. His thinking was original – often only after wrestling with a problem to his satisfaction would he search for academic literature in the field. His writing is always informed by experience, and therefore by the particular circumstances of being an Australian through most of the twentieth century.

In his early years, Donald Horne disdained political processes, while being fascinated by political questions. Later in life he came to embrace political work – never within a party structure, instead through writing and public meetings seeking a vigorous polity, filled with conversation. The scepticism – 'question everything' – learned from John Anderson at Sydney University served him well through a long life, as did an emphasis on individual liberty and toleration, by providing a consistent intellectual stance. Anderson's hostility to the state proved less enduring, and Horne eventually broke with this part of the Andersonian program, at considerable personal cost to friendships and the settled patterns of his first half-century. But he found enjoyment in the unfamiliar challenges of academia, and a renewed sense of purpose through writing and political activism. As Dennis Altman observes, in moving to a university Donald Horne 'continued the conversation with Australia he had started through his journalism'. Late in life this critic of bureaucracy found satisfaction in leading organisations: his chairing of the Faculty of Arts at UNSW, his chancellorship of the University of Canberra, two terms as chair of the Australia Council.

In *Dying: A Memoir,* Horne insisted on 'a last look around', and tackled once again the big issues of criticism, conversation and belief. His final essays could be followed by three questions in three hours, so familiar the range of concerns, so close the nexus between the practical problems of living and the intellectual interest in the culture that gives us meaning.

This journalist-turned-academic urged scholars to seek a popular audience, to see virtue in speaking plainly to create and sustain an intellectual community. His legacy is found in his writing, the institutions he shaped, the people he trained, his encouragement always to be part of the conversation. This was his vision of a public intellectual at work – a role he once doubted was possible in Australia, but eventually embraced with enthusiasm.

It seems impossible to avoid cliché when writing about favourite teachers. All professors become warmly remembered characters, subtly shaping the passing generation of undergraduates, friendly, lively, accessible and tolerant of the gauche. That they may also have been occasionally irritable or bored is forgotten. Yet Donald Horne was always an exceptional teacher, not only in the bare-brick classrooms of Sydney, but in suggesting how intellectuals can contribute to their times.

Discuss.

References at www.griffithreview.com

Glyn Davis is Professor of Political Science and Vice-Chancellor of the University of Melbourne, and a 1981 Honours student supervised by Donald Horne at the University of New South Wales. His essays have featured in *Griffith REVIEW 11: Getting Smart, Unintended Consequences* and *The Lure of Fundamentalism.*

Bruce Dawe

Expectation Valley

As you rein in your bronc on the high ridge
overlooking Hadleyville or Pobrecito or Wrangler
it is coming on dusk or it's already early night
and your eyes squint shrewdly as you take in the scene;
it's been a long ride from Wherever and you wonder briefly
what this miserable apology for a cow-town holds
for a weary suntanned reader who figgers that down there
in a saloon called *Last Chance* or *Lucky Strike*
another dance-hall gal is being brutally manhandled
by some drunken ranch-hand or deputy sheriff
and as you ride in slowly you ease your six-gun-smooth
sensibility in its hog-legged holster thinking to yourself
Just once I'd like to get to page 15 without any of these
doggone heroics and the smell of bar-room powder-smoke
but you guess that ain't on the cards so instead of riding
right on you push through those bat-wing doors
and the saloon goes awful quiet all of a sudden
(as it generally does when Fate, that pernickety little lady,
plays her hand) and your one consolation is knowing
that while Boot Hill is about to be a mite busier for a while
and the town preacher will be exhuming a few old clichés
at least there'll be a persecuted small-rancher's daughter
nestling in your arms by page 186...

Bruce Dawe has won numerous awards for his poetry, including the Centenary Medal for distinguished service to the arts through poetry. Apart from his many books of poems, he has also published a collection of short stories and a book of essays.

MEMOIR

The ace of spades

Tree change in a time of change

Carmel Bird

THE ace of spades is the highest card in the deck, and is also the death card, used as such by American troops during the war in Vietnam. When an artist places this card in a painting, the viewer does well to take notice. And when a publisher puts on the cover of a book an image of a man with an ace of spades in his breast pocket, the reader must pay attention.

My personal library used to contain a paperback copy of *The Lucky Country* by Donald Horne, published in 1964. I am not sure when I first got the book, but it was probably a few years after it was first published. The library has travelled with me for nearly fifty years and has shed some books while acquiring others. The image on the cover of the lost book stays with me – a painting of a man's head by Albert Tucker, a head brutally carved from some hideous yellowy-brown substance, perhaps metallic, with a hawk nose and a grim, humourless prognathous jaw, wearing a battered Stetson with a cockatoo feather stuck in the band. The man is holding a mug of beer in his paw-like hand, and there in his top pocket is the ace of spades. He is a gambling man; he's an Australian. Years after the appearance of the man on the cover of *The Lucky Country*, Malcolm Fraser became the Prime Minister of Australia. I thought the image of the man resembled Fraser, while he in turn resembled an Easter Island statue. I expect all that says is that the man on the cover has a recognisable Australian face, but it was a nice comparison.

Behind the man shimmers a bright blue sky – heaven, you might say – and there are sails of yachts that suggest sharks while also repeating the crisp white collar of the man's open-neck shirt. The sun in the top left-hand corner looks quite pale and small and benign. How I hated that picture when I got the book. Has the great thick blight of the dominant drinking-gambling man with his back to the sea blotted out the carefree summer's day? I am afraid it has. The picture nicely sums up the ironic twist of the title, which arose from the sentence towards the end of the book where Horne says that Australia is a 'lucky country, run by second-rate people who share its luck': fighting words that have been largely forgotten. The title and the cover image play on each

---

PREVIOUS PAGE: Albert Tucker (1914–1999), Painting commissioned especially for the cover of the first edition of *The Lucky Country* by Donald Horne, Penguin Books Australia Ltd, 1964.

other to deliver the cry of the book, which was a wake-up call to Australians to start to understand the 'distinctiveness' of their own society in order for that society to remain 'prosperous, liberal and humane'. In a double irony, the title was taken up as a mantra intended to prove once and for all that Australia is so lucky that it can just sit back, produce the ace of spades, drink up, reap the benefits of luck and enjoy life.

In November 2009, when the federal Opposition was in disarray just before the bill on carbon emissions trading was about to go to the Senate, the image of the Tucker painting kept coming into my mind, and the phrase 'lucky country' kept ringing its hollow ring. Was the very luck on which the country relied finally running out, like sand through the floorboards of each house? In 2009 Australia was being described as the hottest and driest country on the planet, and a great deal of second-rate behaviour and thinking was coming to the fore as the critical vote on the carbon tax bill drew closer. I searched the bookshelves for *The Lucky Country* and that was when I realised it had gone.

I wanted an old copy, one with that man on the cover. So I went to a place called Book Heaven in Castlemaine, Victoria, and there it was. I confess I had forgotten about the beer and playing card. How could I have forgotten the ace of spades? The sweet irony of the second-hand bookshop's name is obvious: Book Heaven. But what was I doing in the old gold-mining town of Castlemaine?

TWO YEARS AGO I left Melbourne for Castlemaine, shedding a thousand books, among which perhaps was *The Lucky Country*. I have spent much of my life writing (in both fiction and non-fiction) about aspects of the distinctiveness of Australia, generally seeking to uncover on the one hand, beauty and goodness; on the other, those forces that play against humanity, often in the very name of prosperity and liberality. I have had a particular interest in policies regarding Indigenous Australians, and also in the racial and religious fabric of this country. I can to an extent trace these interests to having been born in Tasmania during World War II.

When I was a child I was conscious that the island state of Tasmania was a kind of abject Australian joke, not part of a 'lucky' country at all, a place of negative importance nationally and internationally. How interesting it is to see how this perception has changed, with the advent of green politics and powerful political activism of various kinds, as well as clever tourist campaigns. Tasmania is now a destination of choice for people seeking clean air and beautiful wild scenery. My leaving of Tasmania was thus: I was twenty-two, a teacher in the Education Department, going along in lucky-country fashion teaching French and English. Then suddenly I received a transfer to go to a tiny island in Bass Strait, King Island. Now, King Island is world-famous for cheese, but in 1962 it was seen as the young female teacher's gulag. Yes, it could have been a challenge to the brave person I was not. To me, it was a call to arms – I left the state, packing my library of Racine and Voltaire and Rimbaud and Yeats into a big old cabin trunk, and went to teach in a private school in Victoria. I had, in a small way, rebelled. I had gone, as Tasmanians used to say, 'over the other side', meaning mainland Australia, not the afterlife.

I thought of this act of, if you like, disobedience when I read recently in a newspaper the story of a young Melbourne priest who was musing on his vow of obedience. He reportedly said that if his bishop ordered him to move from Brighton to Castlemaine, he would have to go. Perhaps I am reading too much into this, but it seemed to me that he was putting the pleasant life among the sanitised mansions and rose gardens and tennis courts of Brighton against the grim spectre of the bacon factory and the prison of Castlemaine, and was feeling challenged. Of all the places he could have chosen to put up against Brighton, he chose Castlemaine. He caught my attention by that little slip of the pen. Perhaps he was just working his way through the alphabet.

Anyway, he got me thinking about places of obedience and places of choice. I chose to come here to live, making, as it is cutely said, a 'tree change'. Simply stated, since I can pursue my profession of writer just about anywhere, I followed my daughter and her young family here. But why did *they* come to Castlemaine? Well, she and her husband got teaching jobs here, and they thought it would be good to raise children in the country. I shed those thousand books and a lot of furniture and clothes, sold a house and bought a house, and here I am. It has been a short enough journey, from Tasmania to Melbourne to Castlemaine, with a year in LA and a year in Paris thrown in.

Most of my life has been spent in Melbourne, and now that I look around at Castlemaine I can see – in the terrain, the size of the town, the winter cold, the old houses, the old gardens, the pear trees and the prunus trees, the stars in the clear night sky – vestiges of Tasmania in the 1950s.

Perhaps I am just projecting childhood scenes and feelings onto it, but that is my perception. I suppose I am fulfilling some childhood dreams of having a place with a lily pond and a covered walk draped in wisteria – like entering the images on some of my favourite swap cards. The choice of location was made for me by my family, but the choice of residence was my own. In fact, there was very little choice, and ending up with the lily pond and the wisteria vine was a matter of chance. That favourite Australian quality, chance.

The streets of Castlemaine soon tail off into forests and wild places. The town is two hours from the city of Melbourne. Civilisation here winds through the countryside in fairly thin slivers. I can lie in bed and glimpse the Melbourne train as it flashes through the trees in the near distance, running over an old arched brick bridge. I watch the black cockatoos perch in a crackle on the blue spruce outside the bedroom window, and listen sometimes in dismay to their throaty cacophony. Green parrots habitually dangle and twitter on the slender branches of the grey box. Sometimes a kangaroo hops down the road beside the house or takes a short cut through the front garden. And once I found a bewildered koala lurking in the branches of a tall dark cypress. I am reminded at every turn that I have exchanged the streets of Melbourne for life on the edge of the forest, have exchanged the waters of the bay for the dry inland.

In early spring the streets are lined with the dreamy clouds of pink prunus blossoms, and a little later on the verges are washed with waves of the dark golden stars of gazanias. The air is often sweet with the perfumes of many aromatic plants. The drought here is severe and long-lived, so there is an obsession with water. I am obsessed. I grew up in a state that was obsessed with water, to begin with. One of the first things I did here was install a water tank, and then I restored the empty lily pond, removing a dense, dry infestation of dead irises. Living among the irises was the biggest, blackest, knobbliest toad, which I relocated in a deep dark corner of the garden. Since then I have not seen it. I filled the pond and stocked it with water plants and with goldfish which disappeared into the depths, seen only occasionally as a lovely flash in the sunlight.

One day, as I was sitting with friends beneath the wisteria vine beside the pond, I noticed that many of the fish had suddenly decided to swim out in the sunlight and I later discovered that the level of the water in the nearby swimming pool was rapidly dropping. Some of the water from the pool seemed to have moved through the pond, killing off the fish which had multiplied since I had put them there, and which now floated sadly on the surface after their final desperate moment in the sun. Throughout the winter the level of the swimming pool kept falling, owing to the failure of the plug that holds the water in.

During the months when the pool was out of action, the filter pump was turned off. Came the day in late spring when the pool was refilled, I turned on the pump. With a horrible whine the pump, useless, began to give off smoke, for curled up inside it was a dead blue-tongue lizard which had been in residence over the winter months. Stiff and cold and stripy. I buried the blue-tongue and ordered a new pump.

Meanwhile, I restocked the pond with goldfish, in time for the mosquito season. The buds of the waterlilies were just beginning to break the surface of the water. So there I was again sitting happily beneath the wisteria with friends, when a tall heron came swooping gracefully down, silent, alert. He landed on a rock beside the pond, paused, took a quick inventory, but perhaps because we were now watching, flew off. He would be back for the goldfish in due course. The wire mesh below the surface of the water can stop a small child from drowning, but can't stop a heron from fishing.

One of my favourite lines in literature comes from *Alice's Adventures in Wonderland*: 'There was a table set out under the tree in front of the house.' I think of it often when I come out and have tea under the plum tree: the round red teapot and the red-and-white-striped milk jug with its beaded cover to keep out the bugs that might tumble in. There is a cloth on the table, a bowl of red roses, and yes, we sometimes have cucumber sandwiches. Such civilised rituals so close by the busy industry of birds and fish and lizards and toads and bugs. Not to mention spiders and snakes. There is of course no paradise without a serpent as standard issue, whether real or metaphoric. And I realise that Alice was walking in on a *mad* tea party.

I spend a lot of time reading, writing or taking tea under the wisteria's sweet dreamy purple drifts in spring, and under the green umbrella of its leaves in summer. Well, there I was again. It was the day I buried the blue-tongue, and as we sat there, a black swarm of bees moved swiftly overhead, a loud thrumming shadow. For an instant the air was humming with threat; then it was gone. It is a relief and pleasure to see bees, though, since they are endangered, and without them human life will not survive. So if they are going, everybody is going. There are all kinds of superstitions about bees: some say that a swarm overhead is an evil omen; some say it is good. Let's say it's good, then. Will the omen of the bees have the power to counteract the evil promise of the single silent crow – the biggest, blackest, shiniest crow – that took up residence the following day on the blue-tongue's resting place? As I backed away from the crow I saw, among the poppies that were almost flowering, the first ladybird I have seen in two years. It was tiny and shiny and bright, bright glittering scarlet. A busy little bead on the grey-green poppy leaves. Now these bugs *are* a good omen, and the sight of one always lifts the spirit. Except the rhyme you must say if you accidentally kill one is distinctly unsettling as spring turns to summer and the threat of bushfire haunts the heart. Close to the surface of everyday life in rural and not-so-rural Australia lurks the fear of fire. So who wants to hear the words in the rhyme 'Fly away home. Your house is on fire'? The rest of the verse is something I have always found unspeakably awful: 'Your children are gone.'

Something else I have missed since I have been here are the snails. In late spring there was a burst of fierce hot weather. The hardy gazanias by the roadside were suddenly all burnt by the sun. Then there were days and days of black thunderclouds and lightning and lashing rain. And then, one grey day, crawling up the bricks by the front door came a small snot-coloured garden snail. One. I do not wish for snails, but this little creature inching up the wall was the possible harbinger of more sweet rain. Dams and tanks were full and overflowing, and everyone attended public meetings to discuss strategies for the coming fire season. It is so obvious that the patterns of weather in Australia, like elsewhere, have changed, and that extremes of drought, heat and storms are becoming more frequent and more dramatic, and that human behaviour must change accordingly and quickly. Restrictions on the use of water apply not only in the country towns but also in the city. People in the city also now have water tanks. In the 1970s in Melbourne I wanted to put in a tank because it seemed such an obvious thing to do, but council laws forbade it. Times change.

As hot, wet November moved on to December, and summer drew closer and closer, the reports of tragic stories of the early 2009 bushfires kept coming, offering a dreadful background of truth and detail to the hourly twists and turns of the power struggles in the Opposition, mingled with the government's struggle to pass the bill on the carbon emissions tax in the Senate. The two stories seemed to me to be entwined, each embedded in a narrative where the weather is the real villain and chance is driving the plot.

Bushfires are more fierce and more common than they used to be, and I am more alert to them now because I live close to the forest and have a fire plan for the summer. The level of the sea is rising. The polar ice is melting. I have re-read *The Lucky Country*, which I rescued from Book Heaven, and I feel the deep wisdom on Donald Horne's simple enough message of a call to consciousness. But every time I close the book I see the image of the man in the hat and I wonder about the plot. Who will reap the benefits? What are the benefits? What's the weather doing? Is the ugly Australian still holding the highest card, and does he realise it is the death card?

Carmel Bird's latest novel, *Child of the Twilight*, was published earlier this year by HarperCollins. Her essay 'East of the sun and west of the moon' appeared in *Griffith REVIEW 26: Stories for Today*, and 'The legacy of Rita Marquand' was published in *Griffith REVIEW 10: Family Politics*.

Home is where the heart is

A question of belonging II

Cassandra Atherton

COME closer while I tell you this. Let me whisper in your ear. No one likes a dissenter. No one likes a deserter. I can't say this too loudly. So huddle up while I tell you a secret.

I am leaving Dorothea Mackellar's sunburnt country for snowflakes in the north. I'm crossing the equator, because Down Under can never be home to a woman who wants to be on top. I am turning my back on Australia Day for Martin Luther King Day. I may even prioritise Thanksgiving over Christmas. And on the fourth of July I will be out celebrating a different red, white and blue. The greenback might be in strife but the rainbow-fish coloured bills of our currency are a joke everywhere in the world, except New Zealand. 'Advance Australia Fair' doesn't even come close to the 'Star Spangled Banner'. And before you ask, yes, I know all the words. I even know the second verse by heart. So much the worse. We may 'toil with hearts and hands to make this Commonwealth of ours, renowned throughout the lands', but it can't compete with 'Oh, say does that star-spangled banner yet wave / O'er the land of the free and the home of the brave?'

So goodbye to yellow, sun-bleached grass. Goodbye to water restrictions. Goodbye to all that, I say.

WE BOUGHT A house in Salem, Massachusetts, last week – near Pickering Wharf and where the ferry leaves for Boston. Ye Olde Pepper Companie is around the corner and Nathaniel Hawthorne's House of the Seven Gables is down the road.

He told me we didn't have to move right away. But I could tell he was mentally packing his suitcase. And mine. A colleague once said that he was an American trapped in an Australian body. So I guess that part of him was returning to a place he called home. I still call Australia home. And supposedly there is no place like home. Except, perhaps America.

I haven't packed my suitcase yet. I'm not the kind of person who can pack up her troubles in her old kit bag and smile. It will be a wrench to leave. I don't deny it. I won't be able to take things like the dining suite I bought with my first month's pay. Or the partitioned Pilbo coffee table with one missing screw that holds my fondest memories under glass. And what are my fondest memories now? I have been collecting little pieces of Americana. I have gambling chips from Las Vegas and matchboxes from our favourite restaurants in Boston. There is the menu from the place we had dinner at on New Year's Eve in San Francisco and a photo just after he proposed to me at Utopia, in Washington, DC.

The T-shirts I wear and the charms I have on my bracelet will be all wrong when we move to Salem. I need to collect Australiana. Maybe I should buy an Akubra and a Drizabone. I should have an Opera House and Sydney Harbour Bridge charm. What kind of charm do you buy to commemorate Melbourne? The jeweller tells me: 'a tram'.

We live in an apartment in Moonee Ponds. The shopping centre has framed Dame Edna Everage's photograph and displays it outside Kmart. And there is a restaurant called Edna's Table next to the two-dollar shop. It seems most people here don't know about her bitter satire exposing Moonee Ponds as the most ordinary place on earth. There are few things worse than ordinariness. And let's face it, Barry Humphries got as far away from Australia as he possibly could. He returns only to humiliate crowds of adoring fans, for the odd fat cheque. But I like the cafés in Puckle Street. I like the caramel cream cake at Delphi and the calamari salad at the Junction Tabaret. That was enough for him once. He'd put on a Quaddie and we'd play rapid roulette using our favourite numbers. We have different philosophies, though. He thinks if there have been a string of reds in a row, the next will be black. I keep going. I like to roll. Should I risk it all and roll with him?

AT THE WITCH'S Brew in Salem I drink double Scotch and coke while the bartender tells us for the third time how he nearly went to Australia but went to the Bahamas instead. I'd probably choose the Bahamas over Australia for a holiday. I think it's more exotic. But then, Americans generally think Australia is exotic. I think of Australia as the outback, dry and dusty. It's odd that I don't think of the Great Barrier Reef and scuba diving. I think of Uluru and the red earth. And I've never been to the Northern Territory.

The bartender at the Witch's Brew gives me a drink that he describes as a 'heavy pour'. I drink it quickly and order clam chowder. There is nothing finer than Massachusetts clam chowder. There is no equivalent in Australia. Clam chowder is delicious.

He orders bacon, eggs and corned-beef hash. If he were writing this, he would say that there is nothing finer than corned beef hash, that there is no equivalent in Australia and that it is delicious. When people find out we are Australian they ask if we throw shrimps on the barbie. I've never really understood this expression. I always thought shrimps were tiny prawns, most often found in fried rice. So they would definitely fall through the bars on my grill. And before they ask, I tell them that I have always greeted people with the far more American 'Hey', rather than 'G'day'. I think it's because I watch so much American television. I've never been a fan of *Neighbours* or *Home and Away*, and I shudder at the popularity of *Packed to the Rafters* and *Underbelly*. If that is the best Australia has to offer, it is destined for cultural oblivion.

The bartender asks me if I would like another Scotch and coke. He asks partly as a joke, because it is one o'clock in the afternoon, I have already had a pretty potent one and I look young for my age. I give him the thumbs-up. And that appears to be Australian enough to satisfy him.

EVERY MORNING WE walk to the Maribyrnong River. It's about 4,500 steps to the bridge. I know because he always wears a pedometer on his belt. It looks really nerdy and I ask him if he would like a pocket protector so he can wear pens in his pocket to cap off this look, and he smiles. I wonder if he will wear the pedometer in Salem. We pass the man who works at the Junction Tabaret and his dog, Cinnamon. Cinnamon rolls on her back for a tummy rub and I can't imagine not seeing her every day on our walk. Her owner sips strong coffee at Delphi. He is an observer, and sometimes I envy the way he looks so relaxed and content. When I drink coffee I worry I have been away from my email too long. I wonder if I will be the same in Salem. Sometimes I find it hard to sleep in America because, with the time difference, I am sure I am getting important emails that I need to respond to while I am sleeping.

We pass Chiba and I smell the sushi hand rolls. Every morning I think that I will get one for lunch, but I never do. I forget about it until the following morning. We negotiate our way past Stinton's, the card shop, with its oddments for sale on tables and stands, and past Modish, the stationery shop that has tried to copy Smiggle. Then it's over the train tracks and down the hill to the river.

Sometimes we see the Stick Dog, but not very often. He carries his stick in his mouth and, when he gets to the oval, his owner throws it for him and he retrieves it, over and over again. He runs so fast he overshoots the stick and has to turn around and race back to pick it up. But it's the Italian man and his two dogs, Soprano and Bianca, who are my favourites. Soprano, the chubby pug, puffs and snorts his way over to the rubbish dump, while Bianca plays with the birds in the park. Their owner calls them his son and daughter. I think of our ragdoll cats like our children. I feel an affinity with the jolly Italian man. I wonder where he will think we have gone when he doesn't see us anymore. Somehow it is too sad to tell him we are moving. And I realise that my home is a few hokey shops and strangers with their dogs, and I like it.

IN SALEM THERE will be dogs with sticks and far more corny shops to pass on the way to the Common. We will go to the CVS, the drug store, but it won't be as fun. We won't have to stockpile cold-and-flu tablets and aspirin because Australian pharmacies don't stock strong enough over-the-counter medicine; they will always be on hand. I won't have to try every American chocolate bar. Instead, I will crave Violet Crumbles and Chokitos. Sadly, Australia got rid of its own Polly Waffle. And I'll miss Twisties, Tim Tams and Vegemite. But I will be able to eat Lucky Charms every morning for breakfast, and it won't cost seventeen dollars because the box of cereal is imported. Imported things should cost more, but in Australia it is often so much cheaper to buy the Asian option and I can't always afford to buy Australian Made. And sometimes, even though they claim to be, they aren't made in Australia. I wish Dick Smith's Tim Tams tasted as good as Arnott's, but they don't. His peanut butter is pretty good, though.

There will be other strangers to bond with in Salem, and other men drinking coffee in cafés. We will go to the Peabody Essex for an overpriced snack and edge our way past the *Cry Freedom* actors in the square. Maybe after a few years we will roll our eyes and sigh when we hear the trolley bringing tourists. I'll be able to walk more comfortably along the cobblestones in my stilettos, and I might even grow to like the second-hand bookshop, with its books rising like stalagmites from every available piece of floor space. Maybe we will walk past the Elizabeth Montgomery statue and eat at Finz again. He will join the historical society and I might join the book club. I'm not sure about going to see sporting events. I don't go to see sporting events in Australia. I hate the AFL – the players and the way they are worshipped. No one worships people with brains in Australia. I will barrack for the Red Sox. Somehow in America, baseball brings people together. It's refreshing that everyone in the same area barracks for the same team. It will be our new world, but it will be far from home.

Currently I have to time my showers and keep them to four minutes. And I used to love the comfort of a long, warm shower on a cold night or a cool bath on a boiling-hot day. I can't wash my car with the hose. I have to water the garden before 7 am or after 8 pm. No sprinklers. Children in Australia have never known the joy of running under a sprinkler, or a slip-and-slide across the back lawn. I had a clown's head sprinkler and his hat used to rise up when you attached the hose and spin, cartwheeling water across the sky. In primary school, on days over 35°, our teachers used to take us out to the asphalt and spray us with the hose. It was a treat; we loved it. But it's different now. I wish I could lend some of the green of the Salem Common to the nature strips and front lawns down Holmes Road. The platinum grass crumbles into dust when we walk on it. I'm leaving. You won't see me for dust.

LAST WEEK WE bought a house in Salem. House prices are so much more reasonable in America. We bought a beautiful pale-pink condo and we're not afraid of losing money on it. How could we be? In my lifetime the Australian dollar has never even reached parity with the American dollar. When America is having a recession or a depression, we are still somehow doing worse. Or so it seems when I hand over my Australian dollar and get seventy cents back. When the Australian dollar finally hit ninety cents to one American dollar, we transferred our money telegraphically to our lawyer's bank. And now we own a house in Salem with a wooden deck and an attic.

He is excited about the attic, even though we have never seen it. He thinks we can use it for storage – things like our Christmas tree and some books. I wish we could take our fibre-optic Christmas tree that lists to the left. We have had it since we were married. One decoration boasts 'Our First Christmas Together' in a heart. But we can buy another Christmas tree in America, probably a nicer one for less. America has a much better lead-up to Christmas than Australia. Macy's windows are incredible, not like the disappointing Myer windows this year, *Olivia Helps with Christmas*. It wasn't really Christmassy at all. And Dame Edna narrated, despite Barry Humphries hating Australia. Why are we giving him work?

When it snows I am going to stand on the deck of our Salem condo and pretend I am inside a snow globe. Maybe I'll twirl around like Winona Ryder's character in *Edward Scissorhands*. But what if I get dizzy? What if I click my heels together and say 'There's no place like home' and I don't go anywhere, because Salem is my new home? What if I click my heels together and I'm not taken back to the Maribyrnong River, the Puckle Street cafés and the nameless men with their dogs? What if, despite everything, I'm not ready to leave Moonee Ponds?

He reads the Salem news online and researches shipping costs. He's here next to me, so come closer while I tell you this. Let me whisper it in your ear. I can't say this too loudly or he might hear. Huddle up while I tell you a secret: I might just stay.

Cassandra Atherton lectures in Creative Writing and Romanticism at the University of Melbourne. Her first novel, *The Man Jar*, will be published this year by Printed Matter Press. She is currently working on *Wise Guys*, a book examining the role and responsibility of the American public intellectual, and on her second novel, *Cherry Bomb*, set in Japan.

Inside the tent

The legacy of the sixties

Dennis Altman

PUBLIC MEETING
GORDON BARTON
"AUSTRALIA's
WITLESS AND
GUTLESS
FOREIGN POLICY
8·30 PM TUESDAY MARCH 26
WAYSIDE CHAPEL · THEATRE

IN 2009 I attended two large sixtieth-birthday parties. Each celebrated a senior woman academic who had attained considerable recognition and seniority within her profession and the larger intellectual milieu. Both women spoke to mark the occasion: one, of her sense that reaching sixty was a great achievement; the other, that it marked the point to recognise that the end was in sight. Together, the two comments mark the acceptance of a significant generational shift, as the postwar baby boomers give way to a new generation with rather different memories and political influences. Those of us who are now over sixty grew up in the shadow of the Cold War, and the large shifts that make up what is now mythologised as the sixties. We were marching in anti-war protests when Kevin Rudd was starting secondary school.

Many of the same generation were serving in the war against which we were protesting; even in its halcyon days the new left and the counterculture included a minority of young people. Nonetheless, the period marked a fundamental shift in social and cultural attitudes, and its impact remains today. As the baby boomers age, the 1960s has become a major nostalgia industry, and there is a looming sense that the decade was one where the direction of modern history turned irretrievably, with legacies we are still working through today. This is taken for granted in the US: as one conservative wrote, 'To an extent scarcely imaginable thirty years ago, we now live in that "moral and cultural universe shaped by the Sixties".' The mythology of the generation gap spawned by radicalism in the sixties is now a staple of popular culture, as in several recent films based on the Woodstock festival. In Ian Rankin's novel *The Naming of the Dead*, set around the G8 summit in Edinburgh in 2005, a woman policeman is visited by her parents, radicalised in the sixties and now part of the anti-globalisation protest. In the same way the Egyptian author Alaa al Aswany, in *Chicago,* his novel of Egyptians in contemporary America, creates a stereotypical sixties protestor, now an eminent professor, who talks of a time of 'true ideological revolution when progressive values replaced capitalist ideas'.

PREVIOUS PAGE: Sixties anti-war protest meeting poster. www.gallery.rsp.org.au

There is less reverence for the period in Australia, although the social commentator Hugh McKay described the period as 'disrupting the established pattern of cultural baton-passing from one generation to the next'. More common may be George Megalogenis's laconic comment: 'The shriek that greeted the Beatles, the tumult of Vietnam, women's liberation, and full employment can be neatly slotted between these two slumps [of 1961 and 1971–72].'

Yet if the social, cultural and political upheavals of 1968 seemed largely to bypass Australia, the country has changed in significant and radical ways over the past forty years. Without apparently setting out to do so, Australians have reinvented themselves. Some of the changes have met the demands of sixties radicals; others have created new inequalities and problems we could not have imagined. In some ways the present looks very familiar: students who demonstrated against Vietnam found themselves, now in their sixties, marching against sending troops to Iraq. The global recession of 2008 and the looming problems of climate change suddenly made the radicalism of the sixties, long dismissed as irrelevant, seem worth re-examining.

The generation of the sixties was always diverse: more young Australians voted for Menzies in 1966 and 1969 than protested against the sending of troops to Vietnam. Equally, the itineraries of those who were part of the mythical sixties generation have been very different. Some of those associated with radical cultural and political protest have moved to the right, or built successful mainstream political and business careers. Others have remained true to their beliefs, and there are a number of former sixties radicals and hippies to be found living in mud-brick houses in Eltham or on communal farms on the northern New South Wales coast. Less often recognised are the casualties of the sixties, those who were caught up in the major political and cultural events of the time and found their lives disrupted in ways that resulted in depression, dependence and an inability to adjust to later life.

IN MY OWN case I constructed a career as an academic and writer, able to take advantage of the openings that the changes of that period created.

Ironically, I am now part of a system that, through its emphasis on outcomes and evaluation, is foreclosing for new generations the possibilities that allowed some of us to create fulfilling professional lives while retaining some degree of political commitment.

There is very little substantial written about the lasting impact of this period on Australian life. In 1980 Donald Horne published *Time of Hope*, a look back at the years between Menzies and Whitlam when 'some of the established common sense was being upset'. Horne was a political maverick whose politics steadily moved to the left, and who influenced generations of Australian intellectuals and writers. He was interested in this period because he saw it as a time when *everything* seemed to change. (It's worth noting that the book was commissioned by Richard Walsh, who as one of the founding editors of *Oz* magazine was an important part of the cultural changes of the 1960s.) Other than more specialised accounts of particular movements, of which Verity Burgmann's 1993 book *Power and Protest* is the most substantial, little analysis has been added to Horne's.

In retrospect Horne exaggerated the political if not the social changes taking place in Australia. He saw the election of the Whitlam government as changing political debate: 'By the time of the 1972 election it was another country. The maintenance of "economic growth" had disappeared as a political issue.' Perhaps: but it would soon reappear, and economic management was to be central to every election since. Indeed, what is most striking about Horne's evocation of the time is the echoes of his concerns in the current era.

Thus Horne pointed to a questioning of 'developmentalism', and to major shifts in attitudes towards racial, sexual and gender relations. His book reminds us that concerns about consumerism and the environment are hardly new, and generated considerable political debate forty years ago. He was also realistic enough to recognise that the new social movements of the time barely changed basic bureaucratic and capitalist structures, and may in some ways have strengthened them. Horne recognised the strength of institutions in our political culture, and the particular attraction that progress through institutions would have even for those who saw themselves as radicals.

What is most striking about *Time of Hope* is its indifference to the rest of the world, even though in his earlier *The Lucky Country* Horne had been one of the first Australian writers to seriously ponder our relations with Asia. In *Time of Hope* he was very aware of the growing impact of the United States, and the contradiction that many of the cultural ideas imported from the US fuelled protest against Australia's involvement in American military adventures in Indochina. He noted the tentative post-Menzies steps towards closer links with Asia, or at least those Asian countries seen as reliably anti-communist (while Whitlam's visit to China receives a paragraph, there is little sense of just how major a change this prefigured in Australia's relations with the outside world). But Horne was writing before the concept of globalisation had become a framework for understanding the world. He wrote in a tradition that saw the nation state as the primary focus for political action.

Horne ends *Time of Hope* by asking what had changed. Almost thirty years later Raewyn Connell, herself a participant in the radical politics of the period, addressed the same question in reflecting on the new left of the 1960s. Like Horne, she sees the period as one where large numbers of new ideas and possibilities emerged, and describes the new left as 'a collective midwife...a kind of social and cultural catalyst – not a world historical force in its own right but something that helped larger and slower processes along'.

For me, the crucial element of what Horne calls 'time of hope', and Connell 'a startling assertion of vivid life', was the sense of reimagining the world that was expressed through a plethora of social and cultural movements, ranging from Black Power groups to new forms of theatre and music. It is common to dismiss the sixties as inconsequential in Australian life, no more than a faint echo of overseas events. For some, the real shift came in the supplanting of Britain as the most significant cultural influence within Australia, in favour of the United States. Julie Stephens, for example, has argued that the best way to understand the impact of the sixties is to view it through the American experience.

Raewyn Connell draws on a comment by the Yippie leader Jerry Rubin to invoke colour as part of the sixties, and for those of us whose political outlooks were to some extent shaped by this period the sixties, however defined, remain a time of Technicolor brilliance, surrounded by the remembered greyness of the Menzies years and the steady growth of technocratic economic rationalism that came in the 1980s. It is dangerous to generalise about experiences, but for a generation born during the 1940s our school years during the 1950s and early 1960s seemed dominated by a conservative parochialism, where an unreflective anti-communism and slowly growing affluence, symbolised by the arrival of television in 1956 (in time for the Melbourne Olympics), ensured the seemingly endless continuation of conservative governments.

Unlike the United States, where the 1950s also saw significant shifts in civil rights and the beginnings of a counterculture through the Beat generation, there were few signs in Australia before the late 1960s of any revolt against the social and cultural status quo. I have written of the ways in which the stamps produced during the long Menzies years reflected a complacent and parochial view of the world: 'Largely in russet red and royal blue, these are the images of unquestioning respectability: cows and tractors exhorting us to PRODUCE FOOD; homage to the suburban volunteers of Red Cross, Rotary, the YMCA; nativity images of Christmas; and, most laden with symbolism of them all, the Queen's head set in an oval alongside our memorial to the American war effort: this was the Australia Menzies had created, and which we all in our different ways wished to escape.' The fifties were a bad time for stamp design everywhere, but Australia produced some of the very worst.

Despite his strong support of the American alliance Menzies is, of course, heavily identified with Britain and the view that Australia was essentially an antipodean extension of the 'mother country'. That view had been contested already during the nineteenth century, and it could not survive the dual impact of declining British power and large-scale non-British immigration. The historian Henry Reynolds, who grew up a few years ahead of me in Hobart, writes of the excitement at non-Anglo migrants arriving at his school, part of a wave that would in time transform much of Australia. My memories of the 1950s, a decade spent at the only Quaker School in Australia, encompass vignettes of the changes that were beginning to occur. The old trams went, replaced by trolley cars, and with them the unofficial rules whereby single women travelled in the front, men down the back. A couple of cafés opened, serving cappuccinos and – my favourite exotic dish – Russian egg salad. Like many others of my generation, one of my first political memories was the huge Royal Tour of 1954, and during my brief period as a Cub we stood in serried rows in the gardens of Government House to welcome the royal couple. The classes above us rehearsed for months for a schools pageant, and I remember my relief at not being exposed to the relentless drill instructors of the North Hobart Oval.

In 1956 the Melbourne Olympics saw Cold War conflict come to Australia, as Hungarian and Russian water polo players came to blows in the pool. Reports spoke of the crowds of 'new Australians', a term which quietly disappeared from the language once the Whitlam and Fraser governments replaced it with 'multiculturalism'. New Australians were almost exclusively European, and a pervasive racism was part of Australian identity. One of the first signs of a new style of politics was the emergence of a movement opposed to the White Australia policy: the Immigration Reform Movement was founded in 1959 by a group of academics and journalists with links to Melbourne University and the *Catholic Worker*. By the time I was an undergraduate at the University of Tasmania in the early 1960s this was an important issue, and we organised a well-attended debate between the Liberal Senator John Marriott and Professor James McAuley, as well as a visit by federal Labor's deputy leader, Gough Whitlam, who risked expulsion from the party for his opposition to the policy.

Perhaps the first precursors of a new political and cultural era were in popular music, beginning with the period of rock 'n' roll in the 1950s, and the phenomenon of bodgies and widgies. On 1 February 1951 the *Sydney Morning Herald* wrote on its front page: 'What with "bodgies" growing their hair long and getting around in satin shirts, and "weegies" cutting their hair short and wearing jeans, confusion seems to be arising about the sex of some Australian adolescents.' By the mid-1950s there were 'rock and roll riots' in several Australian cities. I was too young to be tempted by what seems now a foretaste of the counterculture, but by the early 1960s British pop music was suggesting new ways of seeing the world, above all through the sensation caused by the Beatles, who visited Australia in June 1964. It is estimated that up to 350,000 people gathered in Adelaide to watch the band arrive, perhaps the largest street gathering in Australian history. Listening to their music today it's hard to recapture the sense of challenge to the old order the Beatles represented, but as Peter Beilharz has noted music was everywhere in that period, and it often expressed an inchoate desire for change that would become expressed in new social and protest movements. *A Hard Day's Night*, which was in cinemas about the time of their Australian tour, marks the transition towards a new sort of cultural politics.

YET IN AUSTRALIA the sixties only began at the very end of that decade. In 1968, while riots and demonstrations threatened governments in France, Italy, the United States, Czechoslovakia and Mexico, the new Gorton government was barely touched by anti-war protest. Arguably more Australians experienced 1968 overseas than here: Carmen Callil, founder of Virago Press, speaks of her experiences in London with 'an Australian mafia…libertarian anarchists' who made their mark in Britain through *Oz* magazine. (*Oz* began in Sydney in 1963 and a British version started in 1967, after co-editor Richard Neville moved to London.) Barry Humphries, already established in London, toured Australia that year with *Just a Show*, featuring Edna Everage.

In Tim Burstall's *Two Thousand Weeks* (1969), the first Australian feature film for a decade, one character says: 'Isolation means that every idea arrives here second-hand, and usually five years out of date.' But the source of these ideas was increasingly the United States, and the emergence of new forms of political and cultural activism in America started to replace the attractions of Earl's Court and the British media. It was perhaps symbolic that the sixties seemed to have been imported to Australia as a rock musical, *Hair,* set in the United States, which opened in Sydney amid huge controversy in 1969. During 2008 a student posted the following on the website for my US Politics course: 'Don't know if Dennis set this up, but this Tuesday's showing of *Hair* in the classroom coincided with the forty-year anniversary of the premiere of the movie in 1968.' It was the fortieth anniversary of the musical, not the film, but the point remains. *Hair* came to Australia the following year, and the thirty-second nude scene was a scandal. The director Jim Sharman speaks of *Hair* and *The Rocky Horror Picture Show* book-ending the era: 'We had lived through the *don't dream it, be it* period and its all too brief *jump to the left*, and were now about to witness a very firm *step to the right* and a return to conservatism in the endless time warp of global politics.'

By 1968 Australia's involvement in the Vietnam War, which had been opposed by the Labor Party from the outset, was dividing the country, with a growing anti-war and anti-conscription campaign. As universities became the sites for anti-war protests, the RSL called for the expulsion of all protesting students. The federal election the following year suggested the long period of conservative rule was declining, as Whitlam won a huge swing to Labor and established himself as Prime Minister in waiting. (Paul Keating entered parliament that year.) That election became famous in Australian mythology through David Williamson's *Don's Party*, which portrayed the emergence of a new generation determined to change Australia. The small numbers of activists who saw themselves at the pioneers of a new Australian identity were overwhelmingly male and Anglo-Irish, and the next forty years would see major growth in diversity as the intellectual and political elites opened up slowly to include women and newer immigrant groups.

The late 1960s were defined by the war in Vietnam in ways very different to the impact of the Iraq war forty years later. The anti-war movement rallied hundreds of thousands of people across Australia in mass Moratoriums, and countercultural and feminist critiques starting cutting across mainstream Australia. In Steven Carroll's 2007 novel of suburban Melbourne, *The Time We Have Taken* (HarperCollins), the older characters are threatened by what seems a tsunami of change. As one muses: 'For Michael, his kind and this Whitlam of theirs are a wave, she imagines, a wave that has been steadily building over the years and will not be stopped. They *are* History, their every word and gesture tells you.' Perhaps the real turning point came in 1970, with the introduction of jumbo jets heralding a new period of mass travel, and the publication of Germaine Greer's *The Female Eunuch*. Tradition was recalled in the celebration of Cook's 'discovery' of New South Wales two centuries earlier, and another Royal Tour, though one with far less pomp and popular interest than that of 1954.

By the end of the decade, changes in the social and ethnic composition of Australia had produced the potential for a rather different radicalism to that which had been based around militant sections of the trade union movement and the Communist Party, largely irrelevant since the denunciations by Khrushchev of Stalin's crimes in 1956. Unlike the United States, there was no

Port Huron document, the founding statement of Students for a Democratic Society, to sum up a new radicalism in Australia. It was easier to retain some faith in electoral politics, for while Labor had been defeated in the elections of both 1966 and 1969 it remained critical of the war in Vietnam, and through its deputy leader, Jim Cairns, was closely linked to the anti-war movement. Some leftists distrusted Whitlam, who was thought too willing to compromise on opposition to the war, but many of us saw in him the promise of radical change and a new pride in being Australian.

The early 1970s was a period of considerable protests, demonstrations and social movement: large number of people marched against the war, there were sit-ins in university offices, consciousness-raising groups, green bans against the razing of inner cities – especially of Sydney. There all took place against the background of larger social and cultural change, which makes it difficult to distinguish what the new movements actually achieved and what was thrust upon us.

The countercultural and new-left politics that developed in this period had both strengths and weaknesses. By re-imagining the very nature of the political they enabled the mobilisation of large numbers of people who would otherwise not have become political activists. Quite extraordinary changes in how we think about cultural, ethnic and gender diversity stem from this period. But in retrospect the new left failed to grasp the ways in which capitalism was also changing, and the seductiveness of consumerism and affluence for the vast majority of people. The constant attacks of the right since the 1980s on 'latte-sipping leftists' demonstrates the failure of the left to capture the cultural agenda, and the irony that its successes in some arenas allowed the right to portray them as dangerous and elitist.

The opinion pages of *The Australian* remain full of attacks on the success of the sixties generation in conquering public space. Thus the former art critic Giles Autry laments the 'abject internal collapse' of western society, which he equates with the success of a whole set of understandings of the world summed up as 'postmodernism', which 'corrodes society largely through assaults on its soft underbelly, principally the effective hegemony it has created in the arts, education and culture generally'. If you start with this premise it becomes very easy to find examples – and *The Australian* has been particularly agitated by politicised readings of literature and history in schools, and the teaching of cultural studies more generally – but evidence that this had changed dominant political understandings is far less apparent. For every postmodern, postcolonial or queer reading of 'reality' shows on television there are many more people who watch such shows as pure escapism, and are probably reinforced in their attachment to an individualistic and acquisitive view of the world. Despite Autry's claim that the left is killing religion we currently have a Prime Minister who is more publicly religious than any of his predecessors, and religious fundamentalisms of various sorts are on the rise.

MANY OF THE new leftists of the sixties did move into various political and civil institutions, seemingly bearing out Pat Buchanan's comment: 'Every great cause begins as a movement, becomes a business and eventually degenerates into a racket.' I find myself spending large amounts of time and energy working through institutions that in different ways are a result of the social changes of the past few decades. Over the past decade I have been an active member of three boards: a university council, the Australian affiliate of a major international development agency and the governing body of the largest association of AIDS professionals in the world.

Although each has its peculiarities, they all represent certain assumptions about complex social organisation that is typical of liberal institutions at the beginning of the century. All, it should be noted, exist within the non-profit sector and have considerable, though very different, relationships with governments. They cover the spectrum of local to global: the university functions under state legislation, though it is heavily dependent on federal funding; Oxfam Australia is part of a confederation that is rapidly moving towards greater consolidation between its national member organisations; and the International AIDS Society is a genuinely international membership organisation, with something like 10,000 members across the world. All are organisations whose mission statements suggest a commitment to social justice and something that an earlier generation would have called 'progress'. All are to some extent representative; that is, I sit on each of their boards as the result of an electoral process, although in no case would I be seen as simply a delegate of my electors. All are likely places for a former activist to find himself, and all have been the cause of very considerable personal frustrations and some sense of achievement.

My dilemmas are one shared, I suspect, by many of my generation. We like to imagine ourselves as radicals, or at least critical thinkers, but we have moved into the lower ranks of the establishment. Objectively, as Marxists used to say, we prop up the system, however much we may imagine we are helping to undermine it. 'Selling out' is not a concern limited to those of us with radical or intellectual claims. At the end of one of his Los Angeles thrillers Michael Connelly writes: 'Bosch knew he would be co-opted...Because [Irving] held the only thing that Bosch had left, that he still cared about. His job. He knew Irving would trade that for his silence. And he knew he would take the deal.'

As I started thinking about the amount of time I spend in meetings, committees and conferences it occurred to me that there should be a major body of work on co-option through institutionalisation. (I am, after all, an academic.) There is only a limited amount, though the political theorist Michael Saward wrote a book fifteen years ago called *Co-optive Politics and State Legitimacy*. But the larger questions of how individuals committed to social change and radical action become incorporated into institutions that in turn develop their own inertia and conservatism is surprisingly under-investigated, though there is some American material on both African-American and environmental politics. Most of the literature tends to be written from the starting assumption that participation in mainstream organisations inevitably leads to some form of selling out; a typical comment comes from an unsigned webpage with the arresting heading 'The Tug of Gravity: Co-option, Absorption, and Shlock Rock'. 'Co-option is a natural product of systems. Which brings us to two rules. Rule one: representatives of the system, no matter how genial, are not on your side. Rule two: there is no such thing as half a loaf. There is no such thing as working within the system. All the alternatives developed by children of the sixties were gobbled up.'

As Michael Barker argues, liberal philanthropy takes radical causes and 'colonizes' them in the interests of perpetuating capitalism. This argument has force, and it occurs in various guises, such as the constant complaint about co-option by consumerism, whereby former radical slogans become advertising gimmicks. But it is worth reversing the argument and asking whether co-option might be a defensible tactic to build political influence and, indeed, effect change.

The development from social movement to institution is a constant one, most obvious in the ways in which the labour movements of the nineteenth century built political parties across most of the industrialised world that in time became part of the dominant political establishment. Australia today is governed by a Labor Party which allows very strong representation of unions within its party structures, but is equally very clearly determined to maintain the supremacy of the parliamentary leadership over the party membership, let alone any sort of social movement. One of the striking differences between the Rudd and the Hawke governments is the lesser role of organised labour, although it would be hard not to argue that Kevin Rudd, like Tony Blair before him, has successfully co-opted all but the most radical sections of the union movement into support of the state.

The new social movements of the 1960s and 1970s inevitably produced their own paths towards co-option through institutionalisation. Australians, as the political scientist Alan Davies used to observe, have a talent for bureaucracy. It is not surprising that Australia pioneered 'femocrats', the neologism coined to describe women who took up positions in government for the purpose of expanding women's equality. (The term is analysed in several books, particularly Hester Eisenstein's *Inside Agitators: Australian Femocrats and the State*, 1996, which may have introduced the term to an international audience.) The Greens began as a social movement born in environmental struggles in the 1970s and 1980s. The party's strongest base was Tasmania, because of the deep divisions around dams and timber, which became national issues on several occasions; the decision to form a political party, and to enter the parliamentary arena, was opposed by a number of environmentalists who feared that having to 'play the game' would reduce the integrity of the movement.

IN A SENSE, this is what the Italian theorist Antonio Gramsci predicted: 'the long march through institutions'. Gramsci argued that real power was exercised through hegemony, the ideological domination possible through non-state institutions such as the church, the educational system and the culture of the workplace. This view of how modern societies operate was developed by Herbert Marcuse through his concept of 'repressive tolerance' and his political reading of Freud's analysis of 'desublimation', summed up in *One Dimensional Man*, which seems largely unread by contemporary radicals.

The right still remembers Gramsci; the British journalist Melanie Phillips referred to him in her crackpot attacks on Barack Obama: 'In both America and Britain, Gramsci's acolytes have been conducting a decades-long march through the institutions. In Britain, they have substantially achieved their aim of subverting western morality and changing the face of British society.' The left now speaks of Gramsci less often, although his ideas have helped shape its ways of seeing the world; even as sophisticated an observer as Manfred Steger writes about 'the rise of the global imaginary' with no reference to Gramsci and one slighting mention of Marcuse.

Co-option operates at a number of levels, both in the ways in which the institutions of civil society (also a term derived from Gramsci) become incorporated into the larger agenda of the state and the ways in which the internal workings of those institutions themselves come to reflect the agenda and assumptions of the dominant system they seek to criticise. An agency like Oxfam constantly needs to balance its desire to remain able to advocate for changes in government policies with the reality that governments will provide much-needed resources for significant development work: whereas Oxfam America refuses any government funding, Oxfam Australia is prepared to use AusAID funds, though it maintains a strict cap on their proportion of total funding. Even this approach would not satisfy the radical critics of development assistance, who argue: 'Foreign aid directed towards NGOs has undermined national decision-making, given that most projects and priorities are set out by the European or US-based NGOs. In addition, NGO projects tend to co-opt local leaders and turn them into functionaries administering local projects that fail to deal with the structural problems and crises of the recipient countries…Rather than compensating for the social damage inflicted by free market policies and conditions of debt bondage, the NGO-channelled foreign aid complements the...neo-liberal agenda.'

The key question is whether we can change institutions faster than they can co-opt us. The danger is that by sitting on committees and working within institutions we strengthen their hegemony, thus making radical critiques all the more difficult. I am reminded of the French term 'recuperation', which the Situationists, a cultural-political movement of the 1960s, proposed to describe the condition whereby radical ideas and movements are incorporated into the mainstream and become commodities to be used by corporations. For a period Benetton advertisements were famous for doing just that.

The particular ways in which interest groups are co-opted into government processes is a form of corporatism that was most evident during the Hawke period, when the Accord provided for representation of unions and businesses alongside government in national economic fora. But this is a strong tradition in Australia, where governments use many advisory bodies made up of the leadership of interest groups both to provide input into policy and to help legitimise government decisions. Recently Penny Wong was able to bring together a large coalition, ranging from business to the Australian Conservation Foundation, behind the (seemingly doomed) proposal for an emissions trading scheme.

This is the dilemma for everyone who seeks political effectiveness. Imagine the agonies for many Indigenous leaders after the announcement of John Howard's intervention in the Northern Territory. The choices they faced were far more complex than the rhetoric on either side usually acknowledged. A senior bureaucrat once justified the inclusion of a maverick scientist on an advisory committee by using Lyndon Johnson's comment that it was better to have him inside the tent pissing out than outside pissing in. Once you accept that the state is made up of myriad different interests and individuals, it is possible to influence policy through careful use of the different levers available, which may include building alliances with people within institutions of both government and business who are willing to contemplate far more radical changes than is recognised by attacks on them as tools of the system.

My own experience of this sort of co-option has been largely in the world of both domestic and international AIDS politics, where I have sat on a number of committees and enjoyed the thrill of ministerial meetings. The world of AIDS politics exhibits both a remarkable degree both of political activism and of inclusion in official decision-making. From the street protests of the 1980s and early 1990s, associated with the self-dramatising projects of ACT UP, to mass action in South Africa organised at the turn of the century by the Treatments Action Coalition against the denialism of President Mbeki and his incompetent health policies, HIV has sparked considerable mobilisation in countries rich and poor. At the same time it has led to the incorporation of activists into major decision-making bodies, with the inclusion of 'civil society representatives' on the boards of several international bodies, and firm commitments for their involvement in a range of national advisory committees.

At one level this is an admirable example of the widening of representation to include those who are most affected. At another it raises questions about how representative such voices can be: the means and criteria for selection will inevitably favour those with the resources to play the system, which means command of English, the language of almost all relevant international meetings. Very small groups of leaders seem to appear at every meeting, with little evidence of their connection to the far broader communities for whom they claim to speak.

Yet for all these problems their absence would leave a significant gap. In my years on the university council I came to believe that the main contribution of those staff and students elected from within the university was to keep the bastards honest; that is, by our presence to remind the external members of council that ultimately the core of any university is its staff and students. In the same way, the presence on AIDS decision-making bodies of someone who is HIV positive, an acknowledged sex worker, homosexual or drug user means certain issues cannot be denied, however weak the claim of that particular person to speak for an entire and ill-defined group.

HOW REPRESENTATIVE ARE those who speak for others, and how far are they able to maintain their radical critique once they enter the system? Members of a board need to balance loyalty to their constituency with loyalty to the organisation as a whole, and the dominant assumption of corporate governance is that an individual's responsibility is now to the institution itself. This becomes apparent to anyone who has sat on any of the myriad committees, boards and advisory structures that are part of the fabric of contemporary life. The dominant language becomes that of the commercial world, and it is assumed that the only relevant skills are those required for corporate boards. Institutional loyalty creates pressure to be supportive of the institution, sometimes to the point of forgetting the reasons you joined the organisation.

One of the unexplored territories of co-option is the impact it has on those who enter the system hoping to change it, and become seen by others as its agents. The public service is full of people who are required to pursue policies with which they disagree, sometimes leading to severe stress, as was known to be the case for many in the Immigration Department under the Howard government. For those who have been elected or appointed to boards there is always the need to restrain our self-importance, the tendency to believe that what we see as crucial – that sneaky question to the CEO, that cunning amendment to the motion – amounts to very little. Some of us adopt symbolic gestures to proclaim our refusal to be co-opted, such as one friend who refused to wear a tie once he started working for a United Nations agency. I'm reminded of the moment in the film *Milk* where Harvey shaves off his beard and starts dressing like the councilman he aspires to be.

After perhaps a quarter-century of working through institutions I still wonder whether it is ever possible to attain other than incremental shifts. Part of the difficulty lies in measuring your achievements, for it is only when others take up radical ideas and they become part of mainstream language that you have changed the debate. It is satisfying to hear people who once opposed a particular suggestion putting it forward as their own, but it is hardly the heady triumph of storming the barricades. There is some pride in knowing that Oxfam played a significant role in creating concepts like 'make poverty history' and 'close the gap', which are now part of mainstream politics.

In Australian politics Peter Garrett is usually chosen to illustrate the dilemma of co-option. The common view is that since entering parliament Garrett has betrayed many of the principles for which he stood as a rock star and an influential, radical environmentalist during the 1980s and 1990s, and has been forced to promote policies he once opposed. As his fellow minister

Lindsay Tanner observed: 'As an activist you don't have much power, and as a politician you operate under heavy constraints.' Garrett tends to avoid too much reflection on the problem, answering questions about it in homilies such as, 'You don't leave your feelings behind you…if you move into jobs which have got additional levels of responsibility, then you act in accordance with the responsibilities of the position.' We are left wondering whether there might be an issue where his conscience demand he no longer stay a member of the government. But what else could someone in his position say?

PAUL KELLY, IN his *March of Patriots*, wrote: 'The deepest fractures in Australian politics are based on generation not party, a universal truth long denied.' It's an attractive claim, and one that seems persuasive in explaining developments such as the collapse of the old ties between Catholics and the Labor Party, and the rise of new social movements in the sixties and seventies. But it's a generalisation that also breaks down pretty quickly, even if you confine your observations to the limited world of Canberra politics: yes, politics is now considerably less male and less Anglo than when Keating and Howard entered it forty years ago, and certain prejudices have now become far less acceptable, even if they are still present. But compare two non-Anglo female politicians of a much younger generation, Natasha Stott Despoja and Sophie Mirabella (née Panopoulos), and it is hard to argue that what united them in age transcends that which divides them in world views.

Political activists are formed by certain shared experiences; World War II and the spectre of appeasement had a marked effect upon the debates over Vietnam in the 1960s, just as memories of the Vietnam War now hover over debates around intervention in Afghanistan. Yet different people will draw very different lessons from these experiences. Barack Obama stressed that he was of a generation too young to have experienced the sixties, and that he could transcend the polarisation that was its legacy. So far events seem to have proven him wrong, and the bitter cultural divisions in the United States that grew out of the divides of the 1960s are perhaps more pronounced than ever.

As I was writing this, I had coffee with a third woman from our generation, one whose achievements more than match those of the ones whose birthdays I'd helped celebrate, but who seemed strangely bitter at how the world has changed. She seemed angry, sharing the common complaint of many former radicals that today's young are apolitical, self-absorbed and uninterested in anything but their own lives. This view too easily ignores the extent to which social movements are as much about individual fulfilment as they are about altruism: those of us who took part in the new left and the counterculture of thirty years ago were as concerned about personal fulfilment as are those who today seek better jobs and their own apartments.

I deeply distrust generalisations about generations: Generations X, Y and Z (will the marketers now return to the beginning of the alphabet for their next category?) are as divided as were the generations of the sixties, where there were pitched street battles between young men in the army and police, and those who opposed them. There may well be common generational experiences mediated through the mass market – popular music and the use of certain forms of technology are the most obvious examples, although even then it is a huge generalisation to assume that the young don't like classical music, or the old don't use Facebook. Yes, polls suggest that people over fifty are somewhat more conservative in their voting patterns and their attitudes to certain social matters, which knocks on the head the self-image of those now well over fifty who cling to the idea of how radical was their generation. But basic worldviews are not defined by generations, and political differences cut across age just as they do across class, gender and ethnicity.

Generational distrust works both ways: there may still be those who claim you can't trust anyone over thirty, but there are at least as many people over sixty – the fastest growing part of the population – who believe that all change is necessarily deterioration. Few are as conservative as those former radicals who cling to their memories of the sixties. But what was crucial about that period was the willingness to rethink all established truths, and to argue for new means of political action. The upheavals of the sixties were simultaneously products of and criticisms of Marxism, and of the whole socialist tradition. Today little remains in popular consciousness of a leftist analysis, let alone the sort of community that it once provided. Radicals tend to be found in specific movements, which speak relatively rarely in common language or see themselves as part of a larger project for radical social change. Even most environmental campaigners behave like single-issue lobbyists, rather than seeking to engage in the rethinking of larger socioeconomic structures that the environmental critique demands. It is an ominous sign that the most inventive accounts of our predicament probably now come in science fiction, which doesn't, by and large, suggest meaningful forms of building political action.

The closest thing to the radicals of the sixties may be found today in the anti-globalisation movement, which quite correctly sees the dominant meanings of globalisation as enforcing a market society based on ever expanding consumption. What strikes me about young activists of today's generation is their far greater sense of universalism, and the commitment to work globally. Street protests at G20 meetings are a small part of this; more interesting are the numbers of people in rich countries who volunteer to work in some of the poorest and most violent areas of the world.

I don't share the pessimism of those veterans of the new left and counter-culture who fear the loss of some sort of essentialist radicalism and assail today's young as self-centred and apolitical. Nor do I believe easy slogans about youth offering all hope for the future; 'youth' is a meaningless term except in demography and perhaps advertising. But it is likely that those of us who have become part of institutions and benefited from the compromises we have made with power over a long period are unlikely to find the radical new ways of seeing the world that the current situation demands. I suspect we won't even recognise the ideas that might reshape our political and social lives even if they were to emerge.

Thus the ultimate way of recreating the spirit of the sixties will be to abandon the nostalgia for a mythologised radical past, and the accompanying culture wars. The sixties remind us that it is possible to radically re-imagine the future, but they don't provide a blueprint for the present. The American civil rights leader Andrew Young once said: 'We can change history through finding the one thing that can capture the imagination of the world. History moves in leaps and bounds.' At the moment we are waiting, breathless, for that 'one thing'.

References available at www.griffithreview.com

Dennis Altman is a professor of politics at La Trobe University, Melbourne. His books include *Global Sex* (University of Chicago, 2001), *Gore Vidal's America* (Polity, 2005) and *51st State?* (Scribe, 2006).

FICTION

STILL HERE

ANNA KRIEN

ENORMOUS things are in the water now. Bull sharks roll below the surface and carp with whiskers like whips slip under the house. A great swatch of brown cloth, the water won't break – it just bulges and inhales as if it were a single living creature. Peter and I make promises, like when the water gets this high – and we mark it on the stilts with blue Texta – we'll leave. But we've made eight blue marks, first from the ground in our gumboots, and the last three Peter hung upside down from the veranda to draw them. Each blue mark disappears overnight, regular enough to make us paranoid that someone is floating past to rub them out, rather than the waters actually rising. And so, on account of our suspicion, we're still here. On his haunches, feet wrinkled and blue from the cold, Peter spits at the water from the veranda. His phlegm clings to the stumps. The air rings with the tinnitus of mosquitoes. The lichen that grew on the shower curtain is spreading all over the walls like a pale green flocking. The carpet squelches under my gumboots. In Beth's old bedroom, the pink paint is lifting off the walls, bubbling like a rash. Her single bed, neatly made with a colourful crocheted rug, stands solid in the water. The stilts at the back of the house have sunk lower than the front, so the rear of the house is filling with water and collecting in the belly of her old wardrobe. Tadpoles dart through the ground-floor rooms of her flooded dolls' house.

Each morning I get dressed in town clothes, as if the water might suddenly recede and I'll be able to do the errands. Peter doesn't bother. He's been wearing the same shorts and T-shirt since the sky broke down. If Beth was here – not as the nineteen-year old university student she is now, whose shoulders stiffen whenever we talk to her, but if she were eight again – she'd have insisted on staying in her room despite the water, and listened to the lap of tiny waves against the skirting boards. She'd have enjoyed the adventure of her bed slowly lifting and floating like a raft. She and the boys could make boats from paddle-pop sticks, and the sample perfume bottles I used to bring home from the chemist would wash up in the corridor with tiny notes inside them. But we haven't heard from Beth for months. Not since Peter pulled out the internet cord in a rage and told her she wasn't welcome home until she took everything – her photos, her poems, *everything* – off the web. I didn't mind it so much. Some things she wrote were hurtful – but we don't know for sure that she was writing about us. I tried to tell Peter that, remind him that she always did have a good imagination. But Peter was furious. 'I am a goddamn English teacher,' he said.

Without telling him, I used the computer at the library to look her up after he disconnected our internet. The photos aren't as slutty as he thinks they are. She looks like she is having fun. And she has hundreds of friends. I study all the boys in the pictures with her and wonder which one is her boyfriend. I opened a Hotmail account and emailed her a few times. I thought we were getting along, but her last email was too much. *Susan told me what happened. Tell Dad he is a hypocrite. No, actually, he's worse than that. He's disgusting. And you're an idiot for staying with him.* It was a cruel email to receive. I deleted it and shut down my account. As for the boys, I don't know if they know. They haven't said anything. I called them and asked them to help after the sandbags we laid out around the stumps kept getting nicked. But they were too busy and couldn't get time off work. I tried to speak to Beth but her housemate said he'd get her and then left me on the line. I don't know if he forgot about me or if she was home and refused to come to the phone, but I sat there for some time, listening to the sounds of our daughter's life. Eventually someone must have seen the phone off the hook and hung it up.

The rescue boats pass us everyday. Once we even saw our cat on it, sitting proudly on the bow. But we can't call out. Peter says what's the point; they're just staying at the community centre, eating and shitting together. We may as well stay put and be civilised about it, he reckons. But it's more than that. No one on the boat even looks at us, let alone checks to see if we're okay. I'm surprised they let our cat aboard.

We can tell who's left. The hovering orange glows of cigarettes and drifts of smoke give them away. Eddie Rollins is in his place behind us; the Bertie sisters across the road; and further down the way Joe Feltham is still there. During the day the boat checks on all three households, trying to persuade them to leave. But so far they've stuck to their guns, probably convinced that if they go they'll never return.

A couple days back, Eddie's wife went with the boat. She has emphysema. The poor woman never smoked a cigarette in her life but got it from Eddie's smoking. Their cockatoo, Frankie, got it too but died pretty quick. For the past three years, Narelle sat at the window with a plastic oxygen mask attached to her face. Eddie had a lit cigarette in his mouth as he helped her down to the boat.

The Bertie sisters must have a stockpile of cigarettes. They light their smokes off each other's, as if to keep some vigil going. A single orange glow leans in, blossoms and then after the brief flare separates into two pulsing lights. My grandpa used to always talk about cigarettes as the perk of serving in Papua New Guinea instead of Europe during the war. 'You could smoke at night because of the fireflies,' he'd say. 'The damn things were everywhere. They made us right jumpy at the start but after a while we stopped shooting at them. We didn't have enough ammunition to shoot at a million specks of orange just in case one of them was a Jap having a smoko.' He laughed as if he were the luckiest bastard in the world because he and his mates could smoke while knee-deep in mud and leeches. Even coming back with one arm couldn't dampen it for him. 'I can still smoke,' he'd say when we pointed this out, holding up a cigarette in his sole hand.

At night we can hear a canoe cutting the water near us, wooden paddles stirring the night. The whirr of fishing line is followed by the plonk of a sinker. Peter and I hold our breath, staring hard at the black, trying to make out the shape of the boat. I rub my calves, using the last of the eucalyptus oil on my shin splints from netball. My muscles are locking up from the wet. Like the worms that showed up at the beginning of the storms, wriggling red all over the footpaths, the veins on my legs are swelling. Some join up like purple bloated streets. The lumpy feel of them makes me sick. Eventually, in the black, a fish is jerked out and slaps against the surface of the flood, trying to get back under its wet covers but it is as if the river has hardened, leaving the fish to the metric clicking of a spinning reel.

The storms began a week and a half ago. Peter kept saying, 'What's everyone complaining about? We *need* the rain.' But anyone who knows anything about farming knows that a flood after a drought is just as bad as no rain. Peter is a typical city man like that. Thinks he knows everything. Or at least, that everything that can be seen can be known. There's something about how a flood can change all that. It has cloaked this town like a sheet over the dead. The spill of water as it coagulated around the cattle, muting the bleats of drowning sheep; the branches of tea-tree rubbing against each other sounding like rusty swings until their roots loosen, let go and tip over. And then silence. That's obvious, I suppose, but it's a different kind of silence to the one we had been getting used to.

Peter emptied out the supermarket a month after it happened. He did the shopping anyway, all five aisles, including the toiletry aisle – which is a first for him – but at the checkout no one would serve him. They had turned off the lights above their registers and put the folded closed signs on their conveyor belts. Then, so they wouldn't have to look him in the eye, they stood outside on the street smoking. Not even Susan, Beth's best friend, served him. After that, Peter didn't bother going back to the high school to clear out his desk. Said he didn't need to be told he was fired. When his graduating class got their marks back – the best final year results in the history of the school – the local newspaper rewrote history by stating the Year 12s were taught by Mr Robbs. Which they are now.

To begin with, people were nice to me. I run – ran – the chemist, so I guess they had to be. It was Peter who was the outsider, after all; I was born in this town. Fourth generation. Girls I'd babysat, braided their hair and coached at netball came into the chemist with their own children and mentioned in loud voices that their husbands had invested in the new units out next to the fake lake with black swans brought in from Adelaide. 'We're looking for tenants,' they said, eyebrows raised at me before enquiring if the costs of goods had gone up recently or had my prices gotten a little bold? When I took the week's takings to the bank Sally widened her eyes at my numbers, even though I'd been banking with her for fifteen years. She said a few times, loud enough so everyone could hear, 'It's not as if you're stuck for choices, Margaret,' banging the notes crisply against her desk, making neat stacks. People call me Margaret now. Sometimes it's Mrs *Cedar*, for real emphasis.

I'D ALWAYS WONDERED about the wives of men in court over some sex scandal, how they dealt with the newspapers and the television cameras, everyone knowing. I studied their expressions on the six o'clock news. Pointy chins jutted forward as they held their husband's hand. I always thought these women were weak, even when it was all over the news – they still believed their husbands. How could they have not known what these men really were?

When Peter and I first met, before the children came along, he had wanted to have sex with me there. He tried a few times but I wouldn't let him. I thought – *I think* – it's unhygienic. Why didn't I know then? It's like Janice used to say: if you don't let them do what they want with you, they'll do it with someone else. But Peter was different. He wasn't from here. He didn't force things like the boys we had grown up with. It's almost like a religion I think now, when I see images of women supporting their husbands. You can't just stop believing in them – especially after twenty-two years and three children. Soon the chain chemist the town had been so against for the past three years opened up in the arcade opposite me and I closed up that same month, arranging a deal with the chain to buy my stock at a loss.

IN THE EVENINGS, when the rescue boats have left, I paddle out on the kids' old boogie board. I touch the marble heads of angels peering above the water line, the tips of their wings poking up like fins, trying to guess which granite curve is my parents' gravestone. I float under the houses of all the people I knew, their pocked dartboards half-submerged like sinking suns, the basketball hoops where the kids mucked around after dinner when it was daylight savings. In the main street I pull myself along by the parking meters until I reach the chemist. There is graffiti on the shop sign hanging over the footpath. Red paint scribbled over the mortar and pestle my father painted when I was a girl. Faded signs for hay-fever tablets and acne cures are still in the window. Peter asks me what I do out here on these night paddles; he says it with fear, like I'm meeting with the rest of the town and conspiring against him. I don't say anything; let him think he's going to get tarred and hung from a tree. Dipping my arms into the water, I feel the odd flank of fish.

I used to tell the kids a great big carp lived in the river and it was his whiskers, not reeds, that lassoed their legs when they went swimming. This carp lived on children whose siblings had not kept an eye on them, because that was all it took, I told the boys, reminding them that Beth was the youngest. A glance at the sky or the small study of an insect, and the carp would rise up, gills full of mud, smacking its Botox lips, wet and hungry. All of our children managed to avoid the carp. They managed to avoid this small town altogether, escaping to the city as soon as they got their P-plates, except for Beth, who was so impatient she left on her learner's licence. The Feltham's little girl wasn't so lucky. Or Mrs Shaw's husband, who got drunk on a forty-degree day and drowned. There was Lucy Stone, who went to school with me. And now Jason. I never thought to tell Peter about the river and its silent takings. It was just a silly story I told the kids to make sure they looked after each other. 'We had been drinking rum and coke but we weren't drunk,' Peter had first insisted to me. 'The others had gone on to the pub to keep celebrating but I didn't join them. I was coming home. You *know* that – I *texted* you.'

He had texted me. At the station Peter made me show the police the message, demanding they read it. Even the woman at the front desk had to read it. *Still celebrating w students be home in half hour*, it said. When the main sergeant shrugged and handed the phone back to me, Peter went crazy. 'This is evidence – shouldn't this be filed somewhere?' In the end one of the policemen put it in a plastic bag and dropped it in a filing cabinet to shut him up. I hated Peter for that. It was my phone. 'What if the kids are trying to call me?' I asked Peter after we left the station. 'The kids don't call you. You call them,' he spat back at me.

The night it happened Geoff phoned me, telling me to bring some of Peter's clothes down to Townsend Road, at the bridge. Geoff had been an outsider like Peter – they bonded over it, Geoff the policeman and Peter the teacher from the city. But this evening Geoff sounded different: not cold, but distant. I know now that, like everybody else, he was probably weighing up his loyalties. When I asked him what happened, if Peter was okay, he said, 'He's okay…Look, you better get down here,' and hung up. The whole road was lit up when I got there, with searchlights and dogs, and I forgot to slow down, still doing eighty kilometres until a man I'd never seen before waved me down furiously. 'Can't you see we've a situation here?' he yelled when I wound down the window. 'If I had any time I'd fine you on the spot. Jesus.' He stormed off and I pulled the car over slowly onto the gravel. There were small groups of police I didn't recognise. The Townsends' house in the far corner of the paddock was lit up, and I could see the kids' faces pressed up against their windows. John was out the front, talking to a policewoman – I started to walk over but then he saw me and scowled. He said something to the woman and disappeared inside.

THE POLICEWOMAN CAME over to me, holding her hand out formally. 'Mrs Cedar?'

I was holding Peter's clothes and by the time I had swapped hands to return the handshake, her arm was back by her side, hitched on her holster. 'What's happened?' I asked her. 'I've Peter's clothes. Where is he?'

The policewoman gently tried to take the clothes from me. 'I'll make sure he gets them. We need to take him back to the station.'

I wouldn't let go. We both held on to the bundle until a T-shirt fell out of the pile and on to the ground. I let go and picked it up, handing it over. 'What's happened? Where's Peter? Can I see him?'

'We're not at a stage to know. A young man has disappeared and we need to talk to your husband about it.'

'Who – which young man? One of his students?' I looked around. 'Who?'

Torchlight was panning the gum trees; the trunks were like white spindly ghosts. Men in black wetsuits slipped in and out of the river, their headlights glowing under the water. Police wearing rubber gloves were picking things up with tongs and putting them into plastic bags, clothes I recognised as Peter's. 'I'm sorry, we can't say who...' the policewoman started – but then I saw Marie Strand kneeling on the muddy banks, her mouth gulping silently. Two policemen were hovering around her, their hands splayed out as if spotting her.

'Jason? Is it Jason?'

Marie's head jerked up and stared at us. The policewoman noticed and tried to pull me away. 'Like I said, I can't say anything at this point.'

'But maybe he's at the pub? Has anyone checked the pub?' I was getting panicky. 'Didn't they all go to the pub?'

A slow howl rose up out of Marie, a guttural sound as she sprung from her haunches towards me. The police grabbed her, held her down. I stared at them. She was screaming. Quiet, meek Marie, who worked every day at the canning factory, was screaming and swearing at me. The policewoman took my elbow and pulled me away. 'A police car will drop him home,' she was saying. 'Go home – get some rest. Things will be clearer in the morning.'

She left me at my car, satisfied after I pulled the car keys out of my handbag and put them in the door. It was then that I saw Peter. He was in the back of the ambulance, the doors wide open – he was wrapped in brown blanket. He looked up and caught my eye. Without thinking my arm shot up and I waved. He stared at me and then looked away. I stood there for a long time, hand in the air.

TWO WEEKS LATER Marie Strand went through Jason's English essays and photocopied Peter's comments. Phrases like 'you have such a beautiful way with words' and 'this is penetrating stuff, Jason' and 'Jason, I think you have real talent – I think if we work together we can get some of your writing published.' It all sounded so predatory. She ran off about fifty copies of his comments and did a letter drop around town. In thick black Texta she wrote at the top of each page *Peter Cedar hunted my son. He is a Killer.*

Things got worse when Jason's VCE external examination results came in, a fortnight after he disappeared. He just scraped a pass in the English exam. Mr Robbs wrote a piece for the local paper after Marie asked him to read Jason's short stories and essays. 'Nothing within these stories indicated to me that Jason had been an exceptional student, let alone a talented writer,' he stated. 'How Peter Cedar had become so enthused over Jason's writing is a mystery to me. It would seem, to me, that he held no *genuine* literary aspirations for this young man, on the cusp of his adult life.'

The evening that was published a rock came through our window. The article was wrapped around the rock. It knocked over a clay vase Beth made in primary school when she was learning how to join coils. Peter was furious. He went outside onto the veranda and yelled that everything this town did was a cliché, that throwing a goddamn rock through the window was a cliché and no one in this town could think of anything original and a goddamn rock through the window was a cliché. I collected the broken pieces of Beth's vase and carried them to her bedroom as he paced and yelled. I lay on her bed and cried. The next night someone threw a garden gnome through the kitchen window. Miraculously, nothing broke except the window, sending shattered glass all over my clean dishes. The gnome lay on the cork floor, nose chipped, staring at us. Peter laughed. 'Well, at least they worked out what a cliché is,' he said proudly, as if he had educated the rock-thrower. After that I slept in Beth's old room and Peter in the boys' bunk bed. Neither of us wanted to sleep in our bed.

ON THE FIFTH night of the flooding I tied the boogie board to our stairs. I tested how many steps were underwater, counting four before clambering back up, my legs dripping and muddy. I'd paddled to the edge of town this time, looked up at the green highway sign pointing towards Adelaide. The roadhouse was ruined; through the windows I could see the tables and bar stools covered in a mould, the fridges and food counter ankle-deep. This was where we used to sit, us girls, and watch people leave town. Especially at graduation time, the place would be feverish with plans of escape, dreams of getting a job and a flat in the city. I'd met Peter there. He was just a boy then. A writer, he said. Hitching his way around Australia. He stayed for a week, camping by the river at a spot I showed him. I went home only once, to pack a bag and leave a note. It was the wildest thing I'd ever done. I honestly thought I was never coming back.

I MISSED HIM then, under the highway sign and drowned roadhouse. I turned the board homewards and paddled. I crawled into the bottom bunk and saw his eyes were woven shut with salt. He'd been crying. He looked so young. I saw our two sons in his face. I put my face in his neck and kissed his skin. 'I'm sorry, I'm sorry,' I said, over and over, prying my arms around him. I lifted him off the mattress and held him. Tears, his and mine, ran down my neck and onto my breasts. 'I'm sorry, I'm sorry,' I kept saying. 'I love you.' And it's true. I still love him. We sunk into each other like we had been starved by the silence. Butting our heads hard. Like horses. For a moment I thought I felt the bunk beds lift, bobbing in the flood, until I cried out, a spasm going through me and into the empty town.

We lay together, on the bottom bunk, for the rest of the wet. Our bodies shifted into their habitual curve around one another, as if in sleep we knew no grudge.

Things will be different when the water recedes, as though sucked away with a straw. The crows will be the first to return. Picking at the bloated flesh of drowned dogs and sheep stuck in the mud, river shrimp and crabs coming out of their mouths. Pecking at the eyes of stranded fish, the silver gills fanned open. The hovering powerlines will return to the ground, and puddles will remain, like a great big mirror has been broken over the town, each reflecting pieces of the sky and passing clouds. They'll find him. Jason Strand. Blue like a swimming pool. Toes and fingers nibbled. Peter's thumbprints all over him. And when the rain stops the streets will fill up with new cars, tyres spinning in the bog. And our house will probably collapse, its knees rotten.

Anna Krien has been published in Griffith REVIEW: Hidden Queensland, The Next Big Thing and Divided Nation, and in the Big Issue, The Monthly, The Age, Best Australian Essays, Best Australian Stories, Voiceworks, Going Down Swinging, Frankie and Dazed & Confused. Her poem 'The Last Broadcasters' won the 2008 Val Vallis Award and her book about the protests to save Tasmania's old-growth forests will be published by Black Inc. later this year.

Out of the ordinary

Bad luck, disaster, democracy

John Keane

THE *Lucky Country* by Donald Horne is among my treasured Australian books. When first tempted to open its covers, as an undergraduate student of politics, long-haired and lined up for conscription to Vietnam, I found myself attracted to the unsettling question posed within the opening pages of its deft description of contemporary Australia: what if things turned out badly? What if disaster struck down the arrogant politicians too set in their ways for the good of their country? What if bad luck suddenly laid its hexing hand on the shoulder of the sun-tanned bloke in an open-necked shirt, the natural-born democrat solemnly enjoying an ice-cream, his kiddie strolling beside him?

Horne never posed things quite so sharply. But from the outset his remarkable book hit readers with a brickbat, with the unsettling thought that the lucky country might not have luck on its side. This most egalitarian of continents, an easygoing country whose soldiers are renowned for the 'lowest saluting rate in the world', happily ignores the problems of the world: 'Australia is not a country of great political dialogue or intense searching after problems (or recognition of problems that exist),' Horne wrote. 'The upper levels of society give an impression of mindlessness triumphant,' he added. 'Whatever intellectual excitement there may be down below,' he continued, 'at the top the tone is so banal that to a sophisticated observer the flavour of democratic life in Australia might seem depraved, a victory of the anti-mind.' Then came Horne's pinching conclusion, the barbed thought that the young and confident Australian democracy, especially its leaders, had such a poor sense of the power of bad luck in human affairs that they had failed to grasp dilemmas and problems for which they had no ready solutions. 'A society whose predecessors pioneered a whole continent now appears to shun anything that is at all out of the ordinary,' he wrote. 'The trouble is that, by Australian standards, almost everything that is now important is out of the ordinary.'

Mindlessness triumphant: what if nothing much has changed in Australia during the past half-century? It has, of course. The country's sense of history, its sensitivity to past sufferings and future uncertainties, and to

---

PREVIOUS PAGE: Frantz Zephirin, *The Resurrection of the Dead*, 2007. Painting reproduced on the cover of the 25 January 2010 issue of the *New Yorker* following the earthquake that struck Haiti on 12 January.

different possible futures, has grown exponentially. So, too, has the quality of its leadership and its sense of interdependence with the wider world.

But let us suppose for a moment that Horne was on to something. Imagine that his profound discomfort with the cluelessness of a democracy confronted by big and threatening problems turned out to have great global relevance in the twenty-first century. Given that democracies such as Australia are already struggling to come to terms with life-and-death matters such as the control of nuclear and bio-chemical weapons, climate change and the wilful sabotage of the biosphere, might it be that they are also courting not-yet-known disasters for which they are unprepared? And the vital question: when compared with alternative political systems, such as those of contemporary China, or Singapore, or Vietnam, is it just possible that democracies are singularly ill-equipped to handle bad luck, and to solve equitably and effectively massive problems that suddenly strike, or that might well be lurking just around the corner?

BAD LUCK, MISFORTUNE, actual or potential disasters: democracies everywhere are today shadowed by them, or so it seems. A mood swing among citizens and their representatives has been underway for some time. Peppered by bad news and short-term panics, and spiced with anxiety and mild melancholia, the atmospheric change is palpable and unprecedented. The apprehension has nothing yet of the biting vertigo and violence that hastened the end of the nineteenth century, with its bourgeois self-assurance and widespread belief in peace and permanent progress; and it is not a throwback to the morbid gloom spawned by the first half of the twentieth century, with its deadly global wars, economic collapse, totalitarian regimes, genocides and nuclear threats. Although linked in various ways to these earlier global disasters, our times are evidently different; their listlessness and dejection are unique. Whether or for how long the mood swing endures, or whether its effects continue to be distributed unevenly across the existing democracies (compare melancholy Germany, Ireland and Britain with the strong sense of promise still alive in India, South Korea and Australia), remains unclear. Yet one thing is certain: more than a few causes and causers are fuelling the atmospheric change that we might call the new apprehension.

Some sense of its complexity can be gleaned from the burgeoning literature on disaster and the misfortunes and dysfunctions that are said to weaken or undermine the capacity of contemporary democracies to define, let alone handle, them. Disaster-watching has become a literary industry with an impressive public following. Viral pandemics and terrorist attacks with hijacked nuclear-tipped missiles are said to be on the list of thinkable disasters that would produce tens or hundreds of thousands – even millions – of fatalities. Also highly ranked is the cultish view that American-led free-market capitalism is once more passing through a period of 'creative destruction', and that this aggressive vampire capitalism thrives on inducing 'shocks' which take advantage of its victims. Forecasts of tsunamis triggered by massive volcanic eruptions and earthquakes, and predictions of catastrophic collisions between the earth and giant extraterrestrial bodies, are favourites on the list. So are the dangerous risks generated by spiralling military spending, disruptions of supply chains, excessive dependence on fossil fuels, climate change and the shameful suffering caused by chronic hunger.

The list cries out for a breakdown analysis. Disasters can strike suddenly or they may be slow-fuse dramas; sometimes, as the citizens of Haiti know from decades of state violence and an afternoon earthquake, people are forced simultaneously to suffer both. Disasters can be triggered by natural changes in our biosphere, such as bushfires in Victoria or hurricanes in Florida, or by famines and genocides and other events for which humans are primarily responsible; in practice, as the calamitous effects of the British bomb testing at Maralinga during the 1950s should remind us, the distinction between 'natural' and 'human' is rarely clear-cut and is becoming ever less meaningful. Whatever their type or form, disasters are always high-impact events. They result in large numbers of victims in the biosphere, and by definition they inflict world-shattering consequences upon the lives and landscapes they touch.

THE GREAT LISBON Earthquake of November 1755 was a template for many catastrophes that followed. The first large-scale disaster whose natural causes and human consequences were recorded in detail, the earthquake (an estimated nine on the moment magnitude scale) consumed Lisbon and surrounding areas in fire and tsunami, misery and disease, death and physical destruction. One hundred thousand souls may have perished. The disaster prompted the invention of cleverly designed earthquake-proof structures (still visible today in the district Baixa Pombalina), frustrated Portuguese colonial ambitions and led to the attempted assassination of King Joseph I.

Unluckily for the Roman Catholic Church, the earthquake struck on the morning of an important religious holiday and turned most of Lisbon's churches into piles of rubble. The bad luck provoked doubts about the Proverbs proverb that luck comes always from the Lord. It triggered bitter battles between theologians convinced that the earthquake was the manifestation of God's wrath and sceptics for whom the ill-timed devastation heaped doubt on the principle that the world was guided by an omniscient and benevolent deity (Voltaire's *Candide* and 'Poem on the Disaster of Lisbon' are perhaps the best-known examples of this suggestion).

The earthquake lent credence to the pagan etymology of the word 'disaster', which had entered the English language – possibly via French – during the sixteenth century from the Italian *disastro*, an 'ill-starred event', from the Latin *astrum*, 'star'. It prompted anguished reflection on the possible causes of natural events (the science of seismology was among its fruits), and called into question the innocence of common metaphors of ground and grounding within the language of philosophy and political thinking. Thanks to a natural upheaval of cataclysmic proportions, things political looked hereon much less governed by certainty.

IN OUR AGE of communicative abundance, the kinds of consequences suddenly sparked by the Great Lisbon Earthquake are amplified by the media hunger for bad news packed off electronically, in real time, around the world. Journalists are generally poor at analysing slow-fuse disasters; they prefer sudden catastrophes. Catastrophism, a term more commonly used by geologists and psychoanalysts, is their bread and butter. One consequence is that sudden disasters seem to be here, there and everywhere. Media coverage makes them feel more immediate, more frequent; it fuels the new apprehension, often by selecting victims with whom audiences can readily identify, so encouraging them to feel, or draw the conclusion, that bad luck and disaster are the whole world's ruinous fate.

Democracies find it hard to turn their backs on the media fixation on sudden disasters. Swept away by tsunamis, incinerated by bushfires and swallowed by earthquakes, famines, genocides, the governments and parties and citizens of democracies find their every move is monitored, their successes lauded, their failures condemned.

So how do democracies generally measure up when coping with sudden disasters? Are their relief and reconstruction efforts more effective and efficient than those of dictatorships whose people face devastation at the hands of a natural disaster, of the kind that confronted the Chinese leadership in the aftermath of the massive earthquake in Sichuan Province in May 2008 and, in the same month, the Burmese military junta following Cyclone Nargis?

There is no simple answer, although it is easy to show two things. One of them – implied but left untreated by Jared Diamond's otherwise fine study of why some societies succumb to disasters, *Collapse* – is that contemporary monitory democracies, defined not just by periodic elections but also by their multiple watch-dog, guide-dog and barking-dog institutions, are in principle much better equipped than other political systems to scrutinise claims about the actuality or probability of sudden disasters. Robust monitory democracies are early warning systems. While never foolproof, in part because they are plagued from time to time by 'echo chambers', 'flat earth news' and other troubling media trends, monitory democracies are generally more sensitive to the criteria for defining disasters. Their mitigation of disaster – for instance, by adopting a version of the precautionary principle – is never straightforward and consistent, but always political.

In the age of monitory democracy, disasters are or should be controversial. Thanks to public monitoring of power we know, for example, that many more people die on our roads or from smoking tobacco than from terrorist attacks. We also sense that it is a tricky business spotting cover-ups by politicians of actual or imminent disasters, or assessing claims by experts about risky trends that may well be leading us toward fatal discontinuities.

The most genuine and reliable disaster forecasts are our very inability to forecast them. That is why democracies, when they have their wits about

them, doubt the wisdom of the tangle-brained, mendacious thinking speci-
fied by the Rumsfeld Rule, a version of the precautionary principle which
states that we know there are 'known knowns' as well as 'known unknowns'.
Democracies cannot know the things that have yet come to pass. They
certainly cannot banish luck from human affairs, if by luck is meant events
that lie outside the horizon of effective predictability. But since there is a
subcategory of luck, the rotten luck that in the extreme can bring disaster to
people, democracies have a definite advantage in tackling its fickle effects.
The openness of democracies ensures that their experts, leaders, journalists
and citizens can make intelligent judgements that warn of actual or imminent
dangers. Such public warnings have more than heuristic value: they mark off
the unusual ability of democracies to guard themselves against bad luck and
bad outcomes, and possible collapse.

The other thing easily shown is that vibrant democracies, because they
contain means of public monitoring and opposition to power, enable individuals and groups to criticise the behaviour of their governments, businesses and
NGOs when faced with out-of-the-blue disasters at home. The public outcries
against the Bush administration's incompetent handling of the devastation
caused by Hurricane Katrina, fuelled by the revelation that the chief of the
Federal Emergency Management Agency was a political appointee and not
formally qualified for the job, are a poignant example.

The irony is that such outcries make democracies unusually vulnerable to
the charge of hypocrisy, to accusations of double standards levelled publicly by
independent monitors, citizens and opposition political parties. Leaders and
governments are lambasted for not doing what they said they would do, or are
slammed by claims that their actions are too slow or at odds with acceptable
standards of justice. When things become acute, charges of incompetence and
hypocrisy hurled at the powerful can fuel embittered resistance, sometimes
to the point, as last happened during the 1920s and 1930s, where democracies
commit 'democide'.

Confronted by cataclysm, panic grips the political elite. Backed by
powerful propertied interests and enjoying some measure of public support,
the political class concludes that democratic power-sharing is a costly waste
of time, ineffective in resolving the crisis and ill-suited to their interests.

Unluckily for democracy, the forces of cynicism and brute power are victorious.

IF DEMOCRACIES FACING sudden disasters at home are vulnerable to democide, how do they fare when facing disasters abroad? The rule is that they are always confronted by a dilemma: if they do nothing they are accused publicly of negligence; whereas, if they choose to act, for instance by dispatching troops or NGO personnel and aid parcels, they become targets of public criticism, allegations that they have contributed to delays, confusion, cock-ups, corruption and loss of life.

This fickle rule certainly applies whenever democracies by their actions or inactions inflict or worsen heartbreaking disasters on other countries and regions. President Bill Clinton's public apology for the failure of the United States to intervene in the Rwandan genocide confirmed this.

Democracies are not disaster-proof. There are times when democracies get things badly wrong. Their early warning systems fail, because they are switched off or defective or pointed in the wrong direction. When for such reasons democracies are blind to the hidden or obvious signs of sudden disaster, either at home or abroad, their panicky political elites can lapse into denial by marching down the road of violence, especially when these same elites themselves begin to feel the pinch of the disaster.

Israel illustrates what can happen when governing elites react against the effects of a sudden catastrophe – the 1948 war and the forcible establishment of the Israeli state – by acting to crush all counterclaims by force, in the process attempting (in May 2009) even to ban public use of the Arabic word for catastrophe, *nakba*, used commonly by Palestinians and others as a description of the 1948 events and their ruinous aftermath.

Such public acts of denial and violence play into anti-democratic hands. They succour the view, traceable to the writings of Carl Schmitt, that disasters spawn breakdowns of law and order that can be repaired only by political means which draw their strength ultimately from the deployment of violence. The priority given to military strategy by the United States after the recent Haiti earthquake is a textbook example of this view, which supposes that emergency situations triggered by sudden disasters demand the suspension of democracy. When devastation strikes, or so it is said, only fools continue to believe that enemies – looters, rioters, criminal gangs, local armies – can be treated as citizen victims, as friends and partners in need of compassion.

The commonsense principle that not all theft is criminal, or that squatting and scavenging are the only way people can survive disasters, is dismissed as claptrap, as a pretext of disorder. Emergencies are said to require tough action. They prove that the ability to distinguish between friend and enemy, and to act forcefully against opponents, is the essence of politics. Disasters make plain that when the world is ripped apart, life becomes a jungle of disagreements and violent conflicts. Disasters reveal an ugly truth: human beings are devilish creatures who are easily driven by force of circumstances to commit devilish acts. That is why those charged with conjuring order from chaos know the true meaning and importance of sovereignty. Sovereign are those (as Schmitt said) who decide things in exceptional circumstances, who aggregate unto themselves an awful prerogative: the unrestrained power 'publicly to dispose of the lives of human beings'.

The argument that political order must trump all other priorities during sudden disasters is clear, but unconvincing. Speedy restoration of civil order often depends upon helping citizens, without delay, to organise themselves into groups dedicated to helping themselves. Civil society against the state is an old slogan, but it sometimes has great purchase in sudden disasters.

When the world crashes down on their heads, people often display great resilience by building self-reliant networks. In Istanbul, squatters elect governments that decide planning and zoning regulations. The illegal markets of Lagos are run by self-governing associations of traders. Women living in Kiberia, the largest mud-hut community of Nairobi, pool their scarce money through 'merry-go-rounds'.

During the early days of the Haiti disaster, the slogan 'Courage, Mon Frère' was widely circulated through the battered slums of Port-au-Prince. The same pattern was evident in the earthquakes that struck San Francisco in 1906 and Mexico City in 1985. Governments under these conditions proved to be worse than useless. Paralysed by panic, corruption and heavy-handed incompetence, they jeopardised the lives of their people, as happened in the aftermath of Hurricane Katrina, when New Orleans citizens trying to rescue their fellows were forced repeatedly to outmanoeuvre police so that they could steer their boats into flooded areas.

Whenever governments misbehave in this way, citizens suddenly find that their fears sprout wings. Defying predictions of chaos they band together, confident in their ability to act together, amicably, generously, as if to confirm the eighteenth-century predictions of William Godwin and others that society could live without political authority. For hours, days and sometimes weeks, civil society outgrows and overthrows state institutions. Amid the earthly hell, the spirit of solidarity prevails.

IT IS NOT always true that disasters afford tastes of paradise on earth; sadly, their sudden strike triggers almost unimaginable mayhem and suffering that rarely come rapidly to an end. The catastrophe lives on inside the victims. Survivors of disasters are often gripped by feelings of confusion, demoralisation and hopelessness. These feelings cut deep, often connecting with earlier disturbing events in their lives. When that happens, individuals are damaged twice over by disasters. Not only are their loved ones lost, their everyday routines wrecked, their possessions destroyed, their homes ruined. Their bonds with others are permanently damaged, sometimes to the point, as happens in severe trauma, that individuals become chronically mistrustful of others.

ARMIES AND POLICE forces are ill-equipped to tackle this damage; so, too, are authoritarian regimes, which force people traumatised by disasters to handle their burdens in private, as best they can, their traps shut by bribes, police harassment and media blackouts. What's done is always done, of course. Yet one way in which living democracies can help heal wounds is to engage in a politics of remembering disasters – and of coming to terms with the follies, arrogance, violence and ruinous effects they unleash on people. The great advantage of democracies is that they are much better equipped to carry out this kind of repair work. Only under democratic conditions can citizens freely carve out spaces in which they can remember, work through and overcome the traumas triggered by the disasters they have suffered.

Sometimes this rule is observed superficially, or by means of sly humour. 'Democracy,' the American comedian Johnny Carson once quipped, 'is the eagle on the back of a dollar bill, with thirteen arrows in one claw, thirteen leaves on a branch, thirteen tail feathers, and thirteen stars over its head. This signifies that when the white man came to this country, it was bad luck for the Indians, bad luck for the trees, bad luck for the wildlife, and lights out for the American eagle.'

Carson meant it. His joke carried a sting in its tail, especially for people trapped in situations where they feel victimised by unnecessary extra suffering. The ongoing work of the International Campaign for Justice in Bhopal and the action of bereaved American citizens who organised themselves after the 9/11 attacks into a coalition for the purpose of forcing Secretary of State Condoleeza Rice to testify before the 9/11 Commission, despite her initial refusal to do so, are recent cases in point.

Every other record that we have of disasters and their traumatising effects, including the terrible long-term violence suffered by indigenous peoples at the hands of their conquerors, shows that people have powerful inbuilt drives to organise and make sense of their experience of catastrophes, to give them meaning, to explain their causes and effects, to bind themselves to disasters by drawing parallels and making links with what came before their onslaught.

Making public sense and alleviating the pain of disasters is near impossible under anti-democratic conditions. Only democratic mechanisms – public apologies, truth and reconciliation tribunals, investigative reports like the Goldstone Report on the Israel–Hamas war in Gaza – can sustain that long, harrowing but necessary process.

IS IT TRUE, as has often been said, that democracies are fixated on the present and blind to the future? How good are they at forecasting potential threats and assessing their veracity? And when it comes to the practical business of handling slow-fuse disasters, such as the long-term, irreversible damage to our biosphere, how competent are they, compared with other political systems?

The topic of bad luck, future catastrophes and democracy is badly neglected in the literature on democracy. The reasons for the lamentable silence are not simply practical, a matter of democrats failing to note or to catch up with events. The silence runs deep, down into the wellsprings of anti-democratic political thinking.

The principal version of such thinking heaps doubt and suspicion on democracy because it is said to suffer from congenital incompetence, a slow-wittedness that stems ultimately from its dependence upon the ignorance of a fickle people. Among the earliest and best-known versions of this suspicion was Plato's rejection of *dēmokratia*. He likened it to a ship of fools sailing into treacherous unknown waters, without a captain or navigational equipment for plotting its position.

From the perspective of this ignorance argument, let us call it, democracy is a slowpoke way of making decisions that at some point naturally result in foolish outcomes, even unmitigated disasters. Modernist versions of the same argument echo loudly through Adam Ferguson's complaint that 'every step and every movement of the multitude, even in what are termed enlightened ages, are made with equal blindness to the future.' The same complaint is evident in Disraeli's remarks against the 'fatal drollery' of democracy; in Mill's anxiety about the age of 'superficial knowledge' and the coming despotism of ignorant public opinion; and in Weber's clever line of attack on democracy in representative, parliamentary form.

Weber's rejection of democracy is especially interesting, if only because it is today so often parroted by people unaware of his bigger (and highly questionable) argument about a global trend towards bureaucracy. The trend, which began in Europe, is peculiar to modern times and irreversible, Weber explained. Complex and risky problems are best defined, handled and resolved by technically sophisticated experts and officials in large-scale organisations. For reasons of administrative efficiency and effectiveness, large corporations managed by executives are now just as much an 'iron necessity' as bureau-cratic command in the field of electoral politics, government administration and military strategy. Winning wars, fighting elections, fending off market competitors and competently administering government all require top-down rule, the concentration of the means of power into the hands of a few people. Weber acknowledged that skilled, devoted, cool-headed political leadership remained important; and he recognised that elections, political parties and parliaments could serve as training grounds for new leaders. But the old democratic vision of self-government by citizens and their representatives was now utterly exhausted. 'Such concepts as "the will of the people", "the *true* will of the people", have long since ceased to exist for me,' he told a former pupil. 'They are *fictions*. All ideas aiming at abolishing the dominance of humans by others are "utopian".'

Recycled versions of the ignorance argument are still alive and well today. Democracy is said to be heavy-footed, reactive, too dependent upon give-and-take procedures, and hence unable to galvanise effectively and efficiently to solve slow-fuse disasters in the making. Most voters are interested mainly in lining their own pockets, so infecting democracies with myopia. Blame is also pinned on democratic mechanisms for their incompetence, their notoriously inefficient and ineffective mechanisms for handling rotten luck and rotten outcomes.

Democratic incompetence is then usually contrasted with the efficiency and effectiveness of alternative ways of making decisions, such as the 'smart power' allegedly employed by the government of contemporary China. 'There is little debate heard in Beijing from op-ed pieces, television talk shows or think-tank forums,' writes Kishore Mahbubani, 'but there is nevertheless a remarkable ability to think outside the box, particularly with respect to long-term planning.'

He adds: 'The typical time horizon in Washington hovers somewhere between the daily spin for the evening talk shows and the next election cycle. In Beijing the clear focus is on where China wants to be in fifty years in order to avoid a repetition of the two centuries of humiliation China experienced before finally emerging as a modern power.' When formulating effective responses to climate change, for instance, democratic impulsiveness and fumbling are reckoned inferior to Chinese smart power, whose acumen and deftness are said to be steeped instinctually in ancient wisdom. 'The pool of historical wisdom that China can turn to is enormous,' says Mahbubani, who goes on to praise the present leadership of China for its 'flexibility', 'better professional diplomacy', 'geopolitical acumen' and unusual propensity for 'keeping a low profile'.

Such nation-centred claims in support of smart power sound rather like those of Edmund Burke, two centuries ago, in defence of landed oligarchy. It is just possible that in spite of their spuriousness (China's obstructive behaviour at the recent Copenhagen conference on climate change was dumb, not smart) these claims will be infectious, partly because they effectively expose major intellectual weaknesses in the inherited stock of reasons used in defence of democratic openness.

MANY PEOPLE ARE today surprised to find that past arguments for democracy sound so antiquated, or downright embarrassing, as when the citizens of ancient Athens commonly justified *dēmokratia* by identifying it with the power and glory of their empire. The subject of disasters forces us to rebuild a boat at sea, to come up with fresh justifications of open communication that make a real political difference in handling cataclysms. Open communication has vital functions during sudden catastrophes. But does democracy make a positive difference when responding to slow-fuse disasters?

Consider the problem of 'strategic misrepresentation' in large-scale construction projects. The euphemism used by planners and planning researchers refers to the way incompetence, long delays and substantial cost escalations typically plague multi-billion-dollar projects, such as new transportation systems, military hardware procurement schemes, giant dams, nuclear-fuelled electricity generation systems and the reconstruction of war-devastated zones. It is as if these and other mega-projects are jinxed by an in-built 'disaster gene' that makes them prone to massive cost overruns and serious shortfalls in benefits to citizens.

Oddly, despite their inefficiency and ineffectiveness, large-scale projects continue to multiply across the world. This 'megaprojects paradox' is explained not just by technical breakthroughs, corporate profit, political power and public prestige.

Strategic misrepresentation also plays a vital role. In plain English: the champions of megaprojects usually lie. Guided by self-interest, the promoters of such projects deliberately conceal risk factors by misinforming governments, publics and the media about the true costs and benefits of projects, in order to get them approved and built. Only democratic openness can stop them in their tracks – so rescuing large numbers of people from the clutches of possible long-term disaster.

The implications are clear: far from operating as a brake on efficiency and effectiveness, as is often claimed, democracy is their vital precondition. And, contrary to a long line of observers, the old griping about the myopia of democracies is losing its grip. The age of monitory democracy no doubt gives a voice to those – cynics, opportunists, stallers and otherworldly abbots – who despite all contrary indications cling to the presumption that everything will turn out well. Yet in the face of reckless projects (Gunns' proposed Bell Bay Pulp Mill is a good bad example) and slow-fuse disasters, such as those fuelled by 'oiloholic' policies, monitory democracies are slowly but surely fostering a sense that life must be lived forwards, that democracy is an exercise in living on the edge of future time, and that voting for posterity is legitimate, and often necessary.

THE PUBLIC SCRUTINY of power is vital for dealing with another source of slow-fuse disasters. No account of the relationship between democracy and long-term catastrophes can be plausible unless it examines the disaster-prone effects of uncontested power. The link is often concealed by people's fascination with powerful men with balls. In the early years of the twenty-first century, there are signs everywhere of a lingering fascination with action-man leaders. In the long run, whatever their achievements, these men always fail. Their arrogance gets the best of them, if only by tempting them into blind and foolish mistakes.

Hubris is the greatest challenge facing any system of concentrated and uncontested power, as the official report on the behaviour of the Bush administration after the invasion of Iraq reminds us. Commissioned by a Bush appointee, the report charts the serious failures of a $100 billion so-called reconstruction project resisted by hostile Pentagon officials and ruined by elementary ignorance of Iraqi conditions, bureaucratic turf wars and spiralling violence caused by worsening local conditions.

There are many lessons to be learned from the disasters of the Iraq invasion, but the one from this report is obvious: democracy is the best available early warning system. Those who ignore that axiom try to wield power freed from the 'burden' of comment and criticism and compromise. They may believe absolutely in the moral and political correctness of their own actions, or in the harmonious effects of annually rising GDP and democratisation. They may suppose that God blesses their power, or that most people can be seduced by turning displays of power into show business. But they are always deeply mistaken.

Power-holders who have little or no sympathy for the rough-and-tumble of democracy, understood as the ongoing public scrutiny, chastening and humbling of power, may accuse it of speaking in tongues. They may say that it produces far too many conflicting points of view that are in any case not of equal worth. They may conclude that open public scrutiny devours far too much precious time, that it breeds confusion, dissent and disorder; or (as is said so commonly in China) that it violates the principles of the Harmonious Society.

In China, smart-power advocates insist that democracy threatens the proven ability of the state to raise standards of material wellbeing and to improve the quality of people's lives. That is why they indict their opponents for plotting chaos, resistance and 'counter-revolution'. It is why, as well, they insist that social harmony requires forceful leadership and intelligent government unconstrained by the vices of party competition, useless parliaments and querulous civil organisations that represent nobody save their own interests, or the designs of 'foreign' powers.

MEASURED IN HISTORICAL terms, most of these well-worn claims are designed to distract attention from the brute fact that in practice power which is unaccountable can have crippling effects, especially in circumstances in which the powerful fall in love with their own judgements. When that happens, the radius of their circle of advisors shrinks. They denigrate, push aside or disappear their critics, and generally become dismissive of all evidence and opinions that run counter to their own views. Silo thinking sets in. They begin to talk hot air; policy failures and enforced retreats either go unrecognised or are interpreted, falsely, as triumphs.

Four decades ago, the American psychologist Irving Janis labelled such behaviour 'groupthink': the tendency of decision-makers operating in group settings to ignore counter-evidence in the interests of keeping their power, towing the line and getting things done. Janis showed how groupthink played a fundamental shaping role in the fiasco of the American invasion of Cuba at the Bay of Pigs.

A theory of democracy and disasters needs to extend this point, partly by drawing upon more recent examples of political decisions and non-decisions protected by groupthink, among them the invasion and occupation of Afghanistan and the negligence of many democratic governments in allowing banking and credit institutions to regulate their own affairs, unhindered by objections and fears that the large-scale 'leveraging' of risk in money markets would result eventually in giant market bubbles, whose bursting, as the world now knows to its cost, led to a great recession.

Policy bungles damage the lives of a growing number of people; for a variety of reasons to do with technological scale, mobility of capital and communicative abundance, their global footprint is widening. These world-wide policy failures drive home the painful truth of the old proverb that fools never differ – that power unchallenged by early warning systems is dangerous, because its vulnerability to groupthink makes it blind to its own dependence upon a universe of great complexity, dangerous unknowns and perilous unintended consequences.

The proverb could be put more succinctly: hubris based on groupthink is the curse of publicly unaccountable power. Or more succinctly still: when devil's advocates go missing, saints commit sins. The only known human cure for their transgressions, which sometimes have deadly effects, is the free circulation of differing viewpoints, courageous conjectures, corrective judgements, checks and balances, the institutional humbling of power.

Robust public scrutiny of power is the wisest way of handling complexity. It is the friend of efficiency and effectiveness, the best means of coping with uncertainty and anticipating, recognising and avoiding mistakes, or of acting to prevent the Big Mistake. That is why, when thinking through the subject of disasters, hubris is a problem for democracy – and why remedies for its malignant effects are constantly needed.

AND SO WE come full circle to Donald Horne's *The Lucky Country* and its concern with the vices of thoughtlessness, political incompetence and arrogance. When weighing up the odds that Australia in the mid-1960s would pull itself together by rejecting second-rate leaders for whom mindless hubris was a way of life, Horne listed the virtues that would be needed to ensure the survival and flourishing of a country that had so far enjoyed, against all odds, gamblers' good luck.

Half a century later, his list remains interesting, for more than antiquarian reasons. Among the prime virtues were the cheeky cheerfulness of country people, 'who acknowledge the possibility of catastrophe – from flood, fire, plague or drought, or the collapse of markets'; widespread public commitment to democratic values such as open-minded, non-doctrinaire tolerance, unpretentious manners and justice for underdogs; and young people's rejection of the prevailing bad habit of speaking of Asia and the Pacific in outdated Eurocentric terms. A visceral scepticism of citizens towards political pomp, social authority and the reckless domination of nature stood highest on Horne's list of virtues. 'It may be the most pervasive single influence operating on Australians,' he noted, before adding a prediction: 'A sceptical people like the Australians is more likely to achieve change organically than by cataclysm: things move along more or less comfortably in their own directions, without the horrifying personal disasters of more catastrophic societies.'

Given that bad luck cannot be wished or legislated away, and that sudden and slow-fuse disasters are coming, as surely as night follows day, might it be that no-nonsense scepticism, commitment to fair play and resilience in the face of bad luck are exactly the kinds of twenty-first-century public virtues that will empower democracies like Australia, by giving them a definite edge on their authoritarian opponents?

References available at www.griffithreview.com

John Keane is professor of politics at the University of Sydney. His most recent book is *The Life and Death of Democracy* (Simon & Schuster, 2009) and his essay 'Monitory democracy and media-saturated societies' was published in *Griffith REVIEW 24: Participation Society*.

ESSAY

The other charge of the Light Brigade

The rage of young men I

Carl Reinecke

UNIONISM IN EXCELSIS—SOLDIERS ON STRIKE

LEADERS OF THE STRIKE.

LATE on a February night in 1916 Ernest William Keefe, a trooper training with the Sixth Australian Light Horse Depot, was shot through the right cheek and killed by the Metropolitan Police at Sydney's Central Railway Station. For much of the day thousands of troops from Liverpool had rampaged through the city in a booze-fuelled rage. After Trooper Keefe was shot, at 10.45 pm, the decade-old station quickly emptied, but gun smoke lingered in the thick summer air. Moments earlier five hundred soldiers and civilians, boots and shouts throwing violent echoes around the tiled cavern of Central Station, came up against a military picket. The angry mob threw stones and bottles, and turned a fire hose on the authorities. A soldier shot a revolver into the air, and those in the picket, which included two police-men, returned fire. According to the police report to the New South Wales Coroner, the picket and police fired fifty shots, seriously injuring seven in the crowd, including a civilian.

Keefe was only nineteen. He was one of the thousands of young men from the city and far-flung country towns who had responded to the recruit-ing marches over the previous three months and the December 'Call to Arms' from Prime Minister William Hughes urging men to join the Australian Imperial Force. Keefe was training in the Light Horse Brigade, which was again making a name for itself in the Middle East. Instead of finding glory or death in battle 'in the greatest war of all time', Trooper Keefe was buried in the Church of England section of Waverley Cemetery, the victim of a battle close to home.

The death of Trooper Keefe marked the end of a strike that had begun almost fourteen hours earlier and caused riotous chaos throughout the city. The seeds of 'the mutiny', as it was called, were sown just before the 9 am parade at Casula Camp, in south-western Sydney, on 14 February 1916 – Valentine's Day.

The AIF had maintained bases in the Liverpool area since 1903, but the camp at Casula was established much later, to accommodate and train recruits before they went to the Great War's foreign battlefields. The overcrowded

---

PREVIOUS PAGE: 'Leaders of the strike', Sydney *Daily Telegraph*, 15 February 1916.
Courtesy of the State Library of New South Wales.

base housed about six thousand troops and was adjacent to the Concentration Camp, which housed thousands of enemy aliens in what some soldiers considered were better conditions. These dusty tent settlements operated with military routine, yet with increasing unease. A Royal Commission had investigated the complaints about overcrowding, lack of ventilation and abuse of alcohol at Casula a few months earlier.

The disquiet at Casula found focus on the morning of 14 February, when the recruits were told their training was being extended by four and a half hours, from thirty-six hours a week. They were angry about the overcrowding and lack of a wet canteen at the camp, and the difficulty of getting leave. The extra drill was the last straw. A report in *The Bulletin* the following day described conditions as 'a dam about to burst' that began 'in cold blood, in bitter sobriety'. The men were hungry for war, not more training, but they wanted to be treated with respect and to receive what they considered to be a fair go.

That February morning thousands of soldiers reached breaking point. They refused the direction to extend training hours and decided to strike. One of the convicted ringleaders, sixteen-year-old Private F Short, later said in his court martial that outside his tent 'there was a big crowd…nearly all the camp. They were going from one tent to another pulling people out. "Now, you have to come with us."' According to Captain Smith, a senior officer at Casula, around midday about 2,500 soldiers out of 5,600 remained at the camp.

The mob marched to nearby Liverpool in full flight. There they swarmed into the pubs and hotels demanding free grog. The *Sydney Morning Herald* reported that at the Commercial Hotel, opposite the Liverpool railway station, the soldiers rolled eleven hogsheads onto the street and drank them dry; the publican estimated that they had stolen a 'hundred gallons' of rum. A bulk store was raided: an axe was used to break down the door and £1,500 of stock was stolen. Several police, including Constable Tillet of Cabramatta, were assaulted. Three hundred soldiers tried to break into a second hotel and then another hotel opposite it. The riot progressed like a tropical storm, with quiet followed by waves of destruction. Captain Smith described the action: 'There would be a lull for a quarter of an hour, then they would continue again. The number would come down to a hundred or a hundred and fifty, and it would suddenly increase again by men coming from different directions, who would form a larger body, and the new lot of men would rush the hotel.'

FROM 1 PM the soldiers started rushing trains leaving for the '50-mile' journey to Sydney – they had long thought they were entitled to free train travel and now took it. Later in the afternoon the police, with the aid of twenty reinforcements from Sydney, managed to keep those remaining in Liverpool out of the other pubs, which lined the streets, and and send them back to Casula.

Shortly before 2 pm the first train arrived at Central Station. Half-drunk soldiers piled onto the main platform and 'quickly formed up in fours'. Organising themselves, they started marching from the platform, heading out of the station and up George Street. The *Sydney Morning Herald* reported, 'Here they made a really fine picture, and keeping good time…the men marched as if on parade.'

In front of the first column the protesting soldiers rigged up a Union Jack, regimental colours and a placard: 'Strike. We won't drill 40½ hours [sic].' Any semblance of discipline among the soldiers, drunk on rum and the luck of getting so far, soon broke down. They raided fruit carts, eating some produce but also throwing it at each other and passers-by. As the troops marched north up George Street, passing vehicles became targets. 'Motor cars, motor bicycles, lorries, drays' were commandeered. There was little the former occupants could do but smile at the long column of men in dungarees and khaki marching down the street, and let them take possession. Many people in the city, though initially frightened, were sympathetic and impressed by the spectacle – thousands joined in the riot later in the day.

By 2.30 pm an estimated three thousand soldiers had reached the city. There they were received by a panicked hundred-strong police force and an even more frightened Cabinet. The Chief Secretary sent regular notes to the Premier describing, with increasing alarm, what was happening as the troops took over the city: 'Three thousand men are now marching down George Street and the military authorities do not know how they got there.'

Four hundred troops marching in rank arrived at the door of the *Evening News* later in the day and demanded that the poster in front of the office declaring 'Riot At Liverpool' be changed to 'Strike at Liverpool', and an apology delivered.

The parade of marching troops continued to thin as groups broke off to raid nearby pubs. Yet the momentum of the day carried many of them on to Circular Quay, before they turned around and took a 'smoko' next to the Domain gates.

AFTER THE REST at the Domain the troops made a run at the Assembly Hotel, opposite the police headquarters. It took a pitched battle with police to get them out. During the afternoon the chaos of the mob turned into a city-wide riot. Hotels were raided and those that were closed had windows broken and charged. *The Bulletin* concluded, 'If all the beer in Sydney had been buried in stone vaults at the moment that the human tornado struck the city, it would have stood a big chance of being torn from its place of seclusion.'

By this stage there were several groups in different parts of the city, as each train from Liverpool deposited between three and six hundred troops. One group rushed towards Broadway and Toohey's Brewery, another marched up Eddy Avenue; two hundred men ran down Shepherd Street. The fruit stalls in the Queen Victoria Building were cleared out and broken.

The riot peaked at 5 pm. A thousand drunk troops in George Street, near Hay Street, almost overwhelmed the few police trying to maintain order. At the Regent Street Police Station about seventy soldiers, some carrying lead pipes, threatened to charge the station and free 'our boys' who had been arrested. Throughout Haymarket the police made baton charges against the troops.

Both the German Club on Phillip Street and R Kleisdorff's tobacco store on the corner of Hunter and Castlereagh streets were attacked. Outside the Criterion Hotel one of the troops, pointing to a name above the sign, shouted 'Here's a German' before the mob got inside and started demanding drinks from that 'German bastard'.

The locus of the riot moved to the Queen Victoria Building by 9 pm. There, about five hundred troops rushed around in a crowd of four or five thousand people. A mob collected across the road, on the Druitt Street side of Town Hall, when three revolver shots were heard and the crowd surged, overpowering the few police and forcing 'many women to take refuge in the grounds of St Andrews Church'.

The military leadership eventually responded, deploying fifteen hundred soldiers as pickets, and the entire Sydney police force joined them in what became a full-scale battle with the mob of striking troops. Police eventually trapped many of them in the city centre.

What happened in the final hours of mayhem, between this exchange in Druitt Street and the death of Ernest Keefe, is unclear. The trail of historical documents peters out. But what is clear is that the riot ended where it started, with the chant 'Will we drill forty hours? No!' answered by rifle fire.

THE FOLLOWING DAY, at 11 am, most of the striking/rioting soldiers reported for a compulsory parade at Casula. In the weeks that followed 279 troops were discharged, thirty-six were convicted in state courts and the ringleaders were sentenced to up to five years of hard labour. Others were sent to faraway battles, and some of those involved in the Liverpool riot went on to fight on the Western Front and in the Middle East. Within months the Casula base was closed and those who had yet to be sent abroad were relocated elsewhere. Within months the Casula base was closed and those who had yet to be sent abroad were relocated elsewhere. The bullet holes at Central were filled with putty and the memory of the Valentine's Day riot slowly evaporated.

Although the battle began as a dispute over working conditions it gave the temperance movement, which had been gathering support for many years, a compelling argument to convince the people of New South Wales to vote in June 1916 for the six o'clock closing of all pubs. *The Bulletin* denounced the link as 'hysterical…pub hours were no more to blame than the railway timetable or the width of the Redfern tunnel'. Yet if the events of Valentine's Day 1916 are remembered at all it is as the trigger for six o'clock closing – a policy that remained law in the state until 1955.

Details of the strike and riot are drawn from records held in the New South Wales and Australian Archives, and from contemporaneous newspaper sources.

References at www.griffithreview.com

Carl Reinecke is studying at the Australian National University. The research and writing of this essay was undertaken in memory of David Patrick (1955-2009).

The angry country

The rage of young men II

Melissa Lucashenko

THIS is what we know about the death of Jai Morcom.

On the morning of 28 August 2009, Jai, a fifteen-year-old Year 9 student, was involved in a fight at Mullumbimby High School, in far northern New South Wales. After being knocked to the ground in an argument about a lunch table just after eleven, he lost consciousness. Other kids told reporters that Jai, lying collapsed on the ground outside the girls' toilets where the fight ended, was 'frothing at the mouth'. First aid was given by a nurse and 000 was called. An ambulance then took Jai to hospital on the Gold Coast.

Two days later the popular young student, never having regained consciousness, was taken off life support. The school went immediately into crisis management, issuing a script for teachers to read out in class concerning the incident, as an urban media pack poured into the quiet rural town, whose population normally hovers around three thousand.

Nearly four months later, in December, police issued a statement asking the Mullumbimby community to come forward with more information. Despite a protracted investigation, with Gold Coast detectives interviewing more than seventy MHS students and staff, no clear picture has yet emerged of why Jai left for school that morning assuring his mother that yes, he had his lunch money, and never returned home.

Despite the fight (variously reported in the national media as a 'brawl', a 'bashing' and a 'savage attack') having occurred during recess, with up to two hundred witnesses in the immediate vicinity, no mobile phone coverage of the fight – as opposed to its aftermath – has been handed to police. Few in the small hinterland town of farmers, hippies and tree-changers are saying anything, and Jai's anguished parents still have no way of knowing exactly how, or why, their son was killed.

A CHILD'S DEATH at a school – any school – is a particular kind of tragedy. Schools are meant to be special places for children. It is the essence of a school, at least in theory, that it nurtures and supports young people as it educates them; aggressive acts are more of an affront at schools than in most other settings. This notion of schools as scholarly safe havens must be tempered by the reality, though, that all high schools contain volatile young teenagers, and that school – particularly schoolyard – conflicts are inevitable. Kids have always clashed in the playground and probably always will. Six short months after Jai Morcom died, another eruption of adolescent conflict saw twelve-year-old Elliot Fletcher fatally stabbed at St Patrick's school in bayside Brisbane. Elliot's death, over which a thirteen-year-old straight-A student has been charged, starkly raises the question of whether adolescent boys may have most of the reasons of adult men to clash, but very few of the negotiating skills which adults are supposed to have developed to avoid disaster.

The harsh reality that no school can ever wholly protect our kids from those who would harm them was abruptly swept aside in the torrent of reaction to Jai's death. Journalists evicted from the Mullumbimby school grounds perched at its gate with telephoto lenses, and headlines blazed 'Schoolboy Beaten to Death During Recess'. Speculation and outright fabrication was published as fact; some of the reportage was sufficiently mendacious to prompt an episode of ABC TV's *Media Watch*.

Unsurprisingly, many in the town and in the media took the line that the death was an outcome of pure thuggery. Bullying became the hot topic that week. Facebook ran wild with hang-'em-high writers urging the cane, military service and the gallows as solutions to endemic 'gang violence' in schools.

Gossip and speculation also whirled about Byron Shire as the school strove to maintain some semblance of authority. In an odd coincidence, the MHS grounds, which border Saltwater Creek, were being fenced with standard issue black six-foot spike-topped panels when Jai's death occurred. This immaculate new security fence was handy in keeping the school ground – previously unfenced and frequently deserted by MHS students streaming to and from the town centre, a few hundred metres away – inviolate from media and other unwanted scrutiny. The irony of a highly visible six-foot steel fence keeping out the dangers of the world, when it was inside the school grounds that Jai had been killed, was not easily missed.

In the immediate aftermath of Jai's death, the security fence kept out everyone but staff, investigating police and those few students who turned

up to class (school attendance records show entire classes absent the following week, with 'unexplained' marked against dozens of names). A friend of
mine who tried to sign his son in to the school was stopped at the gate by
quickly imported security in the first week of September. Eventually the
security guard realised he was a genuine parent, not a predatory journalist,
and allowed him, fuming, into the grounds.

What the new security regime couldn't possibly stop, though, was the
rumour mill, which continues to grind away months later, with devastating
results for community morale. With no charges laid, and an open finding at the
preliminary inquest, Mullumbimby still has nothing concrete to draw upon to
explain the tragedy. An undercurrent of fear is present; I was warned by one
concerned mother close to the incident to 'be really careful' in researching this
story. Every possible scenario to explain Jai's death is being canvassed throughout this small and once close-knit community. A representative sample:

One former Mullum High parent told me the kids believed to be the
perpetrators include 'real head-cases going fast down a real bad road'; another
local added that some are from families suffering mental illness, 'really off
with the fairies'.

No, I was told by a junior MHS staff member, it's impossible to know
who was responsible, since it was a melee – nobody knows exactly what
happened, nor will we ever.

A common conversational thread is that the fight erupted between a
gang of football thugs and a bunch of younger Emo kids. Jai was hit once,
say some, his head striking the wall as he fell, and that was the end of it. Or
perhaps Jai was knocked to the ground and then assaulted multiple times,
kicked and punched by a gang of older boys while unconscious. The autopsy
showed multiple blows to his body, others claim – including Jai's father, Steve
Drummond, in an open letter to the local newspaper, the *Byron Shire Echo*.
Alternatively, the body was unmarked.

One former teacher told me with rolling eyes that the conspiracy theories
have gone so far as to suggest that the Gold Coast Titans football club, based
an hour to the north, has, along with police, had a hand in suppressing the
truth about the death, in order to protect some budding Rugby League talent
in the town.

A disaffected Grade 10 student I picked up hitchhiking towards his new life as an apprentice in a nearby town was strongly attached to the fantasy he recounted: the boy responsible for killing Jai had already been charged, and was now locked up in juvie (neither is true). Furthermore, he said, outlining a sensational picture of hard drug use by students, 'the teachers don't care – they've just given up. They can't control anything.'

What the staff of Mullumbimby High certainly can't control is the demographic mix which turns up on their doorstep each year with the new intake. My daughter attended Mullum High for four years in the mid-2000s. She learned in classrooms where the children of fifth-generation cane and cattle farmers sat next to kids whose parents had fled the cities to find cheap hilly land on which to smoke dope and build permaculture gardens while awaiting world peace. This group is still relatively small in Mullumbimby, which is equidistant between Narrabri and Nimbin on the Rainbow Scale, and is a demographic increasingly squeezed out by the arrival of cashed-up southern yuppies doing a sea change. (House prices in Mullumbimby more than doubled in the past five years).

Nevertheless, the hippies have imparted a distinct counterculture flavour to the town centre, with Santos Wholefoods selling organic everything a couple of doors up from the booming real estate offices, and yoga classes and spiritual healings a dime a dozen. Dreadlocked buskers are common in the main street, and the Mullumbimby Medical Centre may be the only doctor's surgery in the world whose staff – yes, the doctors – have happily posed naked (in a 2003 calendar to raise money for the local hospital). And I somehow think it was a hill-dweller, not a cane farmer, who wrote in the school's condolence book that the attitude of Steve Drummond – in the early days after his only son died, one of forbearance and forgiveness – was 'surely the action of the Buddha and the Christ and the love of the Angels made manifest'.

A good percentage of local alternative lifestylers – who live in the isolated hills surrounding Mullumbimby, popularly supposed to mean 'rounded hills' in Bundjalung, up to half an hour's drive from town on potholed dirt roads that wreck your cheap car – send their kids to the Shearwater Steiner school. The Steiner school sits on its own pretty acreage five kilometres further inland, but it is a private school, and it costs. Those parents who won't, or can't, pay the fees have no other convenient high school to turn to. Once at MHS, the twelve-year-olds from, say, Upper Main Arm are asked to leave behind their primary school uniform – a tie-dyed rainbow T-shirt, shoes optional – and meld into a school population of close to a thousand jostling kids of all descriptions.

UP UNTIL DECEMBER 2009, Richard Heazlewood-Ross was the avuncular and well-liked deputy head of Mullum High. When I spoke to him, he was on the cusp of retirement, looking forward to getting more heavily involved with the marginalised kids who are his passion through the Byron Community College. With the support of Southern Cross University in Lismore, the college operates much like alternative schools in the cities. It remains strongly linked to MHS and delivers its courses through distance education modules. The community college began in Byron Bay, but also operates now through 'The Hut' youth centre in Mullumbimby, staffed part-time by Deb Pearse (a woman who struck me as not so much burnt out as close to incinerated). What kind of kids, I asked Heazlewood-Ross, are shifting across from MHS to study at The Hut? 'The BCC kids are those with mental health issues. Anxiety, agoraphobia. There are sexually precocious girls.' He speaks of teenagers, once capable of seriously destructive behaviour, turning around, finishing Year 10. 'It's a beautiful thing, really – one boy's made a table in woodwork that he wants to donate back to Mullum High.'

The college, Heazlewood-Ross explained, runs on 'the smell of a smell of an oily rag' and is an avenue – realistically the only avenue – for the teenagers who arrive at the school without the skills to survive, let alone succeed, in the classroom at Mullum High. 'They are victims of their home life, and so they come along to us and become victims of the classroom, and that leads to them…well, I don't like to use the word "failing". "Hexagonal pegs" is how one parent described them to me. A lot of them are kids that are difficult for their parents to control. They go out partying, and then it's hard to get to school the next day, so they don't come, and then they get marginalised even more. You've got daughters with AVOs out against their mothers, and the mothers have got AVOs out against the daughters. I mean we've got kids here who go into town at lunchtime and see their mums drunk underneath the Scout Hall. It's no wonder they have trouble fitting in.'

Heazlewood-Ross's deep concern for these struggling kids is palpable. Talking to him, I was reminded of the shock that ran through the school community when he was not awarded the vacant principal's position in 2005. Everyone thought he should have gotten it, my daughter told me at the time – everyone likes him. The job went instead to an outsider to the school, Ian Graham, a quiet, reserved man who in December 2009 took to wearing a red, black and yellow Koori wristband on his right arm, and when asked to describe the mood of the school, told me, 'Settled. Settled – but impacted.'

IMPACTED IS THE word, all right. Tensions ran very high in Mullumbimby in the weeks following the death. Students in the first furious days marched en masse in the street, demanding Ian Graham's resignation, only to be countered by a group of parents and staff vocally supporting the principal. Steve Drummond berated the protesting students, telling them they should be remembering his son in a quiet, respectful manner, instead of having their 'stupid, petty little fights'.

A teenage Halloween dance organised in the Drill Hall a fortnight after the death was marred by brawling outside and in the streets of the town; a boy arrived stoned and carrying a bottle of whisky.

Back at MHS, as floral tributes and graffiti mounted up against the brick wall of the girl's toilets ('We will never forget you Jai'; 'We'll party again don't you worry bro'), the school canteen became a bizarre side issue. A tuckshop revolution ensued when it was found to be tens of thousands of dollars in debt. New managers were appointed in the weeks following Jai's death, and a revised menu of healthy food was promoted by some as the answer to the school's problems.

Much of the local discontent since 28 August 2009 has centred on whether bullying contributed to Jai's death. It could have happened anywhere, say some; table wars are the norm, not the exception, and all schools have fights at some time or another. It was a freak accident, that's all. The town is now deeply split between those who argue that Mullum High is just like every other public high school in Australia and those who see Jai as victim of a 'born-to-rule' football clique clashing with a sub-group of younger kids.

The footy crowd make up their own rules as they go along, some argue, including the mother of a close friend of Jai's: 'It just makes me sick. They think they're above everyone else, just because they play footy. I told [her partner] if he wants our boy to play for the Giants then he's gonna have to take him and sign him up himself and drive him to all the games, 'cos I don't want anything to do with that lot. I didn't want my son to get like they are – to learn to treat women like shit. And I've seen what it's done to relationships between sons and mothers when they do join the club.'

My daughter similarly described the Mullum High pecking order when she was last a student there, in 2006: 'About half the kids were the footy heroes or else they're hangers-on. They're the so-called popular people, loud people that I would avoid and not want anything to do with mostly. Then there was an overlap between them and the surfer kids, and the rest were a pretty diverse bunch. There were a few Emos and some gamers, and the more arty kids, and they all hung together and got called the Emo group.'

Most people from the top echelon – the 'popular' kids – would deign to talk to the ones on the bottom, my daughter told me, but those in the bottom layer were excluded from a particular kind of social life. They weren't necessarily bullied overtly; they just didn't get invited to certain parties. But a small minority of really aggro guys – and their girlfriends – were different again. They would never speak to anyone outside the football clique 'unless they wanted something from them'. My daughter paused here, and then added matter-of-factly, 'or unless the guys wanted to bash the shit out of someone.' This normally happened away from the school buildings, often on the oval across the road when school was over. And while push-and-shove altercations were fairly common at school, serious fights were rare, occurring, she told me, perhaps twice a year.

AT MULLUM HIGH Jai Morcom was involved in the so-called 'table war', where ownership of seating at a long aluminium table was highly contested between groups of boys during recess and lunchtimes. At these relatively unsupervised times, the student population at Mullum divides itself not just by age but also by demographic.

As Heazlewood-Ross explains, this is atypical: 'It's a bit different to other schools, I think. They kind of hang together across grade levels, so you get younger-grade kids mixing with the older ones. The Emo kids hang out in one corner of the school and play cards…you've gotta love that bunch of kids. They're a little bit more sensitive, maybe – the kind of kids who've experienced some harassment…They don't buck the system – they ignore the system. And then there's other groups who have their own particular areas. But it's not strictly a grade division like in most schools…'

What happened on 28 August, he went on to say, was probably that a group of older students had taken offence when the younger Emo group took 'their' table at recess. A spitting match ensued, which quickly escalated. Punches were thrown. After that it gets blurry. Very blurry.

Depending on who you talk to, the table war had been going for a couple of days (the official school line) or for a month or more. The table would be carried in triumph from location to location by the rival groups of kids, and I was told by students that the table war was seen not as bullying, but rather as a big joke. One Grade 8 boy – call him Thomas – told me that he had been sitting on top of the table one August lunchtime when a bunch of rivals 'lifted the table up with me on it and carried it to where they thought it should be'. Not only that but, in the weeks leading up to the death, Thomas (who belonged to neither clique) had been spat on by a member of Jai's inner group. What had his reaction been to having been lifted into the air on the table? 'I just went – oh, great, woo-hoo!' he explained, grinning a wide attractive grin. 'You know, I made a joke of it.' And to being spat on? 'I just ignore it. People try to pick fights with me all the time, 'cos – I don't know why. Maybe 'cos I'm tall. Even tiny little guys' – and here his palm hovered around his waist in demonstration – 'they come up and hit me. People try and start fights with me all the time. It happened in town on Saturday night. I just ignore them.'

For fourteen-year-old Thomas, a stable, loving home and engaged parents have given him the capacity to laugh off his assailants, and to clown, not rage, when the table war erupted beneath him. But stable, loving homes and engaged parents are hardly universal; they may no longer even be the norm. And for older boys accustomed to having their authority recognised on and off the football field, it must have seemed outrageous to be spat on by the school's outsiders – by one of the nerds, Emos and Koori kids who hung together in a distant corner, playing cards, ignoring the system, avoiding the jocks. Male pride can be a terribly dangerous thing and, once unleashed, almost impossible to put back in the bottle without adult help. As an anonymous statement made by one kid the police interviewed reads: '...and we went back to find out why [the spitting had happened] and ask for an apology...an all-in brawl invoked [sic].'

While the author of this statement claims to have been ten to fifteen metres from Jai at all times during the fight, the text also contains the words 'sorry' and 'regret'. The statement, which was published in a Sydney paper, and later posted on Facebook, is adolescent, confused, and reeks of expediency. Penned in the highly charged atmosphere of those early weeks, when revenge attacks threatened, it ends in pathos: 'Two wrongs don't make a right. Peace.'

PROFESSOR ROSS HOMEL teaches criminology at Griffith University. Big schools, he told me over coffee in a Brisbane café, are bad news. Building friendly relationships is paramount in maintaining order among young people, and in big high schools with lots of small feeder schools, these relationships may simply be too many and too hard to manage effectively.

Inside schools and out, youth violence is on the rise in Australia's eastern states, and the figures in the ten-to-fourteen age bracket make for sobering reading. While overall crime rates, including for violent crime, are in decline, probably due to years of sustained economic growth, the youth figures are going in the other direction. The figures are bad but there is plenty of room for optimism, Homel countered, since 'the gap between what we know and what we don't know is much smaller than the gap between what we know and what we actually *do* on the ground.' Atomised modern families are a big part of the problem, as are rampant alcohol abuse, illegal drug use and income inequality, all starkly worse in Australia than in most comparable countries. While the causes of youth violence are multiple and complex, we know a great deal about what helps at-risk teenagers to stay engaged at school and stay out of trouble. Simple interventions like those made by Deb Pearse and others at The Hut can have dramatic effects; where young people feel listened to and valued by adults, tensions quickly dissipate. Kids stay at school.

As much as anything, Professor Homel says, troubled kids need schools they can connect with and then jobs to go to – 'meaningful activity' – just like adults do. And if their dysfunctional families fail them and institutions can't take up the slack, kids need to be provided with a range of different connections to the wider society, avenues they can take into citizenship and belonging. Failing this, they are likely to drift into a downward spiral of grog, drugs, fights, crime. These connections needn't cost a fortune. Sport is one traditional way of bringing young people into generally safe contact with each other (notwithstanding footy's alleged role in Jai Morcom's death) and there are others means, like gaming clubs and art activities, some of which have been offered by Deb Pearse at The Hut over the years.

There is no escaping the hard data showing the need for more interventions such as these. Australian boys – and to a lesser extent, girls – are frequently involved in violent conflict with their peers. Forty-four per cent of Brisbane teens surveyed in 2007 had attacked another person in some way during the previous year (though some of these attacks consisted only of 'throwing something', presumably in some cases innocuous objects like fruit or pens). But in an environment where young men feel cut adrift, abandoned by their fathers especially, a hurled apple can be the only trigger necessary for serious conflict to erupt. 'Some of these kids,' Heazlewood-Ross told me of his Grade 9 boys, 'seem to have such a deep well of anger in them.'

Be it drugs, family breakdown, socioeconomic inequality or some other mix of factors at work, there is a cohort of angry young men and women in the eastern states who apparently regard violence as acceptable, or at least unavoidable, in their young lives.

On the Facebook memorial site 'RIP Jai Morcom', scathing responses to adult bloggers sermonising about kids' violent behaviour brand adult suggestions for reform naive. One boy wrote, 'Kids will never learn we are brout up getting bashed by our rents and watchin our mums get bashed by our faget dads.'

IN THE FINAL quarter of 2009, threats of payback flew around the town as Steve Drummond began to call not for calm but for better explanations, and the police commenced what would turn out to be a tortuously slow investigation. A small group of Jai's young friends – both Kooris and other boys – were taken away by the school's Aboriginal Support Worker, Scotty Sentence, for a weekend camp. The boys came back to town far more settled, most of their talk of revenge evaporated. (Some of this group have since shifted to Byron High, unable to stomach the bad memories at Mullum.) When I visited the school in December, Scotty's predecessor, Steven Strong, showed me plans to have respected local Koori men visit the school and work weekly with all the boys in the younger grades on conflict resolution and identity issues. But interventions to benefit young people and save lives cost money, money that is scarce and hard to find in the public school system. Kings School in Sydney can offer its adolescent boys a top-class education and facilities that include an air-conditioned underground rifle range, but Strong's excellent proposal to give time to troubled boys – one that made Professor Homel nearly leap out of his seat with enthusiasm when I described it to him – remains, as yet, a grossly underfunded dream.

A large mural now decorates the brick wall where Jai lost consciousness on 28 August. The graffiti memorialising him is hidden beneath a songline and kangaroo dreaming painted in mustard and red ochres by Bundjalung leader Uncle Lewis Walker, who along with Maori community leaders held a smoking ceremony for Jai in September. 'It was just an incredible event,' Heazlewood-Ross told me, clearly still moved four months later. 'The most striking thing about it was the presence of Uncle Lewis. He just walked into the school that morning and said: This is what's going to happen here today. This, this and this.' He paused. 'And the *authority* of the man.'

Jai was of Maori descent through his father, and both his parents agreed that an Indigenous ceremony was the best way to remember their son and to help heal the fractured school. More than six hundred staff and students chose to attend the Sorry Business that September morning, sitting in the concrete quadrangle close to where Jai struck his head. The gathering maintained complete silence for the best part of an hour while the white-ochred Uncle Lewis smoked the area, and solemn Maori rituals were carried out. At one point, sitting among tearful friends and students, Steve Drummond broke down, keening in anguish. Uncle Lewis went immediately to kneel at his side and comfort him; as he did so, the male Maori elder stepped forward and sang 'Our Father' to the motionless gathering. Later, staff and students shared a ritual meal of kangaroo and damper, served as per Maori custom, first to the family, and then to the others.

'If you'd told me that our students would sit there with complete attention for an hour, then line up and eat *kangaroo* and damper – well, I would have said you were mad,' Heazlewood-Ross told me, shaking his head. 'What I remember the most was this little ADHD boy of ours who I've never seen be still for more than about thirty seconds. He just sat there' – pointing to the corner of a garden bed – 'and he didn't move a muscle for the whole thing. He was just riveted to the spot. We all were.'

DEB PEARSE, OPERATING The Hut with three functional computers on 'the smell of the smell of an oily rag', told me that she found it a bit curious having to go to Maori and Koori cultures to memorialise Jai. It was as if, she told me, mainstream Australian culture didn't have the right ceremonies to do the situation justice. Aboriginal myself, I was not about to argue with her. I remembered as she spoke that there are no specific words in English for a parent who has lost a child. 'Widow', yes, and 'widower'. And 'orphan' – for one who has lost their parents. But no name for a mother or a father who has had to put a child in the ground. No equivalent to that heartbreaking status label in more than one Indigenous language for a mother whose baby has recently died, which literally translates: she is only empty hands.

Each culture deals with death differently, of course. But across every culture – and probably in every Australian country town of several thousand souls – there remain strong men and women of outstanding leadership ability with the capacity to care for young people, and the willingness to guide them into adult society. Heazlewood-Ross, Scotty Sentence, Deb Pearse, Steve Strong and many others – these people have for years extended an umbrella of deep concern over the troubled young boys and girls of Mullumbimby. It is grossly unfair to think, as did my disaffected hitchhiker, that they don't care, or have given up. They do, and they haven't.

But things are different in Mullumbimby now. A young life is gone, and the town has changed as a result. Angry posters by Steve Drummond (*Truth 4 Jai Part Three*) are plastered on windows and flat surfaces throughout the town: 'There are people responsible. They are not coming forward...the next day after the Drill Hall fighting, two of Jai's friends were attacked by carloads of youths from Mullum...Early this year a boy at Mullum High got taken away by ambulance with concussion, someone had put his head through a brick wall. Jai was not so lucky.'

Innocence has gone from the incense-flavoured township, and been replaced by a lingering suspicion between two tribes. And the language of the school has been forced to change as well. 'When things blew up in the past, I used to use the throwaway phrase *Well, it's not life-threatening*,' Richard Heazelwood-Ross told me soberly as we walked past the spot where Jai had lain unconscious that August morning. 'I don't use that phrase anymore.'

In early March, Steve Drummond delivered 1,400 letters to the Coroner's Court in Sydney, calling for an inquest into his son's death. Still refusing to heed police advice to halt his investigations, Drummond alleged that boys had brought spanners, chains and padlocks to school in August 2009 in an attempt to win the ongoing table wars that culminated in Jai's death. 'It's quite possible that he's been thrown out of the fight and that he may have hit a brick wall,' Drummond concluded. The Coroner will decide whether to recommend an inquest into Jai Morcom's death when all submissions have been considered.

12 March 2010

References available at www.griffithreview.com

Melissa Lucashenko is the author of four novels and the forthcoming *Mullumbimby*, which was extracted in *Griffith REVIEW 28: Stories for Today*. Her essays have also been published in *Griffith REVIEW: Dreams of Land* and *People Like Us*.

REPORTAGE

Joining the pack

The rage of young men III

Helena Pastor

WE sit around the kitchen table like Jesus and his disciples, except there are only six of us and Jesus is drinking too much red wine and swearing a lot. There's Jayne, Simmo, Sally, Geraldine, Flinty and me. And Bernie, of course: our Jesus. We're the BackTrack Crew and I'm the latest ring-in to this gang of youth workers.

Bernie's eyes burn bright but look troubled all the same. For the past week he's been busy talking to the media about his most recent youth-work initiative, the Iron Man Welders. Now he's going through a moral dilemma about being seen as the 'boss man' of BackTrack, the spokesperson with all the answers.

He takes a swig of wine. 'It's hard for me when people ask, "What is it?" Fuck, I don't know.'

At the head of the table, Simmo shifts his half-moon glasses down his nose and moves his chair in closer. His black beanie makes him look like he's about to organise a bank heist. 'BackTrack's a group of people doing shit for youth. I'm here because I like the idea of helping you out,' he says. 'Are you worried it's too Bernie-focused?'

'Yeah.'

Simmo shrugs. 'But I see BackTrack as being Bernie. Some bastard's got to be the leader.'

Bernie runs his fingers through his wavy hair. Although he spent much of his youth as a stockman in Central Australia, his skin is clear and unlined, his face boyishly handsome though he's approaching forty.

He glances around the table. 'Most of you have known me long enough to know that I'm great at flying off on tangents and having all this passion, but if you lot weren't writing the grant applications or helping out where you can, then it would be nothing – just someone with a lot of passion running around chasing his fuckin' tail.'

Maybe so. But he's the one with all the ideas, the ones that work.

'Can I ask a question?' Sally, his sister-in-law, looks like she wants more order in this meeting. 'Don't we have a mission statement or vision or something?'

Bernie gives her a wry smile. 'We do that every time we get together, every time we get pissed.'

Sally laughs, shakes her head like she should have known better.

Then Bernie's wife, Jayne, has her say, elbows on the table. A poncho flares over her arms like dark wings and I notice, not for the first time, her robust beauty; she's a clear-eyed, straight-talking earth mother. 'I'm sure we've answered all these questions before, Bernie. Just keep talking about BackTrack exactly as you have. It's fairly definable – it's us here, in this room. It has been since the beginning.'

Bernie stands, stretches, and goes out to the cold night air, ducking his head as he walks through the back door for a smoke.

THE IRON MAN Welders meet on Sundays in an old council depot on the edge of Armidale, a university town on the northern tablelands of New South Wales. About a year ago, Bernie had a vision of a welding project that would build on the strengths of a group of young men who had dropped out of high school but weren't ready for work. He asked the Armidale community to help out. The local council offered him the depot, which was once a welding workshop and was lying empty, as if waiting for Bernie and the boys to come along and claim it.

There was nothing in the huge shed, not even a power lead. The boys, recruited from a school welding program that Bernie ran the previous year, turned up each weekend and worked hard to clean and create their own workplace. They borrowed nearly everything, from brooms to welding equipment, and started collecting recycled steel for the first batch of products they planned to make and then sell at the monthly markets. Local businesses gave scrap metal; people lent grinders, extension cords and old work boots.

Then the money started coming in. A local builder forked out the first five hundred dollars. The bowling club gave a thousand and a steel-manufacturing business donated a MIG welder. The credit union offered to draw up a business and marketing plan, organised insurance, and contributed a thousand dollars for equipment. Armidale Family Support agreed to keep track of the finances. Hillgrove Mine donated a thousand and raised the possibility of apprenticeships, and the NSW Premier's Department handed over a grant worth five thousand dollars. It seemed like every week Bernie and the boys were in the local paper, celebrating some new success.

A FEW MONTHS ago, I saw a photo of Bernie in the newspaper, surrounded by a group of teenage boys, faces beaming with happiness and pride, and something stirred inside me. I wanted to be part of it: the Iron Man Welders.

The next day I heard Bernie on the radio, seeking community support for the project. 'We'll take any positive contribution,' he said. His words sounded clipped and tight, like he wasn't one for mucking around. 'Whether you've got a pile of old steel or timber in your backyard, or if you've got an idea, or if you like working with young people and you're prepared to come down to the shed and work one-on-one with some of these kids…'

On impulse I rang. I'd never used power tools, let alone done any welding. I liked bushwalking, baking cakes. I enjoyed order, cleanliness, silence. What was I thinking?

Over the past months, though, I've come to feel at home in the shed. Right from the start the boys were gracious in accepting a 42-year-old woman into their grimy world. They find easy jobs for me to do – like filing washers for candleholders or scrubbing rust off horseshoes. I sweep the floor, watch what's going on, listen to what they want to tell me. The fellas who come along are the sort of misfits you see wandering the streets of any country town with nothing to do, nowhere to go. Once, I might have crossed the street to avoid them.

Most of the Iron Man Welders didn't 'engage positively' with the education system. None has finished Year 12; some barely made it through Year 10. One was expelled in Year 11 for 'kissing his missus' in the schoolyard, another told a teacher to 'fuck off' on a ski trip because the teacher wouldn't stop hassling him, and another finished Year 10 at TAFE because he was about to be kicked out of school and reckoned the teachers didn't like him anyway. The welding shed is a different story. They love it. Bernie gives them the chance to take responsibility for their life, to engage on their own terms with the community.

The first Sunday I joined them it was the middle of winter. I walked in carrying a tray of freshly baked brownies. Conspicuous in my new blue King Gee work clothes, I huddled from the cold in the open-sided tin shed. Music blared from an old radio, and thumping and grinding noises came from the machines. Sparks flashed; everyone dragged on rollies, littering every sentence with 'shit' and 'fuck'. Taking a deep breath, I forced myself not to panic.

Thommo, a stocky bloke in his late teens, took me on a tour. His voice rumbled softly, and I could barely hear what he was saying as he showed me the kitchen area, the main workspace and a forge he'd built in a dark side room that brought to mind a scene from the Middle Ages: flickering fire, hammers and anvil, dirt floor, open drain, a rusty tap jutting out from the wall.

He led me towards a shelf at one end of the shed to show me the objects on display, things they were hoping to sell at the markets: a range of candlehold-ers, nutcrackers, penholders, ashtrays and coat hooks made from horseshoes. There was a smartly presented copy of the Iron Man Welders' business plan, and several glass-framed photos: Thommo bent over the anvil, hammering a piece of glowing-red metal; three boys dressed in work gear, looking into the distance like soldiers on the hill at Gallipoli; Bernie and about eight boys slouched in front of his yellow ute; and a young bloke with curly hair using a grinder, a halo of sparks around his head.

Bernie doesn't actually seem to know much about welding. Every now and then I hear him say, 'No point asking me questions about welding shit' – but that could be his way of throwing the decision-making back onto the boys. He knows the basics, like what processes are involved for different jobs, but most of the fellas have the edge on him. Some are doing TAFE certificates in engineering, following on from their school studies.

Along with understanding the welding and power tools, I'm also keen to learn more about boys. You'd think I'd know enough, as I have four of my own. But lately the eldest, Joey, has been giving me plenty to worry about. He left school before finishing Year 10, even though he's more than bright enough. I don't like the way he's drifting through life these days – no job, no direction, living off Centrelink payments, sleeping in till midday. If only he was coming to the shed each week, slowly 'getting his shit together' like the others. 'I'm a lone wolf,' Joey says whenever I pester him about coming down. I think it's time he joined the rest of the pack.

BERNIE SLIDES OPEN the screen door at Simmo's and a cold gust of night air and cigarette smoke blows in with him. He takes his place at the table, ready to carry on with the BackTrack meeting. The crew falls silent when they see his expression. He tells us he's tired of waiting on a funding application that'll secure him a part-time wage for the next two years. He wants to make a roster and call in some other blokes to help ease the load: 'Otherwise it's just relying on me and…'

'It gets real old,' offers Geraldine, with a knowing look.

'Yep,' Bernie says. 'Real old, real quick. And the pressure's on me the whole time. I'm the worst time-manager in Australia, and when we get down to the shed I go righto, I'll get those three started on that, and then I've got to go and pick up Tye or someone else, and I skip up there, and then I get back and Simmo's there and I go oh, great, Simmo must be working with them on that, and then they've drifted off and started fifteen other fuckin' projects, and I go right, Tye, you go and see Simmo and he'll tell you what to do – I've got to go and pick up blah blah blah…I'm a frazzled chook and by the time the day's over I just go what the fuck – we haven't finished anything and we started another thirty things…'

It's true. I've seen how some Sundays are messy and nothing much seems to get finished, but I still reckon Bernie is making great leaps with these boys. And besides, as he often tells me, 'It's not about the fuckin' welding.'

Helena Pastor is writing about the Iron Man Welders as part of a PhD in Creative Research Practice at the University of New England. She was awarded a 2009 ASA mentorship and recently received a Varuna Publisher Fellowship with Griffith REVIEW. Her memoir 'Yahtzee and the art of happiness' was published in Griffith REVIEW 17: Staying Alive.

THE LUNAR COAST

MEGAN McGRATH

I was seventeen when the tide went out. I felt it in my lungs. At the height of its run, my breath snared in my chest. I clutched my school shirt, gasped.

'Lee?' Alex gripped my shoulder. 'What's wrong?'

I saw my agony mirrored in his eyes.

ALEX AND I had grown up on the lunar coast. It was a treacherous northern stretch of coastline, with rocky headlands and monstrous tides. Each day the moon peeled away the sea, exposing an atlas of silver sand spits that spiralled into the sea. Our coast protected ships and deterred them.

We were a fishing village that thrived through the winters when the tides were kind and the sun stayed low. Over the summer season of storms we repaired boats and nets, and re-told stories of great catches and disasters.

Alex and I loved the summers. The days seemed endless and our fathers stayed home. Though not related, we were a family. Our fathers were boyhood friends. They'd lived off the lunar coast, just as their fathers had done, and we would do. They'd taught us to fish, to read the seas and the stars. We were fourth-generation fishermen, or soon would be. The lunar coast was in our blood.

In those summers, salt crunched like gravel at low tide. We'd walk the lunar coast, collecting shells and driftwood and sun-bleached bones. We'd roam the rock pools when the weather was right. The rocks scorching from the sun; the water warm to touch. The rock pools were galaxies all of their own, with weeds and crustaceans and fish trapped within. Worlds interrupted by our touch. We'd catalogue our finds and relay them to our fathers. Our knowledge grew as we did, broadening over the summers.

Alex had the spirit of the sea inside him. Like his father, he was practically made of salt. He was careless in the sun, his shoulders browned to a crisp, his dark hair matted and lips chapped. His feet were broad and tough. I wasn't built for the weather the way he was, and to keep up I wore soft-soled reef boots, zinc cream, swimming goggles. My feet remained pale and wrinkled from the wet.

But out there we were equals.

He was always picking things up, despite my warnings of stingers and barbs.

'What's this?' he'd ask, running his fingers through a tube anemone, delighted by the way it would suck back in.

In those days we were ageless. Time melted away, only to be revealed in the evening by the extent of our sunburn. We were explorers, pioneers, companions and brothers. Every day was like walking on the moon.

BUT WE DID grow up. For so long it felt like it was light years away, then suddenly it was upon us. The rock pools lost their charm. The salt flats seemed less magical. We wanted to take risks, to be challenged and to feel fear.

We found what we were looking for at the headland, where the rocks hollowed out into caverns. There was a vertical cylindrical cave that went right through the headland. We called it the sea shuttle.

When the swells were right we could swim under it, and as a wave came in water would fill the hollow and jettison us to the top. On days with big swells it would almost blow us right into the sky with a whoosh of sea foam and exhilaration.

If we didn't clear the top of the tube, and we rarely did, we would have to grab onto the rocks inside the cave. We had to be swift, and hold strong while the water fell away. If we missed the rocks, and we sometimes did, we'd be sucked out with the swell, tumbled into a whitewash of foam, trapped under the rocks and take water in as breath. While Alex had the courage, I had the lungs and could take two or three rides in a row while he watched enviously from the opening above.

Explaining the cuts on our hands and the scratches on our backs was a nightmare, but the summer was ours and we were delirious with adrenalin. Our fathers would kill us if they knew.

If fishing was the heart of our town, our fishermen were the soul. They were all beanies, whiskers and rubber boots, distinguishable only by the gruffness in their laughs and the kindness in their eyes. We were a superstitious town, like all fishing towns, and Alex and I were regarded with caution. It was said that our families could feel the sea. Sometimes we believed it; sometimes we didn't. Our fathers' boat was one of the few that operated the nets and the long lines alternately. They relied on the weather to dictate their catch. They were both humble and proud. But like all fishermen we were slaves to the sea, and sometimes her master.

THE NIGHT THE tide went out there were big seas. The wind whistled through the weatherboards, and Alex and I stayed awake listening to the reports on the radio. Neither of us mentioned the absence of the moon.

At dawn, we went to the ramps; the air was still thick with foam and mist. Our fathers had already returned with an empty hull. In the eerie morning light I watched them mending the nets. Alex hunched his shoulders against the cold.

'Anything?' I asked.

My father shook his head in that sullen way of his.

Alex's father chuckled his pirate laugh.

'Ah, you can feel it,' he said, pressing his palm to my sternum. Through my jumper I could feel the roughness of his hand. I looked away from the sea, as though my unease was casual, irrelevant.

'You can too, my boy.' He winked at Alex. 'We all can.' He laughed again, but there was a sorrow about him.

My father remained silent, but stopped working on his net for a moment and rubbed his own chest, as if irritated by indigestion.

THE TIDE NEVER came back in. Over time our beach became desolate, shifting from silver to grey, its fine sand becoming pebbled and coarse. The wind stripped the surface, revealing craters and debris.

In the evenings, as the boats set out, I watched the sea birds circling against the sunset. At night they did not return to our shore.

Each day the fishermen left earlier; with further to sail they combined crews, taking fewer boats and more fuel. Our town had retired their nets, relying on the long lines to pull in fish of higher value. But eventually even they became elusive. It was clear the fish had fled the lunar coast. I couldn't blame them.

When enough days had passed, the boats stopped going out all together.

'I think it's time we speak seriously about your future,' my mother said over a dinner of tinned tuna. I'd been set to start my apprenticeship with Alex on our fathers' boat in autumn.

'We were worried something like this would happen,' my father said, not looking at me.

'I know...' I pushed the flakes around my plate. 'I'll go.'

I left for college the following week. Alex didn't even say goodbye.

IT WAS SIX years before I returned to the lunar coast.

Our town had changed dramatically. The boats had all been hauled ashore and lay tilted unsettlingly on the banks, their keels exposed. The ocean-front stores, once hardware and bait shops, now sold ice-creams and sunhats.

I'd heard through my family that Alex had taken a job as a tour guide, driving the coast, pointing out nail-tail wallabies and spinifex.

My parents, with Alex's family, had opened a small bakery on the foreshore and now my mother smelt of pastry. Her hair had grown long and she kept it tied up in a messy knot. I couldn't help noticing she smiled more.

My father hadn't changed much. He sat with Alex's father on our patio, watching the sun bake the beach. I was overjoyed to see them together.

As I sat, he squeezed my shoulder with his large brown hand.

'Seen Alex?' he asked.

'Not yet.'
'You should.'
'I know.'

I MET WITH Alex cautiously at first, over a beer at the tavern, then for dinner with his family. Eventually we began to spend the days together. It was never going to be like the old times, but unlike him I wasn't giving up.

A week after my return, we drove his company four-wheel-drive to the point. We'd only ever walked the coast, but now the distance seemed too far to contemplate.

'Dad said you wouldn't come back until the tide turned,' he said finally, as though the ocean had brought me back, not my family, and not him.

'Has it?'

He said nothing for a while, then smiled. 'I think so.'

We parked on the beach, then climbed the headland; the rocks were brittle, leaving powder on my knees and hands. At the top I looked out over the coast.

'Well?' Alex asked with laboured breath.

'I think you're right.'

The sea was coming back. We watched it for some time, awed, as it rolled back in carrying dried weed and wood, drowning the sand. And then, just a few metres out, that unmistakable flash in the water. There, and there again.

'Did you see that?' I pointed, and Alex followed my gaze.

'It can't be...'

WE RACED TO the beach and peeled off our clothes. We had to get a closer look. Among all the salt and the sunburnt kelp there was a fish. No doubt about it.

'Come on.' He hurried me as I pulled on my boots. While he had never mocked me before, he did now.

'What is all this stuff, anyway?' He snatched at my diving mask and my towel, laughing in the cruel way of a teenager made desperate by age.

I was just another city boy to him now. Our history had fallen with the tide, erased by the time and the distance I'd put between us.

Despite his cruelty, or because of it, I pitied him. Life on the lunar coast had him beat. I was fitter than I had ever been, yet he had developed a paunch. His body sagged in a way I had never imagined it could. Time had been fierce to him.

We entered the water. I waded to my chest before diving in. The water was murky with salt. It flooded my mouth, swelling my tongue. I could hardly see, even through my mask. When I looked back at Alex he had his eyes squeezed shut.

At the headland we bobbed on the surface. The wind had picked up, chopping the water into messy white caps.

'Did you see it?' he asked.

'No.' I spat into the water.

'I think we should check the shuttle.'

I'd forgotten all about it.

WE ROUNDED THE headland and were fully exposed to the wind. The tide was rushing in, as though making up for lost time after half a decade of slack water. It had already moved more than a metre.

I'd expected this landscape to be foreign to me, but as I swam I felt my body guided by the sea. With familiar strokes I pushed under the surface and into the opening of the rocks.

I broke the surface and gasped, holding tight to the rocks. It had been a rough swim, the visibility making it nearly impossible to navigate in the hollow. Still, Alex came up grinning.

'Grab the rocks,' I said, leading him to the wall. 'I can hardly see anything.' We were in a washing machine. The surface churned with foam.

'It's down there,' he said with certainty.

'Did you see it?' My back scraped the rocks as I rose with the next surge of water.

'No, but I feel it.'

'We'll climb out and have another look.'

'We don't have time for that.'

'I just wanted to know what kind it was.'

'Lee, we can't let it get away!' He smiled devilishly before letting go of the rock.

'Alex!' I grabbed at his wrist but he slipped free.

I waited for him to resurface. I calculated the climb to the top. It was just a few metres. I reminded myself I'd done it hundreds of times. I counted to ten. Alex still wasn't back. Shit.

He'd played tricks like this before – pretend there was a giant squid dragging him under, then take hold of my ankle. Or he'd come back up with a handful of sand to rub in my hair. But this felt different.

I put my face in the water. Nothing. I kicked out with my feet, hoping to brush something other than rock. I looked again. It was like swimming in storm clouds. I couldn't see anything.

I took a deep breath and let go of the rocks.

My body plunged into the darkness. I was surrounded by bubbles and foam. Down I went, trusting my memory of the passage. My hands stretched out, feeling nothing but water and rock. I kicked against another surge; I had to stay down until I found him. I felt the pressure on my lungs but knew I could beat it. I reached again, hitting the sand with my shoulder. And then, flesh! I grabbed Alex with both hands and pulled him towards me.

I DRAGGED ALEX up the lunar coast and lay him on his side. Was he breathing? I pulled off my mask and held my ear to his face. I felt the steady thud of his heart under my hand, his breath on my cheek. I stood up and gulped down my own lungful of precious air. I watched the rise and fall of my still-pale chest. I looked at my skinny ankles in my boots. I was dripping, exhausted, alive.

So was Alex.

Only then did I notice the fish clawed in his hand. As though coming out of a coma it began to flap on the sand, its body contorting, frantic, feeble. I knew then why he'd gone back down. This fish, the first to return, was the one thing that could restore him. To catch it would make him a fisherman after all these wasted years.

But the fish needed to be in the sea if we had any hope for the lunar coast. It needed to be alive. I bent to pry it from his grasp, but Alex sprung awake. His eyes jolted open, he looked from me to the fish, first confused, then ecstatic with pride. He raised himself on one elbow, leering at the fish on the sand. With his free hand he grabbed hold of my mask.

'Alex, no!'

He punched down with all his strength. When the mask crushed its skull I felt it in my lungs.

Megan McGrath is a Brisbane-based author. This story won the 2009 State Library of Queensland Young Writers' Award.

'Delicious inside stuff. It makes for an engrossing read and the definitive account.'

MARK BOWDEN
AUTHOR OF *BLACK HAWK DOWN*

'With the surgical skill of a first–rate reporter and storyteller, Sarah Ellison recounts a true story that reads as if ripped from a novel.'

KEN AULETTA
AUTHOR OF *GOOGLED: THE END OF THE WORLD AS WE KNOW IT*

AVAILABLE NOW IN ALL GOOD BOOKSHOPS

Text Publishing, Melbourne Australia
TEXTPUBLISHING.COM.AU

THE GOSPEL ACCORDING TO PHILIP

The remarkable **Philip Pullman** has written
a book that will change the way we think about religion,
about God, and about one of the most enduring
stories of all time.

AVAILABLE
NOW IN
ALL GOOD
BOOKSHOPS

Text Publishing, Melbourne Australia
TEXTPUBLISHING.COM.AU

Save 20% with a 1 or 2 Year Subscription plus receive a FREE copy of a past edition of your choice*

☐ I would like to subscribe   ☐ I wish to give a subscription to: (please tick ✓ one)

Name: _____

Address: _____

_____ Postcode: _____

Email: _____ Telephone: _____

Please choose your subscription package (please tick ✓ one below)

☐ 1 year within Australia: $80.00 (inc gst)   ☐ 2 years within Australia: $150.00 (inc gst)

☐ 1 year outside Australia: $130.00 AUD   ☐ 2 years outside Australia: $250.00 AUD

I wish the subscription to begin with (please tick ✓ one below)

☐ CURRENT EDITION†   ☐ NEXT EDITION

For my FREE copy, please send it to ☐ me   ☐ my gift recipient (please tick ✓ one)

EDITION TITLE* _____

Select from past editions at www.griffithreview.com *While past edition copies remain in stock.*

PAYMENT DETAILS

Purchaser's Address (if not the subscription recipient):

_____ Postcode: _____

Email: _____ Telephone: _____

☐ I have enclosed a cheque/money order for $_____ made payable
to **Griffith REVIEW** (Payable in Australian Dollars only)

☐ **Card Type (please circle one):** Bankcard / Mastercard / Visa / Amex

Card Number: ☐☐☐☐ ☐☐☐☐ ☐☐☐☐ ☐☐☐☐

Expiry Date: __ __ / __ __

Cardholder name: _____

Cardholder Signature: _____

MAIL TO:	**FAX TO:**
Business Manager - Griffith REVIEW	Business Manager - Griffith REVIEW
REPLY PAID 61015	07 3735 3272 (*within Australia*)
NATHAN QLD 4111 Australia	+61 7 3735 3272 (*International*)

● The details given above will only be used for the subscription collection and distribution of Griffith REVIEW and will not be passed to a third party for other uses. For further information consult Griffith University's Privacy Plan at www.griffith.edu.au/ua/aa/vc/pp ● † Current Edition only available for subscriptions received up until 2 weeks before Next Edition release date. See www.griffithreview.com for release dates.

ED28 1153120310